Independent Schools
Examinations Board

MATHS
ISEB Revision Guide
(Third Edition)

Stephen Froggatt
and David Hanson

Independent Schools
Examinations Board

www.galorepark.co.uk

GALORE PARK

Published by ISEB Publications, an imprint of Galore Park Publications Ltd
19/21 Sayers Lane, Tenterden, Kent TN30 6BW
www.galorepark.co.uk

Design and typesetting Typetechnique
Illustrations by Ian Moores

Printed by Replika Press Pvt. Ltd., India

ISBN-13 978 1 907047 01 5

First published 2010, reprinted 2010, 2011

Details of other ISEB Revision Guides for Common Entrance, examination papers and Galore Park publications are available at www.galorepark.co.uk

Front cover photo © GlowImages/Alamy

About the authors

Stephen Froggatt taught Mathematics in Preparatory and Secondary schools for 20 years, during which time he contributed to many websites and articles on teaching Mathematics, and was a regular speaker at Maths teaching conferences. Now he has retired from teaching to pursue a career as a Methodist minister.

David Hanson has over 40 years' experience of teaching and has been Leader of the ISEB 11+ Maths setting team, a member of the 13+ Maths setting team and a member of the ISEB Editorial Board. He has also edited the SATIPS Maths Broadsheet. David recently retired from teaching to run a small shop trading in collectors' items.

Contents

Introduction

This book has been written to help you revise. It is not a textbook, and the emphasis is on reminding rather than teaching you.

The book contains all the revision material you will need for your Common Entrance exam. In addition, Chapters 5 and 6 provide you with some practice in vital skills which will help you pass your exam.

Throughout you will find plenty of 'Test yourself' questions that will allow you to check that you have learned a section properly, and 'Sample questions' with which you practise the kind of questions that you will see in the exam. There are answers at the back of the book.

At the end of each chapter is a summary of what you should have learned. Make sure that you keep track of what you have and haven't covered, and keep practising anything you're unsure of.

Examinations are not designed to trip you up, but to give you a chance to demonstrate what you know and what you can do. Make sure that you have the facts at your fingertips so that you can show yourself off at your best.

Good luck!

The syllabus and your exam

The ISEB syllabus is revised regularly and is based on the programme of study for Key Stage 2 (11+) and Key Stage 3 (13+) of the National Curriculum. The syllabus expects that pupils will be familiar with the skills and knowledge of National Curriculum Key Stage 1 and the National Numeracy Strategy *Framework* for the early years.

If you are taking the ISEB Common Entrance 11+ exam, you will take one paper lasting one hour.

If you are taking the ISEB Common Entrance 13+ exam, you will take three papers:

- a Level 1, 2 or 3 calculator paper lasting one hour.
- a Level 1, 2 or 3 non-calculator paper lasting one hour.
- a mental arithmetic test lasting 30 minutes, which is the same for all levels.

A note for teachers

Sample questions and Test yourself questions have been modelled on ISEB Common Entrance examination questions and, therefore, frequently request the pupil to write on the paper. If you do not wish the pupil to mark this book, these questions are available as downloadable/CD products from Galore Park www.galorepark.co.uk

How to use this book

This book contains several symbols that will help you to revise only what you need to.

First, make sure you know which Level of the exam you are taking. If in doubt, ask your teacher.

- If you are taking Level 1, you do not need to revise anything tagged with the following symbols: ■■□ ■■■
- If you are taking Level 2, you will need to revise everything except the material tagged with the following symbol: ■■■
- If you are taking Level 3, you will need to revise everything in this book.

Symbols such as this **5** refer to National Curriculum levels, a different system used in some schools. Your teacher will tell you if you need to refer to these.

 These symbols in the margin allow you to find the Summary and Test yourself sections quickly. Keep referring to these sections and check that you know what you need to.

In the Summary sections, you may find some points with footnotes ✳. This is because you may be required to know slightly different things depending on which ISEB Level you are taking. Your teacher will explain this if necessary.

Sample questions have marks allocated, eg (2), as they would in the exam.

Tips on revising

Get the best out of your brain:

- Give your brain plenty of oxygen by exercising. You can revise effectively if you feel fit and well.
- Eat healthy food while you are revising. Your brain works better when you give it good fuel.
- Think positively. Give your brain positive messages so that it will want to study.
- Keep calm. If your brain is stressed it will not operate effectively.
- Take regular breaks during your study time.
- Get enough sleep. Your brain will carry on sorting out what you have revised while you sleep.

Get the most from your revision

- Don't work for hours without a break. Revise for 20–30 minutes and then take a five-minute break.

- Do good things in your breaks: listen to your favourite music, eat healthy food, drink some water, do some exercise or juggle. Don't read a book, watch TV or play on the computer; it will conflict with what your brain is trying to learn.
- When you go back to your revision review what you have just learnt.
- Regularly review the facts you have learnt.

Get motivated

- Set yourself some goals and promise yourself a treat when the exams are over.
- Make the most of all the expertise and talent available to you at school and at home. If you don't understand something, ask your teacher to explain.
- Get organised. Find a quiet place to revise and make sure you have all the equipment you need.
- Use yearly and weekly planners to help you organise your time so that you revise all subjects equally. (Available for download from www.galorepark.co.uk)

Know what to expect in the exam

- Use past papers to familiarise yourself with the format of the exam.
- Make sure you understand the language examiners use.

Before the exam

- Have all your equipment and pens ready the night before.
- Make sure you are at your best by getting a good night's sleep before the exam.
- Have a good breakfast in the morning.
- Take some water into the exam if you are allowed.
- Think positively and keep calm.

During the exam

- Have a watch on your desk. Work out how much time you need to allocate to each question and try to stick to it.
- Make sure you read and understand the instructions and rules on the front of the exam paper.
- Allow some time at the start to read and consider the questions carefully before writing anything.
- Read all the questions at least twice. Don't rush into answering before you have a chance to think about it.
- If you find a question is particularly hard, move on to the next one. Go back to it if you have time at the end.
- Check your answers make sense if you have time at the end.

Tips for the Maths exam

- Read the questions extra carefully. It is very easy to miss the word 'not' in a probability question, or the words 'as a percentage' in a number question.

- Show all your working. In a non-calculator question, failure to do this could result in loss of marks; in a calculator question it helps the examiner to check your method even if the final answer is wrong. Candidates often forget that marks can be awarded for working – it's not just about getting the right answer.

- Check that your answer sounds reasonable. A building 7 cm tall, or an average pupil mass of 987 kg, should make you think again. The most common way to get a crazy answer is to forget the units (centimetres and metres in the same question, for example).

- When drawing graphs and doing constructions, use a sharp pencil, and try to be as neat and precise as you can.

Useful resources

Study Skills by Elizabeth Holtom, ISBN: 9781902984599

Junior Maths Book 1 by David Hillard, ISEB: 9781905735211
Junior Maths Book 1 Answer Book by David Hillard, ISBN: 9781905735242
Junior Maths Book 2 by David Hillard, ISBN: 9781905735235
Junior Maths Book 2 Answer Book by David Hillard, ISBN: 9781905735242
Junior Maths Book 3 by David Hillard, ISBN: 9781905735266
Junior Maths Book 3 Answer Book by David Hillard, ISBN: 9781905735297

So you really want to learn Maths Book 1 by Serena Alexander, ISBN: 9781902984186
So you really want to learn Maths Book 1 Answer Book by Serena Alexander, ISBN: 9781902984193
So you really want to learn Maths Book 2 by Serena Alexander, ISBN: 9781902984315
So you really want to learn Maths Book 2 Answer Book by Serena Alexander, ISBN: 9781902984322
So you really want to learn Maths Book 3 by Serena Alexander, ISBN: 9781902984346
So you really want to learn Maths Book 3 Answer Book by Serena Alexander, ISBN: 9781902984353

Mathematics Pocket Notes by David E Hanson, ISBN: 9780903627146

Mathematics Questions at 11+ (Year 6) (Book A Questions) by David E Hanson, ISBN: 9780903627092
Mathematics Questions at 11+ (Year 6) (Book A Answers) by David E Hanson, ISBN: 9781907047152
Mathematics Questions at 11+ (Year 6) (Book B Questions) by David E Hanson, ISBN: 9780903627351
Mathematics Questions at 11+ (Year 6) (Book B Answers) by David E Hanson, ISBN: 9781907047145

Mixed Maths Exercises (Year 6) by Andrew Jeffrey, ISBN: 9780903627030
Mixed Maths Exercises (Year 7) by Andrew Jeffrey, ISBN: 9780903627047
Mixed Maths Exercises (Year 8 Lower) by Andrew Jeffrey, ISBN: 9780903627054
Mixed Maths Exercises (Year 8 Upper) by Andrew Jeffrey, ISBN: 9780903627078
Mixed Maths Exercises Answers by Andrew Jeffrey, (downloadable from www.galorepark.co.uk)

All available from Galore Park: www.galorepark.co.uk

Chapter 1: 11+ Number

1.1 Properties of numbers

Types of number

- You should be familiar with some of the more common words used to describe numbers and their properties.

For this section it really helps if you know your tables well! Let's see why they are so important.

The multiplication table

×	1	2	3	4	5	6	7	8	9	10	11	12
1	1	2	3	4	5	6	7	8	9	10	11	12
2	2	4	6	8	10	12	14	16	18	20	22	24
3	3	6	9	12	15	18	21	24	27	30	33	36
4	4	8	12	16	20	24	28	32	36	40	44	48
5	5	10	15	20	25	30	35	40	45	50	55	60
6	6	12	18	24	30	36	42	48	54	60	66	72
7	7	14	21	28	35	42	49	56	63	70	77	84
8	8	16	24	32	40	48	56	64	72	80	88	96
9	9	18	27	36	45	54	63	72	81	90	99	108
10	10	20	30	40	50	60	70	80	90	100	110	120
11	11	22	33	44	55	66	77	88	99	110	121	132
12	12	24	36	48	60	72	84	96	108	120	132	144

You need to know your tables in several ways. First of all, learn them in columns so that you can list, for example, all multiples of seven. Then, be able to jump in at any point, and know that, e.g. 4 × 8 = 32, without thinking. Finally, you should be able to use it backwards and be able to give all factor pairs of a number (e.g. which numbers multiply to give thirty-six?).

Multiples

Multiples of 3 include 3, 6, 9, 12, 15, 18, ...

Multiples of 6 include 6, 12, 18, 24, 30, 36, ...

Think of multiples as the **results** in the times table of a number.

Factors

Factors of 30 are all the numbers which divide exactly into 30

We can make a factor rainbow.

Notice how they come in pairs.

$$30 = 1 \times 30 \quad \text{or} \quad 2 \times 15 \quad \text{or} \quad 3 \times 10 \quad \text{or} \quad 5 \times 6$$

Think of factors as the **questions** from the times table.

Primes

Quite simply, a prime is a number which has only two factors: 1 and itself.

The first 100 prime numbers

2	3	5	7	11	13	17	19	23	29
31	37	41	43	47	53	59	61	67	71
73	79	83	89	97	101	103	107	109	113
127	131	137	139	149	151	157	163	167	173
179	181	191	193	197	199	211	223	227	229
233	239	241	251	257	263	269	271	277	281
283	293	307	311	313	317	331	337	347	349
353	359	367	373	379	383	389	397	401	409
419	421	431	433	439	443	449	457	461	463
467	479	487	491	499	503	509	521	523	541

Obviously you do not need to learn all these! Try to be familiar with as many as you can, though. At the very least learn the first ten or so, and reach the point where you can recognise all numbers under 100 as either prime or not. Note that 1 is not prime.

Squares, cubes and roots

Any number multiplied by itself gives a **square**. In the factor rainbow this number joins to itself in the middle. Let's try this for the number 36

Notice how the 6 is joined to itself because $36 = 6 \times 6$

Multiply any number (n) by itself and the result is a square number (n^2). Any number multiplied by its square gives a cube number (n^3). It is an extremely good idea to know the squares of at least the first ten numbers and at least the first five cubes. Here are the first fifteen of each:

n	n^2	n^3
1	1	1
2	4	8
3	9	27
4	16	64
5	25	125
6	36	216
7	49	343
8	64	512
9	81	729
10	100	1000
11	121	1331
12	144	1728
13	169	2197
14	196	2744
15	225	3375

n^2 means n to the power of 2

2 is the index number

Similarly, for n^3, 3 is the index number

Remember the connection between squares and square roots.

Cubes and cube roots work in a similar way.

Odd and even numbers and rules

There are several general rules about combining two numbers, depending on whether they are odd or even. You may wish to think about why these rules always work as they do.

odd	+	odd	=	even
odd	+	even	=	odd
even	+	odd	=	odd
even	+	even	=	even

odd	−	odd	=	even
odd	−	even	=	odd
even	−	odd	=	odd
even	−	even	=	even

odd	×	odd	=	odd
odd	×	even	=	even
even	×	odd	=	even
even	×	even	=	even

There are no simple rules for division. Any division could be a fraction which is neither odd nor even.

Negative numbers

● You need to be able to add and subtract negative numbers in context, and sort them into order of size.

Real-life negatives

Where do we find negative numbers in everyday life? Temperatures are perhaps the most common, but we also talk about negative or overdrawn bank balances (in the red), as well as distances below sea level.

Brr! Below zero

Negative temperatures mean ice and snow. -3 °C is 3 degrees below zero and so on. Let's extend the number line downwards to see what's going on.

Put your pencil on 2 °C (as shown).

Now move down 3 degrees and you should end up with your pencil on -1 °C

We write: $2 - 3 = -1$

Check also that: $5 - 8 = -3$

Adding takes us back up again.

$-2 + 6 = 4$

> Adding -1 is equivalent to subtracting 1
>
> $5 + {}^-8$ is equivalent to $5 - 8 = -3$
>
> Subtracting -1 is equivalent to adding 1
>
> $10 - {}^-4$ is equivalent to $10 + 4 = 14$

Putting negative numbers in order

Remember to think of the number line all the time. That way you will correctly say:

-15 is less than -8 which is less than 3 which is less than 11 and so on.

Sample questions

Try these sample questions for yourself. The answers are given at the back of the book.

Some of the questions involve ideas met in earlier work which may not be covered by the notes in this chapter. (See the Useful resources section in the Intoduction if you need to refresh any skills or knowledge.)

1.1 (a) Which of these numbers are divisible by 3? (2)

      15   26   36   45   56   114   1011

    (b) Which of these numbers are multiples of 4? (2)

      6   12   16   18   24   36   52

    (c) Which of these numbers are factors of 24? (2)

      2   3   4   6   8   12   24

1.2 Which of these numbers are prime? (2)

    1   2   3   5   9   13   17

1.3 Here are some number cards.

3	4	6	7	12	18

From the cards, choose:

(a) a multiple of 6 (1)

(b) a factor of 6 (1)

(c) a square number (1)

(d) all the prime numbers (2)

(e) the number which is a common multiple of 4 and 6 (1)

(f) two numbers which have a product of 21 (1)

(g) three numbers which have a sum of 25, using each number only once. (2)

1.4 Write the next two numbers in these sequences.

(a) 15   20   25   30   35   ... (1)

(b) 57   54   51   48   45   ... (1)

(c) 17   13   9   5   1   ... (2)

1.5 Write the next two numbers in these sequences.

(a) 1   3   6   10   15   …   (2)

(b) 2   2   4   6   10   …   (2)

(c) 224   112   56   28   14   …   (2)

1.6 Gina is snorkelling.

(a) She dives to ⁻2 m (2 metres below the water surface) and looks at a shark
    3 metres below her. At what depth is the shark swimming?   (1)

(b) On her next dive, Gina swims −2.3 metres and sees a jellyfish 1.4 metres above her.
    At what depth is the jellyfish swimming?   (2)

1.7 (a) At 0700 one morning, the temperature inside the window was 4 °C and the
        temperature outside the window was 11 degrees lower. What was the
        outside temperature?   (1)

(b) By 0830 the temperature outside had risen to ⁻3 °C. By how many degrees
    had the outside temperature risen?   (1)

1.2 Place value and ordering

Multiplying or dividing by 10 or 100

- You need to be able to multiply and divide whole numbers by 10 or 100 without a calculator.

Multiplying by 10 or 100

Multiplying by 10 or 100 is easy. It can be thought of as:

- writing zeros at the end of the *whole* numbers

- moving digits to the left so they have a higher place value

- moving the decimal point to the right.

Examples

H T U		H T U		H T U
2 3	×	1 0	=	2 3 0
1 7 4	×	1 0 0	=	1 7 4 0 0

Dividing by 10 or 100

Dividing by 10 or 100 can be thought of as:

● removing zeros from the end

● moving the figures to the right

● moving the decimal point to the left.

Remember: whole numbers have a decimal point too – it's after the units digit!

Examples

H T U.t h		H T U		H T U.t h	
2 1 0	÷	1 0	=	2 1	(the same as 21.0)
1 7 4	÷	1 0	=	1 7.4	
3 4 2 0	÷	1 0 0	=	3 4.2	
7	÷	1 0 0	=	0.0 7	and so on

To help you learn, you can play a fun game with your calculator!

Type in a number and then decide between (**×**) and (**÷**) and then between 10 and 100

Have a guess at the answer and then press (**=**)

Were you right?

Ordering numbers

It is important to be able to write a group of numbers in order of increasing, or decreasing, size.

Example

Write these numbers in order of increasing size.

321   123   312   1320   231

Always look at the most significant digit first. In the list above, the numbers all have 3 digits apart from 1320, where the 1 represents 1000

An abacus, drawn or imagined, can help you to understand.

In order of increasing size, the above numbers are

123   231   312   321   1320

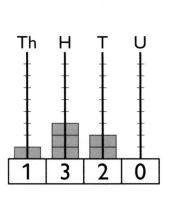

The number line

A number line, either drawn on paper or imagined, is often the best way to help you to order, add or subtract, particularly if you are using negative numbers.

> ### Example
>
> For example, the temperatures at midday on three days were −3 °C, 2 °C and −5 °C. What is the difference between the highest and lowest of these temperatures?
>
>
>
> *Answer: Count up from −5 to 2: the difference is 7*
>
> Here are three more number lines using different scales:
>
>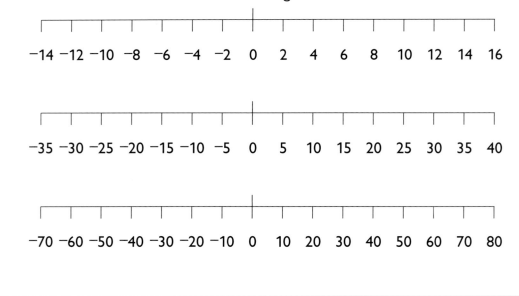

Sample questions

Try these sample questions for yourself. The answers are given at the back of the book.

Some of the questions involve ideas met in earlier work which may not be covered by the notes in this chapter. (See the Useful resources section in the Introduction if you need to refresh any skills or knowledge.)

1.8   (a)   Write in numerals (figures) the number three hundred and nine.   (1)

      (b)   Write in words the number 147   (1)

1.9   The value of the 6 in 3061 is 60 (6 tens).

      (a)   What is the value of the 7 in 207?   (1)

      (b)   What is the value of the 3 in 1304?   (1)

      (c)   In the number 175.73 how many times greater is the value of the 7 on the left than the 7 on the right?   (2)

1.10   Put a decimal point in each of these numbers so that the 3 has the value of three tenths.   (3)

      2 1 3   5 3 0   7 8 3 5

1.11   (a)   Multiply 307 by 10   (1)

      (b)   Divide 307 by 100   (1)

1.12   (a)   How many times more than 120 is 12 000?   (1)

      (b)   How many times more than 3.05 is 3050?   (1)

1.13   (a)   On the number line, the number 2 is shown as a black dot.

         Mark clearly with a cross (X) the number which is 7 less than 2   (1)

      (b)   On the number line below, mark clearly with a cross the number 0.4   (1)

      (c)   On the number line below, mark clearly with a cross the fraction $\frac{3}{4}$ (1)

1.14   (a)   On the number line below, mark clearly with an asterisk (*) all the integers such that * < 4   (2)

      (b)   On the number line below, mark clearly with an asterisk (*) all the integers such that * > ⁻3   (2)

1.15 (a) Write these numbers in order of increasing size. (2)

231 312 213 321 132

(b) Write these numbers in order of decreasing size. (2)

7.3 6.37 7.91 7.36 8.1

1.3 Estimation and approximation

Rounding numbers

It is very useful to be able to 'round' a whole number to give an approximate value.

To help you round, draw a vertical line after the digit you are rounding to. If the number after the line is 5 or more, then round **up**. If the number after the line is 4 or less, then round **down**.

- Round **up**: add 1 to the digit before the vertical line and replace all digits to the right of the vertical line with zeros.

- Round **down**: simply replace all digits to the right of the vertical line with zeros.

Examples

(i)   Round 1327 to the nearest ten   1 3 2|7
      Round up   1 3 3 0

(ii) Round 3029 to the nearest thousand   3|0 2 9
      Round down   3 0 0 0

(iii) Round 1250 to the nearest hundred   1 2|5 0
      Round up   1 3 0 0

An abacus can help you to understand rounding.

Example

Round 6435 to the nearest ten.

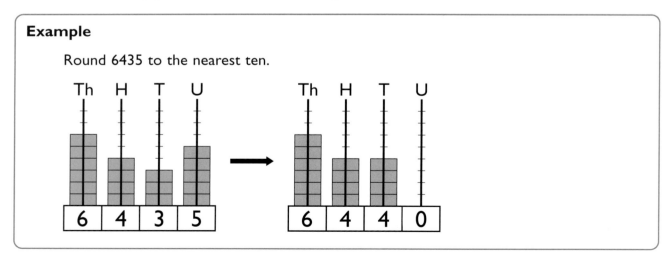

We use the same rules when rounding decimals to the nearest integer (whole number).
The only difference is that we do not replace the figures to the right of the point with zeros.

Examples

    (i)   Round 3.7 to the nearest integer   4

    (ii) Round 4.4 to the nearest integer   4

    (iii) Round 4.5 to the nearest integer   5

    (iv) Round 4.49 to the nearest integer   4

Sample questions

Try these sample questions for yourself. The answers are given at the back of the book.

Some of the questions involve ideas met in earlier work which may not be covered by the notes in this chapter.

1.16 (a) Estimate the position of 3 on this number line. Mark it with a cross.   (2)

      (b) Estimate the position of 60 on this number line. Mark it with a cross.   (2)

1.17 (a) Write 274 to the nearest ten.   (1)

      (b) Write 751 to the nearest hundred.   (1)

      (c) Write 9.85 to the nearest whole number.   (1)

1.18 (a) Estimate (do not calculate exactly) the result of this calculation: (1)

      2998 + 4003

      (b) Estimate the result of this subtraction: (1)

      11 002 − 4997

1.19 It has taken Katie about half an hour to read 20 pages of her adventure story book. The book has 405 pages. About how many hours will it take Katie to read the whole book?   (3)

1.4 Fractions, decimals, percentages and ratio

Fractions

In a fraction, the bottom number (the **denominator**) tells us how many pieces a whole has been divided into, and the top number (the **numerator**) tells us how many of the pieces we have.

In $\frac{3}{4}$ we have three of the four pieces.

In $\frac{3}{5}$ we have three of the five pieces.

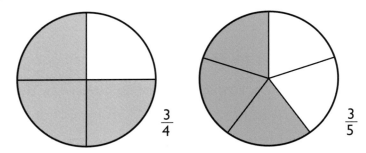

Imagine a cake being cut up. You would eat more cake if you ate three of four pieces than if you ate three of five pieces!

Fractions and decimals

To change a fraction to a decimal, we change it to an equivalent fraction with a denominator (bottom number) of 10 or 100

Examples

   (i) $\frac{1}{2}$ is the same as $\frac{5}{10}$ 0.5

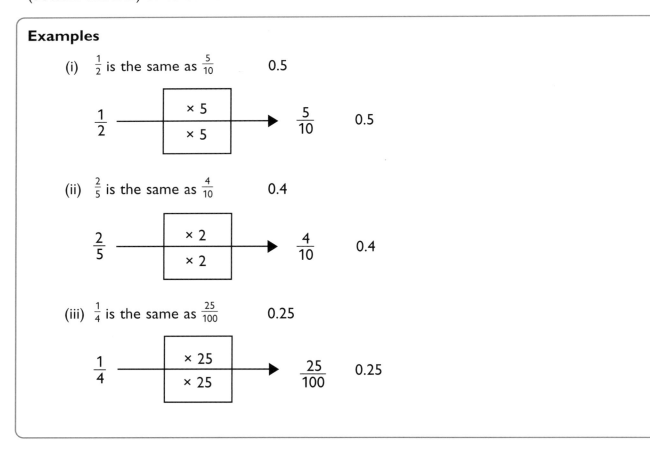

   (ii) $\frac{2}{5}$ is the same as $\frac{4}{10}$ 0.4

   (iii) $\frac{1}{4}$ is the same as $\frac{25}{100}$ 0.25

Decimals and percentages

To change a decimal to a percentage, we simply multiply by 100

Examples

    (i)   0.5 = 50%

    (ii) 0.4 = 40%

    (iii) 0.25 = 25%

The fraction wall

- You need to understand the approximate sizes of the most common fractions and their percentage equivalents.

A good way to see how fractions and percentages compare is by using the 'fraction wall':

whole						1 (100%)				
halves		$\frac{1}{2}$					50%			
thirds		$\frac{1}{3}$			$\frac{1}{3}$			$33\frac{1}{3}$%		
quarters		$\frac{1}{4}$		$\frac{1}{4}$		25%			25%	
fifths		$\frac{1}{5}$	$\frac{1}{5}$		$\frac{1}{5}$		20%		20%	
sixths	$\frac{1}{6}$		$\frac{1}{6}$		$\frac{1}{6}$		$16\frac{2}{3}$%	$16\frac{2}{3}$%		$16\frac{2}{3}$%
eighths	$\frac{1}{8}$		$\frac{1}{8}$	$\frac{1}{8}$		$\frac{1}{8}$	12.5%	12.5%	12.5%	12.5%
tenths	$\frac{1}{10}$	$\frac{1}{10}$	$\frac{1}{10}$	$\frac{1}{10}$	$\frac{1}{10}$	10%	10%	10%	10%	10%

Using a ruler held vertically, it is now easy to see that (for example):

$\frac{2}{6} = \frac{1}{3}$, or $\frac{8}{10} > \frac{3}{4}$

Ratio

Fractions (such as $\frac{3}{5}$) compare the number of parts we have (in this case 3) to the total number of parts in the whole (in this case 5).

Ratios can do the same thing, but they can be much more useful.

Look at this group of shapes.

There are four squares and three circles.

The fraction of the shapes which are square is $\frac{4}{7}$

The ratio of the number of squares to the total number of shapes is 4 : 7 but with ratio, we can go further.

We can also say that the ratio of the number of squares to the number of circles is 4 : 3

Some fractions can be simplified.

Example

$\frac{6}{9}$ can be simplified to $\frac{2}{3}$

Some ratios can be simplified in the same way.

Example

10 : 8 can be simplified to 5 : 4

Sample questions

Try these sample questions for yourself. The answers are given at the back of the book.

Some of the questions involve ideas met in earlier work which may not be covered by the notes in this chapter. (See the Useful resources section of the Introduction if you need to refresh your skills or knowledge.)

1.20 In this strip of squares, two of the five have been shaded to show the fraction $\frac{2}{5}$

   $\dfrac{2}{5}$

Sketch a similar diagram to show the fraction $\frac{5}{8}$ (2)

1.21 Find $\frac{3}{4}$ of 56 cm. (2)

1.22 Slimy the slug was 60 mm long at the beginning of July. At the end of the month he was $1\frac{1}{4}$ times as long. How long was Slimy at the end of July? (2)

1.23 Gill's aunt gave her £45 and asked her to save two-thirds of it. How much did Gill save? (2)

1.24 (a) Which is bigger, $\frac{1}{6}$ or $\frac{1}{7}$? (1)

(b) Which is bigger, $\frac{3}{4}$ or $\frac{2}{3}$? (1)

1.25 Lachlan has drawn a machine which finds equivalent fractions.

$\frac{2}{3}$ ──→ [× 4 / × 4] ──→ $\frac{8}{12}$

(a) Fill in the details to show how the machine can change $\frac{1}{2}$ into sixths. (2)

$\frac{1}{2}$ ──→ [ ] ──→

(b) Fill in the details to show how the machine can change $\frac{3}{4}$ to twelfths. (2)

$\frac{3}{4}$ ──→ [ ] ──→

1.26 Complete the table, showing the equivalent fractions, decimals and percentages. (9)

Fraction (in simplest form)	$\frac{1}{2}$				$\frac{3}{10}$
Decimal		0.75		0.7	
Percentage	50%		40%		

1.27 Sally has five cats and two dogs.

(a) What is the ratio of the number of cats to the number of dogs?
Give your answer in the form _ : _ . (2)

(b) What is the ratio of the number of dogs to the total number of pets? (2)

S   Summary

Remember that you should be familiar with all of the material in National Curriculum Key Stage 1; for example, rounding integers to the nearest 10 or 100

You should also now be able to do the following:

1.   Recognise and describe number patterns and relationships, including multiples, factors and squares.   **4**

2.   Understand the concept of a prime number.   **4+**

3.   Order, add and subtract negative numbers in context.   **5**

4.   Use your understanding of place value to multiply and divide whole numbers by 10 or 100   **4**

5.   Round numbers efficiently.

6.   Recognise approximate proportions of a whole and use simple fractions and percentages to describe these.   **4**

Use the glossary at the back of the book for definitions of key words.

TY   Test yourself

Before moving on to the next chapter, make sure you can answer the following questions.

The answers are at the back of the book.

1.   Here is a number grid.

1	2	3	4	5	6
7	8	9	10	11	12
13	14	15	16	17	18
19	20	21	22	23	24
25	26	27	28	29	30
31	32	33	34	35	36

(a)   Circle 3 and then every third number.

(b)   Put a cross on 4 and then every fourth number.

(c)   What can you say about the numbers which are circled and also have a cross?

2. Here is part of a multiplication square which has been partially completed.

×	2	3	4	5	6	7	8
2				10			
3	6						
4							
5		15					
6							
7							
8							

(a) Carefully shade in all the multiples of 9

(b) Put a circle around all the square numbers.

(c) If the square were completed, which numbers would appear most often?

3. (a) What is a prime number?

(b) Without looking at the table on page 2 write, in order, the prime numbers up to at least 30

4. Jasmine has three number cards.

(a) Using all of these cards, Jasmine can make three-digit numbers such as 354

(i) List, in order of increasing size, all six of the three-digit numbers which Jasmine can make.

(ii) Round each of the numbers in part (i) to the nearest ten.

(iii) How many of the numbers you made in part (i) are divisible by 3?

(iv) Which of the numbers you made in part (i) are multiples of 5?

(v) Write down the number which is a hundred times the size of the largest number you made in part (i).

(vi) Write down the number which you get if you divide the smallest number in part (i) by ten.

(b) Using pairs of the same cards, Jasmine can make three proper fractions: $\frac{3}{4}, \frac{3}{5}$ and $\frac{4}{5}$

Which is   (i)   the smallest

           (ii)   the largest

of these fractions?

Hint: it may help to change each fraction to a percentage.

Chapter 2: 13+ Number

2.1 Properties of numbers

Prime factorisation

- You need to know how to express any number as a product of its prime factors.

Of course, you can't go much further unless you know what the prime numbers are. Check the table on page 2 in Chapter 1, or at least remember that the first five primes are 2, 3, 5, 7 and 11

Procedure

1. If you can, divide by 2 and keep dividing by 2 as many times as possible.

2. Then divide by 3 as many times as possible.

3. Then divide by 5, 7, 11 etc. in turn, each as many times as possible until you reach 1

4. Write the original number as a product of all the primes that went into it, in order.

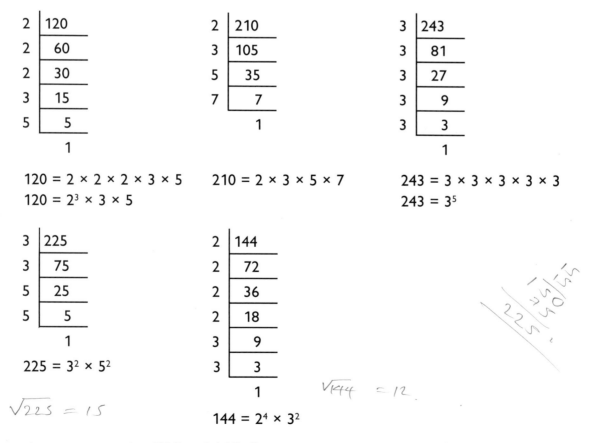

2	120
2	60
2	30
3	15
5	5
	1

$120 = 2 \times 2 \times 2 \times 3 \times 5$
$120 = 2^3 \times 3 \times 5$

2	210
3	105
5	35
7	7
	1

$210 = 2 \times 3 \times 5 \times 7$

3	243
3	81
3	27
3	9
3	3
	1

$243 = 3 \times 3 \times 3 \times 3 \times 3$
$243 = 3^5$

3	225
3	75
5	25
5	5
	1

$225 = 3^2 \times 5^2$

$\sqrt{225} = 15$

2	144
2	72
2	36
2	18
3	9
3	3
	1

$144 = 2^4 \times 3^2$

$\sqrt{144} = 12$

These last two examples (225 and 144) illustrate an important point: **if the prime factors all appear an even number of times, then the original number was a square number and vice versa.**

The **highest common factor (HCF)** of two or more numbers is the largest factor of the numbers. It helps to consider the numbers as products of prime factors.

For example, 12 may be written as $2 \times 2 \times 3$ and 20 may be written as $2 \times 2 \times 5$. The HCF of 12 and 20 is 4 (2×2).

The **lowest common multiple (LCM)** of two or more numbers is the smallest multiple of the numbers.

For example, the LCM of 12 and 20 is 60 ($2 \times 2 \times 3 \times 5$).

Addition and subtraction with negative numbers

- You need to be able to give short answers to questions involving negative numbers.

We use these rules to deal with positive and negative numbers:
- adding a **positive** is just ordinary adding
- adding a **negative** is equivalent to subtracting
- subtracting a **positive** is just ordinary subtracting
- subtracting a **negative** is equivalent to adding

Let's try a few questions.

$12 + {}^-3$ is the same as	$12 - 3 = 9$
$12 - {}^-3$ is the same as	$12 + 3 = 15$
${}^-5 + {}^-4$ is the same as	${}^-5 - 4 = {}^-9$
${}^-5 - {}^-4$ is the same as	${}^-5 + 4 = {}^-1$

Multiplication and division with negative numbers

- You need to be able to multiply and divide using various combinations of positive and negative numbers.

Positive or negative?

To put it simply, numbers below zero are negative, and numbers above zero are positive. Negative numbers always have that little negative sign ($^-$) in front of them to show everybody who they are.

Multiplication with negative numbers

We know that when we multiply two positive numbers we get a positive answer, so it would seem likely that if we multiplied a positive by a **negative** number, the answer would change to negative too. And that's what happens.

$7 \times 4 = 28$
$7 \times {}^-4 = {}^-28$

The same is true if we multiply a negative number by a positive number. $-3 \times 8 = -24$

Predictably, perhaps, multiplying a negative number by another negative $-5 \times -9 = 45$
number makes the answer positive.

Division with negative numbers

Division follows very similar rules to multiplication. A positive number $72 \div -8 = -9$
divided by a negative number, or vice versa, gives a negative answer,
but one negative number divided by another makes the answer positive. $-56 \div 7 = -8$

$-16 \div -2 = 8$

Summary

We can put all this information into a table which works for both multiplication and division.

multiply or divide this ⟶ by this ↓	positive	negative
positive	**+**	**−**
negative	**−**	**+**

Sample questions

Try these sample questions for yourself. The answers are given at the back of the book.

Some of the questions involve ideas met in earlier work which may not be covered by the notes in this chapter.

2.1   Write down:

(a)   the **sum** of 13 and 29   42   (1)

(b)   the **difference** between 7 and 23   16   (1)

(c)   the **product** of 8 and 9   72   (1)

(d)   the **remainder** when 11 is divided by 4   3   (1)

(e)   the **square** of 8   64   (1)

(f)   the **square root** of 16   4   (1)

(g)   the **cube** of 4   64   (1)

(h)   the **cube root** of 8   2   (1)

(i)   **3 to the power of 4**   12 ✗ $3^4 = 3 \times 3 \times 3 \times 3 = 81$ (1)

3^4 10^7 2^2 8^3

21   2×2 $8 \times 8 \times 8$

2.2 Look at these numbers.

1   3   15   18   21   39   56   60   81

From the list, write down:

(a) a multiple of 13   *39*   (1)

(b) a factor of 12   *3*   (1)

(c) the product of 8 and 7   *56*   (1)

✳ (d) the square root of 9   *~~81~~ 3*   (1)

(e) a cube number   *1*   (1)

(f) a prime number.   *3*   (1)

You may use a number more than once if you wish.

2.3 (a) List the **prime numbers** between 30 and 50   *31, 37, 41, 43, 47*   (3)

(b) Which number can be written as the **product of primes** $2^3 \times 3 \times 5$?   *120*   (1)

(c) Write 2790 as a product of primes, using index notation.   *$2 \times 3^2 \times 5 \times 31$*   (3)

2.4 (a) Write these numbers in order of increasing size: *$-3, -2, -1, 0, 3, 5, 7$*   (2)

$^-2$ 3   0 $^-3$ 5 $^-1$ 7

(b) Find the value of each of the following:

(i) $^-3 + 5$ = *~~m18~~ 2*   (1)

(ii) $1 + {}^-4$ = *-3*   (1)

(iii) $^-2 - 1$ = *-3*   (1)

(iv) $3 - {}^-4$ = *7*   (1)

(c) Find the value of each of the following:

(i) $^-2 \times 5$ = *-10*   (1)

(ii) $5 \times {}^-4$ = *-20*   (1)

(iii) $^-3 \times {}^-4$ = *12*   (1)

(iv) $^-4 \div 2$ = *-2*   (1)

✳ (v) $2 \div {}^-4$ = *$-\frac{2}{2}$*   ✳   *$-\frac{1}{2}$*   (1)

(vi) $^-6 \div {}^-2$ = *3*   (1)

2.2 Place value and ordering

Multiplying and dividing by 10, 100 and 1000

- You need to be able to multiply and divide any number by 10 or 100 or 1000 without a calculator.

First remind yourself of the basics on pages 6–7 of Chapter 1.

Rule 1: Multiplying by 10 moves the decimal point **right** (or the digits **left**).

Rule 2: Dividing by 10 moves the decimal point **left** (or the digits **right**).

×	100	is	×	10	done twice
×	1000	is	×	10	done three times
÷	100	is	÷	10	done twice
÷	1000	is	÷	10	done three times

Examples

2.7	÷	10	=	0.27		1.23	×	10	=	12.3
2.7	÷	100	=	0.027		1.23	×	100	=	123
2.7	÷	1000	=	0.0027		1.23	×	1000	=	1230
0.05	×	10	=	0.5		98.7	÷	10	=	9.87
0.05	×	100	=	5		98.7	÷	100	=	0.987
0.05	×	1000	=	50		98.7	÷	1000	=	0.0987

It is an extremely bright idea to make up lots of examples with your calculator. You'll soon be able to get 100% correct!

Ordering and rounding decimals

● You need to be able to put decimal numbers in order and round them to any number of decimal places.

Ordering decimals

This is made much easier by remembering that you can always write zeros at the right-hand end of any decimal number without changing its value.

0.5 is the same as 0.50 and 0.500 and 0.5000 and ...

Example

Sort these numbers into increasing order of size:

2.71   0.721   0.17   0.7   1.271   1.72

1. Ignore the decimal parts of each number initially and put them in whole number order.

    0.721   0.17   0.7   1.271   1.72   2.71

2. Make all the decimal parts the same length by writing extra zeros where necessary.

    0.721   0.170   0.700   1.271   1.720   2.710

3. Sort the decimal parts without disturbing the whole number order.

    0.170   0.700   0.721   1.271   1.720   2.710

4. Remove the extra zeros.

    0.17   0.7   0.721   1.271   1.72   2.71

With practice you will develop your own short cuts to this procedure, until you can do the entire sort in your head. It's a handy little skill to acquire!

Rounding to two decimal places

Draw a vertical line after the second decimal place to separate the second and third positions. If the number after the line is 5 or more, then round **up**. If the number after the line is 4 or less, then round **down**.

Round **up**: add 1 to the digit **before** the vertical line.

Round **down**: remove all digits **after** the vertical line. Don't do anything else!

Examples

$3.24 | \textcircled{7} 1$
$\rightarrow 3.2\mathbf{5}$

$2.47 | \textcircled{1} 3$
$\rightarrow 2.47$

Similarly:

2.95 → 3.0 to 1 d.p.

2.718 18 → 2.7182 to 4 d.p.

Sample questions

Try these sample questions for yourself. The answers are given at the back of the book.

Some of the questions involve ideas met in earlier work which may not be covered by the notes in this chapter. (See the Useful resources section of the Introduction if you need to refresh your skills or knowledge.)

2.5 (a) Find the value of each of the following:

   (i) 5.07 × 10 $= 50.7$ (1)

   (ii) 5.07 ÷ 100 $= 0.050507$ (1)

   (iii) 0.507 × 1000 $= 507$ (1)

   (b) Use the fact that 8.2 × 13.5 = 110.7 to write down the value of each of the following:

   (i) 82 × 1.35 110.7 (1)

   (ii) 0.82 × 13.5 11.07 (1)

   (iii) 820 × 0.001 35 $= 1.107$ (2)

   ✳ (iv) 11 070 ÷ 13.5 $= 0.82$ 820 (2)

2.6 (a) Write the following in order of increasing size: (2)

   2.13   3.21   3.12   2.31   1.32 $1.32, 2.13, 2.31, 3.12, 3.21$

   (b) Use the correct symbol (<, >, ≤ or ≥) to make each of these statements true:

   (i) 0.023 $<$ 0.203 (1)

   (ii) $\frac{3}{4}$ $>$ $\frac{1}{2}$ (1)

   (iii) x is a number greater than or equal to 4, so x $\geq$ 4 (1)

   (iv) y is a number less than or equal to ⁻3, so y $<$ ⁻3 (1)

2.3 Estimation and approximation

Significant figures

- You need to know about rounding numbers, significant figures and approximating.

Remind yourself about rounding decimals by turning back to page 24.

In many situations, particularly when interpreting a full calculator display, care has to be taken that the answer quoted is given to an appropriate level of accuracy. What is appropriate? Well, usually the figures in the question indicate the sort of accuracy which is required. For example, finding the circumference of a pond 4.5 m in diameter would not need such an accurate answer as if the pond were given as having a diameter of 4.512 271 9 m. Common sense is usually the best guide!

Significant figures in whole numbers

All the figures in a whole number are significant, except sometimes for zeros at the end. Thus 4500 is written to 2 significant figures, but 4000 is only to 1 significant figure. Similar ideas for rounding decimals apply when rounding whole numbers.

Examples

Round the number 23 456 to

(i) 3 significant figures   2 3 4|5 6
     Round up   2 3 5 0 0

(ii) 2 significant figures   2 3|4 5 6
     Round down   2 3 0 0 0

Significant figures in decimals

All the figures in a decimal are significant, except for zeros at the **beginning**. Thus 0.52 and 0.000 052 are both to 2 significant figures, but 0.005 200 52 is to 6 significant figures. (You must include the zeros in the middle.) Similarly, 0.052 000 is to **5** significant figures, since only zeros at the beginning are not significant.

Example

My calculator display gives the answer to a problem as 47 176.455 55
Write this to 3 significant figures   4 7 1|7 6 . 4 5 5 5 5
Round up   4 7 2 0 0

Notice that, as with all rounding situations, the result is the same order of magnitude (rough size) as the original number. Here both numbers (47 176.455 55 and 47 200) are roughly 47 000 (to 2 significant figures). Don't make the common mistake of leaving out the vital zeros before the decimal point. The answer is **not** 472!

Approximation and estimation

Sometimes we want an approximate idea of the answer to a calculation, perhaps because we are in a hurry or because we want to check that the answer we have already worked out is about right. Whatever the reason, we can find a rough answer by rounding each number to 1 significant figure and calculating the result, either on paper or using a calculator.

Example

$$\frac{(417.6 \times 2.91)}{(50.8 + 9.73)} \quad \text{becomes} \quad \frac{(400 \times 3)}{(50 + 10)} \quad \rightarrow \quad \frac{1200}{60} \quad = 20$$

This compares well with the exact answer which is . . . . Well, I'm sure you can work it out for yourself!

Sample questions

Try these sample questions for yourself. The answers are given at the back of the book.

Some of the questions involve ideas met in earlier work which may not be covered by the notes in this chapter.

2.7   (a)   Round:

    (i)   545 to the nearest hundred *500* (1)

    (ii) 395 to the nearest ten. *400* (1)

  (b)   Write:

    (i)   81.49 to 1 decimal place (1 d.p.) *81.5* (1)

    (ii) 81.49 to 3 significant figures (3 s.f.) *81.5* (1)

2.8   Estimate, to 1 significant figure:

  (a) 5.95×7.02 *40* (1)

  (b) $81.3 \div 8.98$ *9* (1)

2.4 Fractions, decimals, percentages and ratio

Calculating *A* as a fraction of *B*

- You need to be able to compare two numbers using fractions and percentages.

This method is very easy!

Example

A gardener planted 30 seeds and 12 failed to germinate.
What is this as a fraction?

What is 12 as a fraction of 30? Simple! $\dfrac{12}{30}$ That's it!

Now we can simplify this fraction in order to write it in its lowest terms:

$$\dfrac{12}{30} \xrightarrow{\;\div 2 \text{ top \& bottom}\;} \dfrac{6}{15} \xrightarrow{\;\div 3 \text{ top \& bottom}\;} \dfrac{2}{5}$$

In general, to write *A* as a fraction of *B*, just write it as $\dfrac{A}{B}$ and simplify as we did above.

Percentages

You want it as a percentage? Just make the fraction out of 100

$$\dfrac{2}{5} \xrightarrow{\;\times 2 \text{ top \& bottom}\;} \dfrac{4}{10} \xrightarrow{\;\times 10 \text{ top \& bottom}\;} \dfrac{40}{100} \xrightarrow{\;\text{which is}\;} 40\%$$

Remember that the **original** value or amount is the one which we call 100% when working out profits and discounts, or increases and decreases.

Example

A dress is reduced in a sale from £18 to £14.40

What is this as a percentage?

A reduction from £18 to £14.40 is a reduction of £3.60 on the original amount of £18

As a percentage of £18 this is calculated as follows:

$$\dfrac{3.60}{18.00} \xrightarrow{\;\times 100 \text{ top \& bottom}\;} \overset{20}{\dfrac{360}{1800}}_{(100)} \xrightarrow{\;\div 18 \text{ top \& bottom}\;} \dfrac{20}{100} \xrightarrow{\;\text{which is}\;} 20\%$$

$45\% = \dfrac{45}{100} \qquad 50\% = \dfrac{50}{100} = \dfrac{1}{2}$

Calculating a fraction or percentage of a quantity

- You have to know how to calculate a fraction or a percentage of a quantity without a calculator.

Remember that a fraction is simply a division into equal portions. To find a fraction of something, you simply have to divide the quantity up into the correct number of portions, and then take the number of portions which are required.

Example (using fractions)

Find $\frac{3}{4}$ of £1.80

The first thing to notice is that we want to divide the money into four equal portions (quarters); then we want three of these portions.

To find $\frac{1}{4}$ of £1.80 we simply divide it by 4. Always **d**ivide by the **d**enominator!

$$\begin{array}{r} 0.45 \\ 4\overline{\smash{\big)}\,1.80} \end{array}$$

so $\frac{1}{4}$ of £1.80 is 45p.

Now, $\frac{3}{4}$ is 3 lots of $\frac{1}{4}$,

therefore $\frac{3}{4}$ of £1.80 is £1.35 (3 × 45p).

Memory aid: DIVIDE by the DENOMINATOR, then TIMES by the TOP.

An easy trick with percentages is to base all your working around the calculation of 10%, which is simple to find since it is just one-tenth. 5% is then half of it, 20% is double it and so on.

Example (using percentages)

Find 35% of 140 kg

	10% of 140 kg is 14 kg (one tenth)
Therefore:	5% of 140 kg is 7 kg (half of 10%)
	30% of 140 kg is 42 kg (3 × 10%)
Therefore:	35% of 140 kg is 49 kg (5% + 30%)

Another trick is to use percentages of 100 which, of course, don't even need to be worked out! If you want to find 36% of 50 cm, just use the fact that 36% of 100 cm is 36 cm, and then halve it to get 18 cm. Similarly, to find 17% of 200, just say '17% of 100 is 17', and then it's clear that 17% of 200 must be 34

Fraction, decimal and percentage equivalents

● You need to be able to transfer easily between fractions, decimals and percentages.

Here is a cunning little diagram which has helped many children through the fraction/percentage/decimal maze. I hope it helps you too!

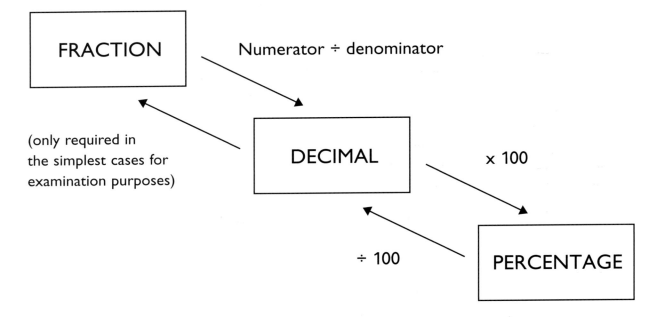

Example 1 (writing a fraction as a decimal and as a percentage)

$\frac{3}{4}$

Write the fraction $\frac{3}{4}$ as a decimal and as a percentage.

$3 \div 4 = 0.75$ or $4 \overline{\smash{\big)}\,3.00}$ = 0.75   if you are doing it by hand.

Now to write 0.75 as a percentage, we simply multiply by 100: $0.75 \times 100 = 75\%$

Example 2 (ordering fractions, decimals and percentages)

Place in increasing order of size: 0.9   78% $\frac{4}{5}$ $\frac{7}{8}$

Method

Write as decimals:	0.9	0.78	0.8	0.875
Sort the decimals:	0.78	0.8	0.875	0.9
Rewrite as they were	78%	$\frac{4}{5}$	$\frac{7}{8}$	0.9

Addition, subtraction, multiplication and division of fractions

● You need to be able to add, subtract, multiply and divide fractions and mixed numbers.

A reminder of the basics

1. You cannot add or subtract two fractions with different denominators. You must make the denominators the same first.

2. To make two denominators the same, find the smallest number into which both denominators divide (the lowest common multiple or lowest common denominator) and use equivalent fractions to scale up the two fractions accordingly.

3. When adding mixed numbers, work out the whole number part first and then add the fractions. When subtracting, multiplying or dividing fractions, convert mixed numbers into improper 'top heavy' fractions before proceeding. This can make subtractions easier; for multiplication and division it is vital.

The following table shows the sorts of calculations you can expect to meet at each level.

	Level 1	**Level 2**	**Level 3**
+	$\frac{3}{7} + \frac{2}{7} = \frac{5}{7}$	$1\frac{1}{2} + \frac{2}{3} = 2\frac{1}{6}$	
−	$\frac{8}{11} - \frac{5}{11} = \frac{3}{11}$	$1\frac{1}{3} - \frac{3}{4} = \frac{7}{12}$	
×		$\frac{3}{5} \times \frac{2}{3} = \frac{2}{5}$	$1\frac{1}{3} \times \frac{3}{4} = 1$
÷		$\frac{3}{4} \div \frac{2}{3} = 1\frac{1}{8}$	$2\frac{1}{2} \div 1\frac{3}{4} = 1\frac{3}{7}$

Example 1 (addition)

$3\frac{3}{4} + 2\frac{4}{5}$ is the same as $5 + \frac{3}{4} + \frac{4}{5}$

Now, $\frac{3}{4} + \frac{4}{5} \rightarrow \frac{15}{20} + \frac{16}{20} = \frac{31}{20}$ or $1\frac{11}{20}$

So $3\frac{3}{4} + 2\frac{4}{5} \rightarrow 5 + 1\frac{11}{20} = 6\frac{11}{20}$

Example 2 (subtraction)

$3\frac{3}{4} - 2\frac{4}{5}$ First change to improper fractions $3\frac{3}{4} - 2\frac{4}{5} = \frac{15}{4} - \frac{14}{5}$

Remember, the denominator stays the same. To find the new numerator, use the word formula:
new numerator = whole number × denominator + old numerator

Then proceed as usual $\frac{15}{4} - \frac{14}{5} \rightarrow \frac{75}{20} - \frac{56}{20} = \frac{19}{20}$

Example 3 (multiplication)

$3\frac{3}{4} \times 2\frac{4}{5} \rightarrow \frac{15}{4} \times \frac{14}{5}$ cancel 5s $\rightarrow$ $\frac{3}{4} \times \frac{14}{1}$ cancel 2s $\rightarrow$ $\frac{3}{2} \times \frac{7}{1} = \frac{21}{2}$ or $10\frac{1}{2}$

Example 4 (division)

$3\frac{3}{4} \div 2\frac{4}{5} \rightarrow \frac{15}{4} \div \frac{14}{5}$ invert the second fraction $\rightarrow$ $\frac{15}{4} \times \frac{5}{14} = \frac{75}{56}$ or $1\frac{19}{56}$

Calculating with ratios

● You need to understand different ways of calculating with ratios.

It often helps to think of ratios as parts, and to begin by seeing how many parts are involved altogether. That way they become fractions.

Example 1

[handwritten: 2 + 5 = 7]

Share £42 in the ratio 2 : 5

[handwritten: A   B]

2 parts + 5 parts = 7 parts altogether, so each part is $\frac{1}{7}$ of £42, in other words £6

Answer: 2 parts = 2 × £6 and 5 parts = 5 × £6

      So £42 shared in the ratio 2 : 5 is £12 : £30

[handwritten: 12 : 30]

[handwritten right side: 75 : 25,   3 : 1,   30,   3 : 2,   18 : 12,   = 5]

Example 2

A class contains boys and girls in the ratio 3 : 2

If there are 12 girls, how many boys are there?

First be clear that because of the order of the words, the 3 in the ratio goes with *boys* and the 2 goes with *girls*. We are told that the 2 in the ratio represents 12 girls, so each part of the ratio represents 6 children.

Answer: The number of boys is 3 (from the ratio) multiplied by 6 (the number of children per part). So there are 18 boys in the class.

Adapting a recipe

Sometimes you have to change the quantities in a recipe so that it serves a different number of people. Ratios to the rescue!

Example 3

[handwritten left margin: 6, 300, 720, 180, 6 and 1, 50, 120, 30, 1, 6]

Apple Pie (serves 4)	Adapt this recipe	Apple Pie (serves 5)
200 g shortcrust pastry	for 4 people to	250 g shortcrust pastry
480 g cooking apples	serve 5 people.	600 g cooking apples
120 g brown sugar		150 g brown sugar
4 cloves		5 cloves

We first calculate one person's share (dividing by 4) and then multiply this by 5, as has been done above. This method is called the **unitary method**, and can be used for either increases or decreases.

Sample questions

Try these sample questions for yourself. The answers are given at the back of the book.

Some of the questions involve ideas met in earlier work which may not be covered by the notes in this chapter.

2.9 (a) Write the **fraction** representing 5 parts of a whole containing 8 parts. $\frac{5}{8}$ (1)

(b) What fraction of this rectangle has been shaded? (1)

$$\frac{8}{20} = \frac{4}{10} = \frac{2}{5}$$

(c) Using the words **denominator** and **numerator**, name the parts of the fraction $\frac{2}{3}$ *numerator* *denominator* (1)

2.10 (a) Change the fraction $\frac{3}{5}$ into:

(i) an **equivalent** fraction with denominator 10 $\frac{6}{10}$ (1)

(ii) a **decimal** (decimal fraction) 0.6 (1)

(iii) a **percentage**. $\frac{6}{10} \times 10 \quad \frac{60}{100} = 60\%$ (1)

(b) Write the fraction $\frac{18}{30}$ in its **simplest form (lowest terms).** $\frac{9}{15} \quad \frac{3}{5}$ (1)

2.11 (a) (i) Write the **improper fraction** $\frac{17}{5}$ as a **mixed number.** $3\frac{2}{5}$ (1)

(ii) Write the mixed number $2\frac{2}{5}$ as an improper fraction. $\frac{12}{5}$ (1)

(b) Write the mixed number $1\frac{3}{4}$ as:

(i) a decimal 1.75 (1)

(ii) a percentage. 175% (1)

2.12 Calculate

(a) $\frac{3}{13} + \frac{7}{13}$ $\frac{10}{13}$ (1)

(b) $\frac{1}{2} + \frac{2}{3}$ $\frac{3}{5}$ $\frac{3+4}{6} = \frac{7}{6}$ or $1\frac{1}{6}$ (1)

(c) $1\frac{1}{3} + \frac{3}{4}$ $\frac{4}{3} + \frac{3}{4}$ $\frac{16+9}{12} = \frac{25}{12} = 2\frac{1}{12}$ (2)

(d) $\frac{7}{8} - \frac{3}{8}$ $= \frac{4}{8} = \frac{1}{2}$ (1)

■■□ (e) $\frac{2}{3} - \frac{1}{2}$ $\frac{4-3}{6} = \frac{1}{6}$ (1)

■■□ (f) $1\frac{1}{3} - \frac{3}{4}$ $\frac{4}{3} - \frac{3}{4}$ $\frac{16-9}{12} = \frac{7}{12}$ (2)

2.13 Calculate

■■□ (a) $\frac{3}{4} \times \frac{2}{3}$ = $\frac{6}{12} = \frac{1}{2}$ (1)

■■■ (b) $1\frac{1}{4} \times \frac{2}{3}$ = $\frac{5}{4} \times \frac{2}{3} = \frac{10}{12} = \frac{5}{6}$ (2)

■■□ (c) $\frac{1}{2} \div \frac{2}{3}$ $\frac{1}{2} \times \frac{3}{2} = \frac{3}{4}$ (2)

■■■ (d) $1\frac{1}{3} \div 2\frac{3}{4}$ $\frac{4}{3} \div \frac{11}{4} \Rightarrow \frac{4}{3} \times \frac{4}{11} = \frac{16}{33}$ (3)

2.14 (a) There are 11 pupils in a school team. Six are boys. Write the ratio $6:5$

(i) boys to the total $6:11$ (1)

(ii) boys to girls $6:5$ (1)

(iii) girls to boys. $5:6$ (1)

(b) Write the ratio 8 : 12 in its simplest form. $2:3$ (1)

■■□ 2.15 To make six chocolate crunchies, these quantities are used.

To make six crunchies
Cornflakes	150 g	600g
Chocolate	125 g	500g
Honey	10 ml	40ml
Sultanas	25 g	100g

Rewrite the recipe to make 24 chocolate crunchies. (4)

S # Summary

Remember that you should be familiar with all of the material in Chapter 1.

You should also now be able to do the following:

1. Understand prime factors and express a number as a product of primes, using index notation. **5+**

2. Order, add and subtract negative numbers in the abstract. **5+**

3. Use your understanding of place value to multiply and divide whole numbers and decimals by 10, 100 and 1000 **5**

■■□ 4. In making estimates, round to one significant figure and multiply and divide mentally. **7**

5. Reduce a fraction to its simplest form by cancelling common factors and solve simple problems involving ratio and direct proportion. **5**

6.   Calculate fractional or percentage parts of quantities and measurements, using a calculator where appropriate.   **5**

■■□ 7.   Be aware of which number to consider as 100 per cent, or a whole, in problems involving comparisons, and use this to evaluate one number as a fraction or percentage of another.   **6**

✳ 8.   Understand and use the equivalences between fractions, decimals and percentages, and calculate using ratios in appropriate situations.   **6**

✳ 9.   Add and subtract fractions by writing them with a common denominator.   **6**

✳ 10.   Multiply and divide fractions, including easy mixed numbers.   **6+**

■■□ 11.   Understand and use proportional changes, calculating the result of any proportional change using only multiplicative methods.   **7**

Use the glossary at the back of the book for definitions of key words.

Test yourself

TY

Before moving on to the next chapter, make sure you can answer the following questions. The answers are at the back of the book.

1.   Complete this jumbled multiplication table as quickly as you can. Record your time in minutes and seconds. (A time of less than 2 minutes is quite good!)

×	4	9	2	5	8	6	1	3	7
3							3		
9									
8									
2									
6									
5									
4									
7									
1									

✳ **Footnotes**

8. ISEB Level 1 only requires a limited amount of conversion between fractions, decimals and percentages. ISEB Levels 2 and 3 require the full conversion of all three, and the ability to order them.

9. and 10. ISEB Level 1 requires the addition and subtraction of fractions only with the same denominator. It does not require the multiplication and division of fractions. ISEB Level 2 requires the addition and subtraction of both fractions with different denominators and mixed fractions. It also requires the multiplication and division of proper fractions only. ISEB Level 3 requires the addition and subtraction of both fractions with different denominators and mixed fractions. It also requires the multiplication and division of both proper and mixed fractions. (Refer to the table on page 31)

2. Look at these numbers.

4   5   8   16   19   27   30   32

From the list, choose a **different** answer for each of the following:

(a) a prime number 19

(b) the square root of 16 4

(c) a factor of 15 5

(d) a multiple of 4 16

(e) a square number 27 16

(f) a cube number 8

3. Look at the eight directed number cards below.

$^-4$ $^-2$ 5   8   6 $^-5$ 4 $^-3$

(a) What is the sum of all eight cards? 25 9

(b) Choose two cards which have a sum of zero. $-4, 4$

(c) Which two cards give the lowest product? 8×-5

(d) Using all eight directed number cards once only, fill in the gaps in the calculations below.

(i) -4 + 5 = 1

(ii) 6 − 4 = 2

(iii) -5 × -3 = 15

(iv) 8 ÷ -2 = $^-4$

4. (a) Express the number 630 as the product of prime factors, using indices. $3^2 \times 5 \times 7 \times 2$

(b) Evaluate $2^3 \times 3^2 \times 5 \times 7^2$ $17,640$

5. (a) Write the following numbers in order of size, starting with the smallest:

6.606   6.6006   6.066   6.660 $6, 6.066, 6.6, 6.606, 6.66$

(b) What is the difference between the largest and the smallest of the numbers in part (a)? 0.660

6. By first writing each number correct to 1 significant figure, estimate the value of the following:

(a) $\dfrac{59.3 \times 30.4}{5.75}$ = 300

(b) $\dfrac{41.7 \times 3.2}{0.63 \times 49.4}$

36

7. Complete the following table to show rows of equivalent fractions, decimals and percentages:

Fraction	Decimal	Percentage
$\frac{7}{20}$	0.35	35%
$\frac{1}{4}$	0.25	25%
$\frac{6}{5}$	1.2	120%
$\frac{3}{20}$	0.15	15%

(handwritten: $\frac{60}{50}=\frac{120}{100}$ $\frac{6}{5}$)

(handwritten right margin: $13 \times 5 = 65$, $\frac{15}{100}$)

8. (a) Express 26% as a fraction in its lowest terms.

    (handwritten: $\frac{26}{100}=\frac{13}{50}$)

   (b) Write $\frac{13}{20}$ as a decimal.

    (handwritten: $\frac{13}{20} \times 5 = \frac{65}{100} = 0.65$)

   (c) Calculate $\frac{2}{3}$ of £4.80   *(handwritten: £3.20)*

   (d) Express 0.54 as a fraction in its lowest terms.

    (handwritten: $\frac{54}{100} = \frac{27}{50}$)

   (e) Find 15% of £40

    (handwritten: $10\% = £4$ $5\% = £2$ ANS = £6)

9. (a) Last year in Roley there were 50 reported cases of 'flu. This year the number dropped by 12%. How many cases have been reported this year?   *(handwritten: 44)*

    (handwritten: $10\% = 5$, $2\% = 1$, $12\% = 6$)

   (b) When a farmer digs up 120 kg of potatoes, he finds that 20% are rotten. Of the remaining healthy potatoes, 12.5% are too small to sell. What is the mass of healthy potatoes large enough to sell?

    (handwritten: 80% 500d $80\% \times 120 = 96$ kg $96 \div 8 = 12$ kg   84 kg)

   (c) At a party, 15 children share three identical cakes equally. What fraction of a cake does each child receive?   *(handwritten: $\frac{1}{5}$)*

   (d) My cat, Tabitha, eats $\frac{3}{5}$ of a tin of cat food each day. How many days does a pack of six tins last Tabitha?

    (handwritten: $5 \times 6 = 30$ 10 days $3\overline{)30}$)

10. Shirts are normally marked at a price of £45 each.
    In a sale I paid £36 for a shirt.

   (a) How much money did I save?   *(handwritten: £9)*

   (b) What was the percentage discount for the sale?   *(handwritten: 20%)*

   SALE
   All shirts
   were **£45**
   now **£36**

    (handwritten: $100\% = £45$ $80\% = £36$ $\frac{9}{45} = \frac{1}{5}$)

   On a second shirt, I was offered a further 10% discount on the sale price.

   (c) How much did I pay for the second shirt?   *(handwritten: £32.40)*

   (d) What was the overall percentage reduction on the original marked price for the second shirt?

    (handwritten: 72% / 28%)

    (handwritten working: $0.6 \times 50 =$ $0.6 \times 10 = 6 \times 5 = 30$ $42 \times 3 = 126$ £36   £36 - 10% $10\% = £3.60$ £32.40 $45\overline{)3240}$ £2 $\frac{3240}{45} \times 100 = 72\%$ $\frac{30}{45} = \frac{2}{3} = 66\%$)

37

■■□ 11. (a) Evaluate:

  ✓ (i) $\frac{1}{4} + \frac{1}{6}$

  ✓ (ii) $\frac{3}{4} - \frac{1}{6}$

  (b) Evaluate

  ✓ (i) $\frac{1}{3} \times \frac{3}{4}$

  ✓ (ii) $\frac{1}{3} \div \frac{3}{4}$

■■■ (c) Evaluate

  (i) $2\frac{1}{3} \times 1\frac{3}{4}$

  (ii) $2\frac{1}{3} \div 1\frac{3}{4}$

Handwritten working:

$\frac{3+2}{12} = \frac{5}{12}$

$\frac{9-2}{12} = \frac{7}{12}$

$\frac{3}{12} = \frac{1}{4}$

$\frac{1}{3} \times \frac{4}{3} = \frac{4}{9}$

$\frac{7}{3} \times \frac{7}{4} = \frac{49}{12} = 4\frac{1}{12}$

$\left(\frac{7}{4}\right)$ $\frac{7}{3} \times \frac{4}{7} = \frac{28}{21} = \frac{4}{3} = 1\frac{1}{3}$

12. One sunny day, a man stood near to a tree.
    The shadow of the tree was 10.8 metres long.
    The shadow of the man, of height 1.8 metres, was 2.7 metres long.
    What was the height of the tree?   *7.2m*

13. The sizes of the angles of a quadrilateral are in the ratio 1 : 2 : 1 : 2

  (a) Calculate the size of each angle.   *90° 60 60*

  (b) What shape is the quadrilateral?   *Rectangle*

14. A blend of coffee is made up of three parts Brazilian and two parts Honduran by weight.

  (a) How many grams of each type of coffee are there in 200 g of the blend?

  The costs of Brazilian and Honduran coffee are in the ratio 3 : 5
  Brazilian coffee costs £12 per kilogram.

  (b) What is the cost of a kilogram of Honduran coffee?   *£20.*

  (c) What should be the cost of a jar containing 200 g of the blend? Give your answer
      correct to the nearest 10 pence.   *£3.00*

Handwritten margin working (top right):

14a

200g

5 part

3 × B + 2 × H

40g per part

B = 120g

H = 80g

£12 = 1kg. [B]

£1.20 < 100g

24p = 20g

£14.4 = 120g [H]

£20 = 1kg

£2 = 100g

£1.60   80g

120

Lower working:

1 : 10
100 : 1000
1,000,000 : 10,000,000

10.8 m

2 : 3

7.2m : 10,8m

1·8 | 2.7
18 : 27
2 : 3

6 : 9   27m
18 : 27
2 : 3   38
20 : 30

B | H
3 : 5
12   20

H: 1.60
B: 1.44
£ 3.04

03.6 × 2 =
3) 10.8

2 : 3
8 : 12
40 : 60

Chapter 3: 11+ Calculations

3.1 Number operations

The number line can be very useful in understanding the number operations.

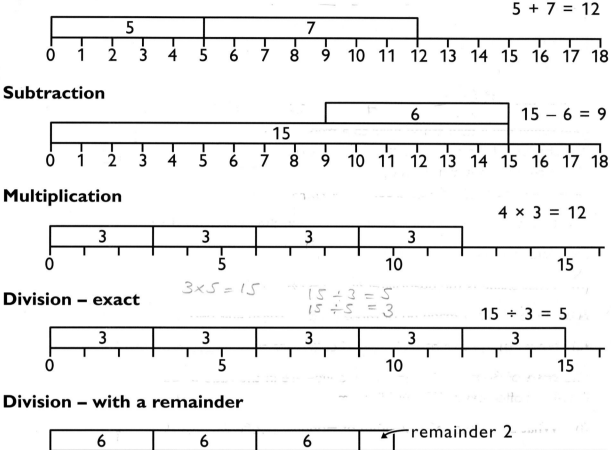

Addition

$$5 + 7 = 12$$

Subtraction

$$15 - 6 = 9$$

Multiplication

$$4 \times 3 = 12$$

Division – exact

$3 \times 5 = 15$

$15 \div 3 = 5$
$15 \div 5 = 3$

$$15 \div 3 = 5$$

Division – with a remainder

remainder 2

$$20 \div 6 \rightarrow 3 \text{ remainder } 2$$

It is also useful to see what happens with square numbers and prime numbers.

Square numbers

$$5 \times 5 = 25$$

Prime numbers

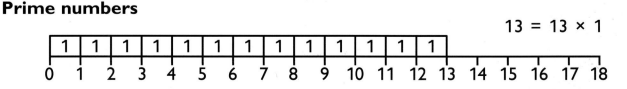

$$13 = 13 \times 1$$

Sample questions

Try these sample questions for yourself. The answers are given at the back of the book.

Some of the questions involve ideas met in earlier work which may not be covered by the notes in this chapter. (See the Useful resources section in the Introduction if you need to refresh any skills or knowledge.)

3.1   On the number line below, show the addition fact 6 + 11 = 17   (2)

0 1 2 3 4 5 6 7 8 9 10 11 12 13 14 15 16 17 18

3.2   On the number line below, show the subtraction fact 16 – 9 = 7   (2)

0 1 2 3 4 5 6 7 8 9 10 11 12 13 14 15 16 17 18

3.3   On the number line below, show the multiplication fact 7 × 2 = 14   7 + 7   (2)

0 1 2 3 4 5 6 7 8 9 10 11 12 13 14 15 16 17 18

3.4   On the number line below, show the division fact 18 ÷ 6 = 3   (2)

0 1 2 3 4 5 6 7 8 9 10 11 12 13 14 15 16 17 18

3.5   On the number line below show what happens when we divide 29 by 5   (2)

0   10   20   30

29 ÷ 5 = 5 r 4

3.6   Here is an addition fact:

16 + 7 = 23   7 + 16 = 23 ; 23 – 16 = 7 ; 23 – 7 = 16

Using the same numbers (16, 7 and 23) in each fact, complete the three related addition/subtraction facts.   (3)

3.7   Here is a multiplication fact:

6 × 7 = 42   42 ÷ 7 = 6 ; 42 ÷ 6 = 7 ; 7 × 6 = 42

Using the same numbers (6, 7 and 42) in each fact, complete the three related multiplication/division facts.   (3)

9 × 45
450 – 45 = 405

9 × 122   1220
              122
             1098

320 × 5
3200 ÷ 2 = 1600

320 ÷ 5 =
32 × 2 = 64

11 × 313 = 3130
              313
             3443

40

3.2 Mental strategies

Mental strategies

- For mental arithmetic tests, you need to have a range of strategies for speeding up calculations in your head.

Change the question!

When working out 7 × £2.99 it is much easier to change it to 7 × £3 and then subtract those seven extra pennies at the end to get £20.93

Subtraction and addition in stages

If you want to subtract something awkward like 54, then it is usually easier to subtract in two or more stages: first subtract the 50, then subtract the 4

Adding in stages is surprisingly similar...

Subtraction and addition in partnership

It is often a really good idea to use a combination of adding and subtracting to make the calculation easier. For example, when subtracting 17, it is probably easier to subtract 20 then add on 3 to the result.

The famous five

Multiplying by five is equivalent to multiplying by ten and then halving the answer. Dividing by five is equivalent to dividing by ten and doubling the answer. You need to try this out to see just how quick this is!

10 − 1 = 9

OK, so you knew that (I hope!) but it does give us a very handy way of multiplying by 9: just multiply by 10 then subtract the original number.

10 + 1 = 11

You can probably see where this is going ... To multiply by 11, just multiply by 10 then add the original number.

Last digit delights

The last digit in any product is the product of the last digits in the two numbers being multiplied. So, for example, we know that 24 × 312 must end in an 8 since 8 is the result of 4 × 2 in the original question.

Playing rough

Always get a rough answer before you work anything out to give you a quick check that you haven't messed it up completely!

Sample questions

Try these sample questions for yourself. The answers are given at the back of the book.

Some of the questions involve ideas met in earlier work which may not be covered by the notes in this chapter. (See the Useful resources section of the Introduction if you need to refresh your skills or knowledge.)

Note: For all questions in this section you should do no written working, but simply write the answers. Do all the calculations in your head. Check that each answer is sensible.

3.8   Fill in the missing numbers.

    (a)   4 × 19 =   (1)

    (b)   7 × 31 =   (1)

    (c)   29 × 5 =   (1)

    (d)   11 × 17 =   (1)

3.9   There are 254 children in a school. One day 59 were absent. How many children were at school that day?   (2)

3.10   There are 37 people on a bus. At the next stop 19 of them get off and 11 get on. How many people are now on the bus?   (3)

3.11   What is the cost of 11 chocolate bars costing 43 pence each?   (2)

3.12   What is 9.5 × 4?   (2)

3.13   Sarah left home at 0845 and cycled for 35 minutes to reach her friend's house. At what time did she arrive?   (2)

3.14   What is the smallest number, greater than 200, which divides exactly by 3?   (2)

3.15   A known division fact is 32 ÷ 8 = 4

    Use this fact to help you to find the answers to the following:

    (a)   320 ÷ 8 =   (1)

    (b)   32 ÷ 80 =   (2)

    (c)   3200 ÷ 80 =   (1)

    (d)   32 ÷ 0.8 =   (2)

    (e)   3.2 ÷ 8 =   (2)

42

3.16 (a) Anne used her calculator to share £52 between 8 people.
This was her calculator display: **6.5**
How much money did each person receive? ~~£6.50~~ £6.50 (1)

(b) Barney's calculator shows this result: **30**
Which number had he multiplied by 4? 7.5 (2)

(c) Carrie's calculator shows this display: **-4**
Which number did Carrie subtract from 7? 11 (2)

3.3 Written methods

Addition and subtraction of decimals to two places

● You need to be able to add and subtract decimals to two places without a calculator.

There is really only one thing to remember here.

Line up the decimal points! (or if you prefer) **Line up the units digits!**

Addition

Let's try adding three numbers together, bearing this rule in mind:

> **Example**
>
> | U . t | | U . t h | | U . t h | | U . t h |
> |-------|---|---------|---|---------|---|---------|
> | 2 . 1 | + | 0 . 2 1 | + | 2 . 1 2 | | 2 . 1 |
> | | | | | | | 0 . 2 1 |
> | | | | | | + | 2 . 1 2 |
> | | | | | | | 4 . 4 3   Correct! |

43

Subtraction

This is very similar – just make sure that you line up those decimal points. Remember also that writing zeros at the end of a decimal does not change the number, and that putting .0 or .00 on the end of a whole number is OK too.

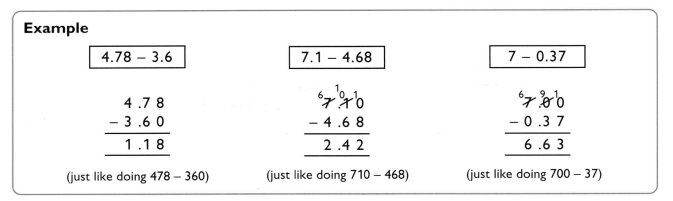

Example

| 4.78 – 3.6 | 7.1 – 4.68 | 7 – 0.37 |

$$\begin{array}{r} 4.78 \\ -\ 3.60 \\ \hline 1.18 \\ \hline \end{array}$$

(just like doing 478 – 360)

$$\begin{array}{r} 7.10 \\ -\ 4.68 \\ \hline 2.42 \\ \hline \end{array}$$

(just like doing 710 – 468)

$$\begin{array}{r} 7.00 \\ -\ 0.37 \\ \hline 6.63 \\ \hline \end{array}$$

(just like doing 700 – 37)

Multiplication and division by a single-digit number

● The first thing to do after you have learned your tables is to learn to multiply or divide any large number by a single-digit number.

Short multiplication – multiplying by a single-digit number (e.g. 126 × 7)

The two favourite methods are the compact and partitioning methods:

Compact

$$\begin{array}{r} 126 \\ 7 \\ \hline \mathbf{882} \\ \scriptstyle 1\ 4 \end{array}$$

Partitioning

$$100 \times 7 = 700$$
$$20 \times 7 = 140$$
$$6 \times 7 = \underline{\ 42}$$
$$\mathbf{882}$$

Short division

Simple short division	Division with remainder as a decimal
$384 \div 6 = 64$ $$\begin{array}{r} 064 \\ 6\overline{)3\,3\,8\,^{3}\,^{2}4} \end{array}$$ The zero above the three is important because it acts as a place holder and stops us getting a crazy answer such as 640 or 604! It is always a good idea to write it in.	$384 \div 5 = 76.8$ $$\begin{array}{r} 076.8 \\ 5\overline{)3\,^{3}\,8\,^{3}\,4.\,^{4}0} \end{array}$$ As before, we must write the zero above the three. We also write in **two** decimal points, one above the other, so that we can continue the division beyond it.

Check by multiplying	**Division with remainder as a fraction**
64 6 ――― **384** 3 2 Obviously this should take us back to our original number. And it does!	$384 \div 7 = 54\frac{6}{7}$ 054 remainder 6 7 $\overline{)384}$ 3 3 Since we were dividing by 7, the remainder is put over 7 to make the fraction.

Long multiplication

● You need to be able to multiply a three-digit number by a two-digit number without a calculator.

We shall take the example 126 × 64 and work it through, explaining every stage in detail.

Procedure

1. Write the two-digit number underneath the three-digit number, lining up the units column as if it were an addition problem.

      1 2 6
   ×   6 4

2. Multiply the three-digit number by the **units** digit of the two-digit number, working from **right** to **left**, with carrying where necessary.

      1 2 6
   ×   6 4
      5 0 4
      1 2

3. Put a zero in the units column of the second row of working. Multiply the three-digit number by the **tens** digit of the two-digit number, again working from **right** to **left**, with carrying if it is needed.

      1 2 6
   ×   6 4
      5 0 4
   7 5 6 0
   1 3

4. Add together the two rows of working to obtain the final answer.

      1 2 6
   ×   6 4
      5 0 4
   7 5 6 0
   8 0 6 4
   1

Notes

You can, if you wish, multiply by the tens digit first, but it is still a good idea to keep two separate rows of working. The reason we write a zero in the units column in step 3 is because we are really multiplying by 60, not by 6, so writing the 0 effectively does the multiplying by 10 for us.

Sample questions

Try these sample questions for yourself. The answers are given at the back of the book.

Some of the questions involve ideas met in earlier work which may not be covered by the notes in this chapter.

Note: When answering these questions, you are expected to show clearly all your working, even if you could do them in your head.

3.17 (a) Add 77 to 48   125. ✓   (1)

   (b) Subtract 19 from 102   83   (2)

3.18 (a) Add 2.9 + 4.6   7, 5   (1)

   (b) Subtract 3.75 from 12.2   8.45   (2)

3.19 (a) Which number is 3.7 less than 10.4?   6, 7   (1)

   (b) What must I add to 9.6 to get 14.1?   4.5   (2)

3.20 (a) Multiply 18 by 7   126   (2)

   (b) Multiply 312 by 13   4,056   (2)

3.21 (a) Divide 1205 by 5   241   (2)

   (b) Divide 1001 by 7   143   (2)

3.22 Write these decimals in order of increasing size.   (2)

   2.31   1.23   3.12   1.32   2.13   1.23, 1.32, 2.13, 2.31, 3.12

3.23 (a) What is the total cost of six pens costing £2.75 each?   £16.50   (2)

   (b) Share £2 between seven people as best you can.

      (i) How many pence will each person receive?   28   (2)

      (ii) How much will be left over?   4p   (2)

Summary

Remember that you should be familiar with all of the material in National Curriculum Key Stage 1.

You should also now be able to do the following:

1. Understand fully the four operations (addition, subtraction, multiplication and division) and the associated language.

2. Use a range of mental methods of computation with the four operations when solving number problems (including mental recall of multiplication facts up to 10 × 10 and quick derivation of corresponding division facts). **4**

3. Check the reasonableness of your results by reference to your knowledge of the context or to the size of the numbers. *[handwritten: GUESTIMATE]* **4**

4. Interpret calculator displays. **5**

5. Use efficient written methods of addition and subtraction and of short multiplication and division (including addition and subtraction of decimals to two places, and ordering decimals to three places). **4**

6. Use all four operations with decimals to two places (where multiplication and division are always by an integer less than 10, and rounding to the nearest integer). **5**

7. Use and understand an appropriate non-calculator method for multiplying any three-digit number by any two-digit number. **5**

Use the glossary at the back of the book for definitions of key words.

Test yourself

Before moving on to the next chapter, make sure you can answer the following questions. The answers are at the back of the book.

1. Brian has multiplied 197 by 15 and has written the answer **incorrectly** as 1182

    (a) Suggest at least two reasons why Brian should realise straight away that his answer is incorrect. *[handwritten: 200 × 10 (!) = 2000 !! Last digit / unit) answer must be a 5 or 0]*

    (b) What should the answer be? *[handwritten: 2955]*

    (c) Suggest what error Brian made.

2. Calculate the square of 19 *[handwritten: 361]* *[handwritten: 238]*

3. Which number between 240 and 250 divides exactly by 7? *[handwritten: 245]*

[handwritten working:]

$$34 \text{ r } 2$$
$$7 \overline{\smash{)}24^30}$$

$$197 \times 10 = 1970$$
$$197 \times 5 = 985$$
$$\underline{2955}$$

$$\begin{array}{r} 197 \\ -15 \\ \hline 182 \end{array}$$

$$\begin{array}{r} 1970 \\ 985 \\ - \\ \hline 985 \\ +197 \\ \hline 1182 = 6 \times 197 \end{array}$$

$$19^2 = 19 \times 19$$
$$= 20 \times 19 = 190 \times 2 =$$
$$19 \times 10 = 190 \times 2 = 380$$
$$361$$

4. Jasmine still has her three number cards!

3   4   5

Jasmine arranges her cards into a two-digit number and a single-digit number, for example, 35 and 4

She then finds the product of these two numbers, so 35 × 4 is 140

Which similar grouping of the cards will give

(a) the smallest product   34 × 5 = 170   =   135 [3 × 45]

(b) the largest product?   54 × 3   = 43 × 5 = 215

5. Diana used her calculator whilst doing some shopping, to keep a record of how much money she would have left.

First she entered 20, since she started with a £20 note. She subtracted the cost of each item as she put it into her shopping basket.

Just before she reached the checkout she pressed [=] and was surprised to see this display.

⁻0.03

Assuming that she had pressed the keys correctly, what does this mean?

34
× 5
170
  2

54
× 3
162
  1

43
× 5
215
  1

3¹

34 × 5 = 170
54 × 3 = 162

35 × 4 = 140

45 × 3 = 135

43 × 5 = 215

£20

−3

−4

23p

1 @

48

Chapter 4: 13+ Calculations

- Before you start this chapter, it might be a good idea to have another look at Chapter 3, particularly the section on mental strategies. You might also like to answer questions 3.8 to 3.16 again.

4.1 Written methods

Multiplication and division of decimals to two decimal places

- You need to be able to multiply and divide decimals to two decimal places without a calculator.

This is very similar to working with whole numbers – once you can do one you can do the other.

Multiplying

1   Add together the **numbers** of decimal places in the two numbers being multiplied.

2.   Rewrite the questions without the decimal points.

3.   Multiply the whole numbers in the usual way.

4.   Count back the correct number of decimal places and put the decimal point in the answer.

Example (multiplying decimals)

Calculate 2.3 × 4.76 without using a calculator.

2.3	×	4.76	
1 d.p.		2 d.p.	Total: 3 decimal places

```
        4 7 6
  ×       2 3
      1 4 2 8
      9 5 2 0
    1 0 9 4 8
```

Rewrite and calculate as a long multiplication without the decimal points.

Count back three places and rewrite the decimal point, giving the final answer **10.948**

Dividing

1   Write the division as a fraction, with one number above the other.

2.   Multiply top and bottom by 10 (if either number is to 1 d.p.) or by 100 (if either number is to 2 d.p.).

3.   Cancel down the fraction in the usual way to simplify it as much as possible.

Example (dividing decimals)

Calculate 3.15 ÷ 4.2

First write as a fraction $\dfrac{3.15}{4.2} \times \dfrac{100}{100} = \dfrac{315}{420}$

Notice that we multiply top and bottom by 100 because the first number has two decimal places. Now cancel down to produce the simplified answer.

$\dfrac{315}{420}$ cancel 3s $\rightarrow$ $\dfrac{105}{140}$ cancel 5s $\rightarrow$ $\dfrac{21}{28}$ cancel 7s $\rightarrow$ $\dfrac{3}{4}$

Pencil and paper multiplication and division

● You should be able to multiply and divide two numbers using pencil and paper methods.

Believe me, if you know your tables up to 10 × 10, then you can multiply any two numbers up to 100 × 100. Actually you can multiply any two numbers as big as you like!

Short multiplication usually refers to multiplying by a single-digit number. Long multiplication is used when multiplying by a number with two or more digits. Short division and long division work the same way.

There are many methods of multiplying two numbers, and you probably know at least two. Look in the following section for some crazy methods which are fun to try.

Whenever you multiply or divide, always make an estimate first to help you check your answer!

Division always divides people into two groups. Those who get the right answer and those who don't. If you want to be in the first group, here are some things to remember:

● Practise by doing a multiplication question 'in reverse'.

● You can always get there by repeated subtraction if you're desperate (this method is sometimes known as 'chunking').

● Always check your answer by multiplying back again.

● Check that your answer is close to your original estimate.

● You can write any division question as a fraction and just cancel it down until you get your answer.

Decimals

Those who treat decimals as whole numbers are missing the point. Provided you put that point back again afterwards, though, it's the best way to do them.

How many decimal places do you make in the final answer?

When you **multiply** two decimals, you **add** the number of decimal places.

When you **divide** one decimal by another, you **subtract** the number of decimal places.

Quick example: 6.71 (2 d.p.) and 1.1 (1 d.p.)

671 × 11 = 7381 so put 3 decimal places (2 + 1) in to get

6.71 × 1.1 = 7.381

671 ÷ 11 = 61 so put 1 decimal place (2 − 1) in to get

6.71 ÷ 1.1 = 6.1

Long multiplication (alternative methods)

● It's useful to know a variety of methods for multiplying two numbers using pencil and paper. Here are some interesting ways of finding 387 × 52 which are fun to try.

The Elizabethan method ('Napier's Bones')

Write the two numbers across the top and down the right. Multiply each pair of digits in the grid. Add along the diagonals and the answer appears around the other corner!

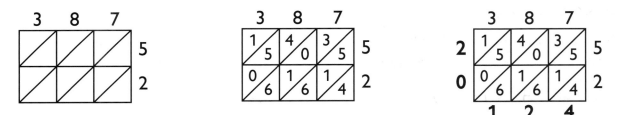

(Add from the right and work backwards. Don't forget to carry the digits where a diagonal sum gives more than 10

So, 5 + 1 + 6 gives 12; carry the 1 to add in the next diagonal to the left, giving
1 + 3 + 0 + 1 + 6 = 11

So 387 × 52 = 20 124

The Egyptian method

Make two columns. On the left write 1 and on the right write the larger number of the two. Keep doubling both. You get your answer by adding a clever selection of the rows.

1	387	I don't need to go any further because doubling 32
2	774	would give me 64 and I don't need to go past 52.
4	**1548** *	Now I choose the rows for which the **left** numbers
8	3096	add up to 52, then add up the numbers on the **right**.
16	**6192** *	
32	**12 384** *	

*52 = 32 + 16 + 4 so I just add up 12 384 + 6192 + 1548 = 20 124 as above.

The Russian peasant method

Make two columns, with one number in each column. Double the numbers on the right and halve the numbers on the left (ignoring remainders). At the end, cross out the rows in which there is an **even** number on the left, then add up the remaining numbers on the **right**.

~~52~~	~~387~~
~~26~~	~~774~~
13	1548
~~6~~	~~3096~~
3	6192
1	12 384

Now there's a surprise! It's the same numbers left as with the Egyptian method! Can you see why?

Using one calculation to find the answer to another

● You need to be able to use multiplication and division facts to calculate related problems.

Variations on the original problem are achieved using a combination of two procedures:

1. Changing the order of the numbers in the question and answer.

2. Multiplying or dividing any of the numbers involved by powers of 10 (i.e. 10 or 100 or 1000 etc.)

Example 1

Given that 5 × 7 = 35, **write down** the answers to the following:

(The phrase *write down* means that you shouldn't need to do any detailed calculations.)

(i) 35 ÷ 7   *5*   (ii) 50 × 700   *35,000*   (iii) 350 ÷ 0.05 *= 7,000*

Answers

(i) 35 ÷ 7 = 5

This is just a restatement of the original problem, in a different order.

(ii) 50 × 700 = 35 000

If the question is multiplied by 10, so is the answer. This has been done three times here: 5 × 10 and 7 × 10 × 10, so the answer is 35 × 10 × 10 × 10

(iii) 350 ÷ 0.05

First use the fact that 35 ÷ 5 = 7 and think of the division as a fraction.

350 ÷ 5 = 70   Multiplying the **numerator** by 10 multiplies the answer by 10

350 ÷ 0.5 = 700   Dividing the **denominator** by 10 multiplies the answer by 10

350 ÷ 0.05 = 7000 Dividing the denominator again by 10 multiplies the answer by 10 once more.

Example 2

Given that 58.7 × 89 = 5224.3, **write down** the answers to the following:

(i) 5.87 × 8900   (ii) 52 243 ÷ 58.7   (iii) 5.2243 ÷ 0.089

Answers

(i) 5.87 × 8900 = 52 243

One number has been multiplied by 100 and the other has been divided by 10; the net result of this *tug of war* is × 10

(ii) 52 243 ÷ 58.7 = 890

We know that 5224.3 ÷ 58.7 = 89 (the original problem). Therefore 52 243 ÷ 58.7 is 10 times bigger.

(iii) 5.2243 ÷ 0.089 = 58.7

We know that 5224.3 ÷ 89 = 58.7 (the original problem). Both numbers in the division have been divided by 1000. If both numbers in a division are multiplied or divided by the same amount, then the answer stays the same. If you think about it, this is what equivalent fractions are all about!

Sample questions

Try these sample questions for yourself. The answers are given at the back of the book.

Some of the questions involve ideas met in earlier work which may not be covered by the notes in this chapter.

Note: In this section you should not use a calculator. It is particularly important that you show all your working.

4.1 (a) Add 190.5 + 2909.6   *3100.1* (2)
(b) Subtract 2909.6 − 190.5   *2719.1* (2)
(c) Multiply 365 × 72   *26,280* (2)
(d) Divide 24 144 ÷ 48   *503* (2)

4.2 Evaluate, showing all your working:
(a) 3.95 + 0.471   *4.421* (2)
(b) 3.95 − 0.471   *3.479* (2)
(c) 7.12 × 0.5   *35.6* (2)
(d) 7.12 ÷ 0.5   *0.1424* (2)

4.3 Evaluate:
(a) 16 − 9 ÷ 3   *13* (1)
(b) 3 + 7 × 4   *31* (1)
(c) 7 + 5 × 7 − 19   *23* (2)
(d) 2 + 3 × (4 − 5)   *−1* (2)

4.4 Given that 34 × 75 = 2550, find:
(a) 17 × 75   *1275* (1)
(b) 68 × 0.75   *5106* (2)
(c) 2550 ÷ 17   *140* (2)
(d) 510 ÷ 3.4   *40.8* (2)

4.5 By first writing each number correct to 1 significant figure, estimate the answer to
(a) $\dfrac{3.95 \times 19.4}{9.8}$ (3)
(b) $\dfrac{7.98}{2.03 \times 3.92}$ (3)

4.6 (a) Calculate the total cost of buying 12 football shirts at £37.95 each.   (3)
(b) When 16 people go to the theatre, the total cost of the tickets is £287.20
What is the cost of each ticket if they are all the same price?   (3)

4.2 Calculator methods

Interpreting calculator displays

Money, time, distances etc. – we know the difference but the poor calculator doesn't have a clue. It operates a simple RIRO rule (Rubbish In Rubbish Out) which means that it cannot think for itself!

You could ask your calculator to work out £3 + 12 minutes – 4 bananas and it would tell you that the answer was 11, but that's just making the calculator look stupid.

Calculators sometimes give rounding errors, and you need to be careful with money and time answers. Always think of the context of the question.

3.7   £3.70 not 3 pounds and 7 pence

4.25   4.25 hours = 4 hours 15 minutes (not 4 hours 25 minutes)

5.3   If we have worked out how many tins of paint we need then the answer is 6 not 5 since 5 would not be enough!

41.99999999999   This recurring decimal seems to suggest that the real answer is actually 42 after all!

Calculating fractions and percentages with a calculator

- You have to know how to calculate a fraction or a percentage of a quantity using a calculator.

Did you know that every calculator has an *OF* button? No, not *OFF* – *OF*.

It looks like this: **X**   of

Let's see how it works.

Using a fraction calculator

Most fraction calculators have a button which looks something like this: $\boxed{a^b\!/\!_c}$

Let's work out $\frac{2}{3}$ of 72

If we don't have a fraction key on the calculator, we can use the division key instead:

2 $\boxed{\div}$ 3 $\boxed{\textbf{X}}$ 72 $\boxed{=}$ 48.

   two-thirds   of   72   equals   48

Percentages

Percentages are just as easy. Remember that % means *out of 100* and you have a fraction again, or a decimal if you prefer. We'll find 75% of 108

75 $\boxed{\div}$ 100 $\boxed{\times}$ 108 $\boxed{=}$ *81.*

or simply

0.75 $\boxed{\times}$ 108 $\boxed{=}$ *81.*

Sample questions

Try these sample questions for yourself. The answers are given at the back of the book.

Some of the questions involve ideas met in earlier work which may not be covered by the notes in this chapter.

Notes

- In this section a calculator is essential for most questions. You will be told if you should **not** use a calculator.

- Unless instructed otherwise, or the answer is exact, write all the figures shown in the calculator display first and then write the answer to 3 significant figures.

Remember:

- Different calculators work in different ways and you should have absolute confidence in your own calculator and your ability to use it.

- The calculator will respond faultlessly to the instructions given to it, so it is very important that you give it the appropriate instructions.

- In most cases, it is important to write more than just the 'answer' and you should say what you are doing.

- It is a good idea to know roughly what the calculator answer is likely to be before you start and to do a check after the calculation.

4.7 Calculate:

(a) $3.95 - -7.83$ (1)

(b) $\dfrac{6.9 + 8.2}{3.9}$ (1)

(c) $\dfrac{6.45}{0.95 - 0.08}$ (1)

(d) $\dfrac{4.09 + 6.23}{3.97 \times 0.21}$ (1)

4.8 Calculate:

    (a) $(29 + 413)^2$ (1)

    (b) $\sqrt{11.45}$ (1)

    (c) $\sqrt[3]{1.65}$ (1)

    (d) $7\frac{1}{2}$ divided by $2\frac{3}{4}$, leaving your answer as a fraction.   (1)

4.9 Calculate:

    (a) the area of a circle which has radius 5.8 cm   (1)

    (b) 47 000 × 80 000   (1)

4.10 Write an appropriate answer for each of these calculator displays:

    (a) calculation involving **money** (£, GBP)   (1)

        10.8

    (b) calculation involving **time** (in minutes)   (1)

        15.2

    (c) calculation involving **time** (in hours)   (1)

        4.75

    (d) calculation involving **number of minibuses** needed for a school trip   (1)

        3.8

    (e) calculation involving **fractions**   (1)

        2 ⌐ 7

4.11 Write an appropriate answer for each of these calculator displays:

    (a) calculation involving **fractions**   (1)

        1 ⌐ 3 ⌐ 5

    (b) calculation involving very **large distances** in miles   (1)

        4.5 9

    (c) calculation involving **small lengths** in centimetres   (1)

        5.07 -03

    (d) calculation involving **sharing 8 cakes between six people**   (1)

        1.333333333

    (e) calculation involving **division**   (1)

        9.999999999

4.12 (a) Writing down all the figures shown on your calculator, find the value of (2)

$$\frac{27.3 - 5.4}{3.8}$$

(b) Write your answer to part (a) correct to 3 significant figures. (1)

(c) Write your answer to part (a) correct to 1 decimal place. (1)

4.13 Brian's calculator display is shown here, after he has done a multiplication.

61.755

(a) Write the number shown in the display correct to 2 decimal places. (1)

(b) Write the number shown in the display correct to 1 significant figure. (2)

(c) Which number did Brian multiply by 3.45? (2)

4.14 (a) (i) Writing down all the figures on your calculator, evaluate (2)

$$\frac{123.9 \times 0.03}{207.5}$$

(ii) Write your answer to part (a) (i) correct to 1 significant figure. (1)

(b) (i) Writing down all the figures on your calculator, evaluate (2)

$$\frac{30.98}{371.5 - 456.5}$$

(ii) Write your answer to part (b) (i) correct to 3 decimal places. (1)

■■□ 4.15 Look at this calculation:

$$\frac{287.3}{31.1 + 9.6}$$

(a) **Without using a calculator**, and showing all your working:

(i) rewrite the calculation shown above, giving each number correct to 1 significant figure. (2)

(ii) evaluate your answer to part (a) (i). (1)

(b) (i) Using a calculator, and writing down all the figures displayed, evaluate the original calculation. (1)

(ii) Write your answer to part (b) (i) correct to 1 significant figure. (1)

(iii) Write your answer to part (b) (i) correct to 2 decimal places. (1)

4.3 Checking results

Inverses and approximations as checks

- You should know how to check your answers by using inverses and approximations.

Inverses can be thought of as opposites. There are lots of opposite pairs in mathematics, but let's start with the most important four:

The inverse of this:	+	−	×	÷
is this:	−	+	÷	×

Checking using inverses

1.   We have just done the calculation: $257 - 78 = 179$
      We check the subtraction by **adding**: $179 + 78 = 257$ OK!

2.   We have just done the calculation: $108 \div 3 = 36$
      We check the division by **multiplying**: $36 \times 3 = 108$ OK!

Estimation and approximation

Imagine that on your calculator you are working out 28.7×5.42
and you obtain from the calculator display the answer 697.554

A quick approximation will tell you that this can't be right!

28.7 is roughly 30, and 5.42 is roughly 5, so the answer must be about 150

Better try again!

Getting the right answer

Checking your results often involves making use of mental strategies (see page 41), including:

- making approximations to get an idea of the 'size' of the result
- using inverse operations (working backwards)
- looking at the units digit following a multiplication.

If your check suggests that an error has been made, this could be because you have:

- entered the wrong number into the calculator (very easy to do, particularly when you are in a hurry!)
- given the calculator inappropriate or incomplete instructions, such as failing to press $=$ at the right time
- set out written calculations incorrectly, such as forgetting 'carrying digits' or failing to take account of place value
- made 'zero' errors, such as leaving them out or putting in extra
- made a simple 'tables' or other computation error.

Of course it is best to avoid making errors in the first place.

You are less likely to make errors if you:

- have a rough idea of the result before you start
- set out written working clearly
- write down intermediate calculator results.

Handwritten notes (top right):
Small volume = 0.5 × 0.5 × 0.5
= 0.125 m³
Large volume : 4 × 2 × 1 = 8 m³
8 m³ ÷ 0.125 m³
= 8000 m³ ÷ 125 m³
= 64

A final word of caution!

If your check suggests that you may have made an error, don't forget that the error may be in your check!

If your check confirms that your original answer is likely to be correct, then that is probably fine. If your check casts doubt upon your original answer then it is safer to check again before changing your answer!

Sample questions

Try these sample questions for yourself. The answers are given at the back of the book.

Some of the questions involve ideas met in earlier work which may not be covered by the notes in this chapter.

Note: Questions 4.16 and 4.17 involve the use of mental strategies and should be done entirely in your head – write down only the answer.

4.16 (a) I invest £800 at 5% interest. How much interest do I earn in a year? (1)

Handwritten: 5% = £40   £840

(b) Tommy played in four soccer matches. The figures show the number of goals he scored in each match. How many goals does he need to score in his next match to make his mean number of goals four per match? (1)

3   0   5   2   *10 = 16*   *6*

(c) A recipe says that 6 kg of flour will make 12 loaves of a certain size. How many kilograms of flour do I need to make 20 loaves of the same size? *10 kg* (1)

Handwritten: 3 kg = 6   6 kg = 12

(d) On a trip to Edinburgh, Len spends £14.40 on the train, £8.00 on a taxi and £2.60 on a bus. How much does the journey cost him altogether? *£25.00* (1)

Handwritten (left margin):
14.40
8.00
+ 2.60
25.00

(e) The information shows the charges for parking in a car park for different lengths of time.

0–2 hours	90p
each extra hour or part hour	40p

If I arrive at 0930 in the morning and leave at 1345 the same day, how much do I pay to park? *£1.80   4¼ hr.* (1)

Handwritten (left margin):
1,
4hr 15
2hr 15
90p   1hr 15
40p
40p   15 min
10p   0 min
40p = 60 min

Handwritten (bottom):
90p
1.20
£2.10

5 hrs charge

4.17 (a) This calculation is used to find the total cost in pounds of some items in a sale.

$$\frac{11 \times 15}{0.3}$$

Calculate the total cost. (1)

(b) Tina is 13 years old. Five years ago her sister was half Tina's age. How old is Tina's sister now? (1)

(c) An A6 sheet of paper, a quarter the size of this page, has an area of about 150 cm². What approximate area **in square metres** could be covered by 100 sheets of A6 paper? (1)

(d) How many cube-shaped boxes of edge half a metre can I fit into a case measuring 4 m by 2 m by 1 m? (1)

(e) The circumference of Ed's cycle wheel is 249 cm. Estimate, to 1 significant figure, how many times the wheel goes round while he cycles 10 km. (1)

4.18 When Mrs Watt goes shopping she keeps a mental note of the approximate total of the items as she puts them into the trolley. If the item cost is less than 49p she ignores it, if it costs 50p to £1.49 she counts it as £1, if it costs £1.50 to £2.49 she counts it as £2 and so on.

Here is one of Mrs Watt's shopping bills.

SHERRY	£5.39
MILK	£0.86
6 EGGS	£1.50
TIGER ROLLS	£0.55
MILK	£0.45
FELIX POUCH	£3.43
FELIX POUCH	£3.43
REDUCED ITEM	£1.01
REDUCED ITEM	£0.39
PUN PEACH	£1.00
SHORTBREAD	£0.81
BISCUITS	£2.93
REDUCED ITEM	£0.91
GO CAT	£2.55
GOCAT COMP V	£2.36
BABY ACC	£0.70
HANDWASH	£1.00

(a) Use Mrs Watt's mental strategy to find the approximate total cost of the items in her trolley. (2)

(b) Use your calculator to find the exact cost of the items. (2)

4.19 (a) Julian has thought of a number. When he adds 3 to his number, then multiplies by 4 and finally subtracts 6, he gets 30
Megan says that the number Julian thought of is 6
By means of a flow chart showing the inverse operations, or otherwise, show Megan how to check. (3)

6

(b) Moira has thought of a number. When she subtracts 4 from her number, then divides by 3 and finally adds 11, she gets 45
John says that the number Moira thought of is 109
Check to see if John is correct and, if he is not, say what Moira's number is. (3)

108

$45 - 11 = 34 \times 3 = 102 + 4 = (106)$

S Summary

Remember that you should be familiar with all of the material in Chapter 3.

You should also now be able to do the following:

1. Use all four operations with decimals to two places (including rounding to 1 or 2 decimal places). **5**

2. Understand and use an appropriate non-calculator method for solving problems that involve multiplying and dividing any three-digit number by any two-digit number. **5**

■■□ 3. Understand the effects of multiplying and dividing by numbers between 0 and 1 **7**

■■□ 4. Solve numerical problems involving multiplication and division with numbers of any size, using a calculator efficiently and appropriately. **7**

5. Check your solutions by applying inverse operations or estimating, using approximations. **5**

Use the glossary at the back of the book for definitions of key words.

$109 - 4 = 105 \div 3 = 35 + 11 = (46)$
$108 - 4 = 104 \div 3 = 34\frac{2}{3}$
$106 - 4 = 102 \div 3 = 34 + \frac{45}{35} \quad 35 + 11 = 46$

$\begin{array}{r} 35 \\ 8\overline{)10^{0}5} \end{array}$

x = the number.

$4(x + 3) - 6 = 30$

$4x + 12 - 6 = 30$

$4x + 6 = 30 \quad (-6)$

$4x = 24$

$x = 6$

$x = 2$
$(2 + 3) \times 20$
$4 + 6 = 10$

62

Test yourself

Before moving on to the next chapter, make sure you can answer the following questions.

The answers are at the back of the book.

1. Showing all your working, evaluate:

   (a) 6.04 + 3.5

   (b) 6.04 − 3.5

   (c) 6.04 × 3.5

   (d) 6.04 ÷ 4

2. Showing all your working, evaluate:

   (a) 31.47 + 17.58

   (b) 31.47 − 17.58

   (c) 6.79 × 0.35

   (d) 6.79 ÷ 0.35

3. Showing all your working, calculate:

   (a) 4 + 5 × 6

   (b) (10 × 4.99) + (5 × 0.85) + (3 × 2.05)

   (c) 3 × 4 + 6 − 5 × 2

4. (a) Showing all your working, calculate

   (i) 3.6 + 6.6 ÷ 5

   (ii) 1.9 + 2.9 × (3.9 − 4.9)

   (b) What is the difference between your two answers in part (a)?

5. (a) Look at this calculation:

   $$\frac{39.7}{8.9 \times 9.1}$$

   Without using a calculator, and showing all your working,

   (i) rewrite the calculation shown above, giving each number correct to 1 significant figure

   (ii) evaluate your answer to part (a) (i).

   (b) (i) Now, using a calculator and writing down all the figures displayed, evaluate this calculation.

   $$\frac{19.6}{3.8 \times 5.1}$$

   (ii) Write your answer to part (b) (i) correct to 2 significant figures.

   (iii) Write your answer to part (b) (i) correct to 3 decimal places.

6. (a) (i) Writing down all the figures shown on your calculator, find the value of

$$\frac{47.9}{8.1 \times 0.8}$$

(ii) Write your answer to part (a) (i) correct to 3 significant figures.

(b) (i) Writing down all the figures shown on your calculator, find the value of
$20.7 \div (9.37 - 2.6)$

(ii) Write your answer to part (b) (i) correct to 3 decimal places.

Note: Questions 7 and 8 involve the use of mental strategies and should be done entirely in your head – write down only the answer.

7. (a) In Rugby Union, a converted try is worth seven points. A penalty is worth three points. In a match, a team scores two converted tries and four penalties. What is the team's total score? $14 + 12 = 26$ points

(b) The total cost of a coach trip for 20 people is £2300 £115
How much will each person pay if the cost is divided equally between them?

(c) Tiles are sold in packs of ten and cost £9 per pack. I estimate that a bathroom requires 150 tiles. How much will the tiles cost? £135

(d) A pudding which feeds four people requires 240 ml of milk. How much milk is required if the pudding is to feed six people? 360 ml

(e) Find the value of 99^2

8. (a) A fire destroyed 60 out of the 240 paintings in a gallery. What percentage of the original number of paintings was destroyed by the fire? 25 %

(b) The masses of three packets are 55 g, 35 g and 60 g. What is the mean mass of the packets? 50 g

(c) The cost to enter an adventure park is £16 per person. There is a reduction of one quarter for parties of ten or more. What is the total cost for a group of ten people to go to the adventure park? £120

(d) Calculate, in hectares, the area of the rectangular field shown. 4.5 hectares

300 m

150 m

not to scale

1 hectare = 10 000 square metres

64

(e) I need to attend a meeting at my bank, which is 10 minutes walk from the bus stop in Dimwich, at half past ten. What is the latest time I can catch the bus in Waledale?

Waledale depart	0740	0820	0910	1000
Ploptown arrive	0825	0905	0955	1045
Dimwich arrive	0855	0935	1025	1115

10.30 am

Chapter 5: 11+ Problem solving

Note: The material in this chapter is not detailed in the ISEB syllabus but it is included here to help with learning and practising important skills needed in examinations.

5.1 Decision making

Choosing a strategy

When tackling a problem, it is important to decide on a suitable strategy. This is largely a matter of common sense, but you could consider the following strategies.

Making an organised list (listing all possible outcomes)

> **Example**
>
> How many different integers (whole numbers) could you make using the three number cards below?
>
>
>
> There are obviously three single-digit numbers: 1, 2 and 3
>
> There are six two-digit numbers: 12, 13, 21, 23, 31, 32
>
> There are also six three digit numbers: 123, 132, 213, 231, 312, 321
>
> So, altogether, you could make fifteen different integers.

Trying a practical approach (drawing diagrams etc)

> **Example**
>
> How many diagonals does a regular pentagon have?
>
> Doing a rough sketch should help you.
>
>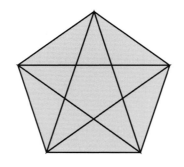

Guessing and checking (trial and improvement)

Example

Amy is thinking of three different positive integers and has given these clues:

The product of the numbers is 72 and their sum is 18

What are Amy's numbers?

You know that 72 is 2 × 36 and 36 is 3 × 12, so you could guess that the numbers are 2, 3 and 12

Unfortunately, this cannot be correct since the sum of 2, 3 and 12 is 17, not 18

What would be your next guess?

Trying a simpler example (trying easier numbers etc.)

Example

How many pound coins could you place in a single layer on a tennis court?

You might like to start by seeing how many pound coins you could fit into a 10 cm square. It would also be a good idea to see how best to arrange the coins – rows and columns may not be the best way!

Looking for a pattern

Example

Here are some 'steps' made from matchsticks.

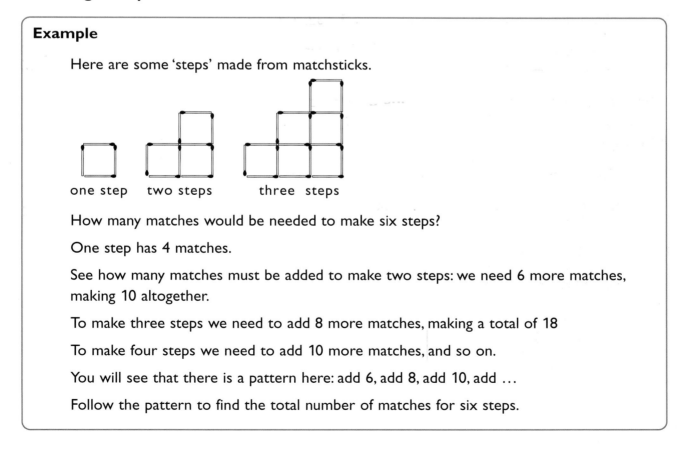

one step   two steps   three steps

How many matches would be needed to make six steps?

One step has 4 matches.

See how many matches must be added to make two steps: we need 6 more matches, making 10 altogether.

To make three steps we need to add 8 more matches, making a total of 18

To make four steps we need to add 10 more matches, and so on.

You will see that there is a pattern here: add 6, add 8, add 10, add …

Follow the pattern to find the total number of matches for six steps.

Sample questions

Try these sample questions for yourself. The answers are given at the back of the book. The sample questions in this chapter are not reflective of typical examination questions as the material is more concerned with practising important skills.

Some of the questions involve ideas met in earlier work which may not be covered by the notes in this chapter.

5.1 Decide which method you might best use to solve each of the following problems.

You do not need to solve the problems! Just write M, MJ, PP or C.

- M   mental – entirely in your head
- MJ   mental with jottings – perhaps writing down an intermediate result
- PP   pencil and paper – setting out a calculation (such as a long multiplication) on paper, or doing a drawing
- C   calculator – only if all other methods are unsuitable!

(a) What is the cost of ten stamps costing 61 pence each?   (1)

(b) How many diagonals does a heptagon have?   (1)

(c) What is the product of 47 and 29?   (1)

(d) Which number multiplied by itself is 841?   (1)

(e) How many DVDs costing £8.99 each could you buy for £100, and how much change would you receive?   (1)

5.2 Which equipment would you use, and how would you use it, to solve these practical problems?

(a) Find the height of a friend.   (2)

(b) Find the distance around your waist.   (2)

(c) Find the temperature of water in a washing up bowl.   (2)

(d) Find the volume of water in a washing up bowl.   (2)

(e) Find the length of time it would take you to hop 100 metres.   (2)

(f) Find the mass of a baked bean.   (2)

(g) Find the area of the sole of your foot.   (2)

5.2 Reasoning about numbers or shapes

When solving puzzles and problems about numbers or shapes, you may need to:

- make use of a variety of strategies
- make use of your knowledge and experience
- make careful observations
- do more thinking than writing
- ask yourself questions, such as 'What if …'
- be prepared to try a different strategy if you seem to be getting nowhere.

Sample questions

Try these sample questions for yourself. The answers are given at the back of the book.

Some of the questions involve ideas met in earlier work which may not be covered by the notes in this chapter.

5.3　The sum of two numbers is 109
One number is 9 less than the other.
What are the two numbers? (2)

5.4　Gina has three coins in her pocket. She has a total of 62 pence.

(a)　What are the three coins? (1)

She buys a pen costing 53 pence, handing over two of her coins. The shopkeeper gives her two coins as change.

(b)　Which coins does the shopkeeper give her? (2)

5.5　Robbie has thought of a number and has given these clues.
The number
- is smaller than 50
- is one less than a multiple of 6
- is **not** prime.

What is Robbie's number? (3)

5.6　Lynn has thought of two numbers.
The product of her numbers is 36
The difference between her numbers is 5
What is the sum of her numbers? (3)

5.7 (a) The shapes A, B and C have been made by joining together two congruent tiles like this one.

(i) Which shape has reflection symmetry only? (1)

(ii) Which shape has rotation symmetry only? (1)

(iii) Which shape has no symmetry? (1)

(b) On a square dotted grid or squared paper, using the same simple tile, draw your own shapes, D with reflection symmetry and E with rotation symmetry. You may use more than two tiles if you wish. (4)

5.3 Real-life mathematics

Everyday situations

Many examination questions concern everyday situations including, for example:

- shopping
- DIY tasks
- holidays
- journeys
- cooking with recipes.

The mathematical knowledge and skills involved can be from all areas including, for example:

- money and currency conversions
- fractions, decimals and percentages
- measurement
- ratio
- bearings
- data tables, graphs etc.

Sample questions

Try these sample questions for yourself. The answers are given at the back of the book.

Some of the questions involve ideas met in earlier work which may not be covered by the notes in this chapter.

5.8 Janet has £4.20 and John has £1.40 more than Janet. They decide to buy a DVD costing £6.80 and share the money that is left equally.
How much money will each of them have when they have paid for the DVD? (3)

5.9 Mrs Smith buys three pints of milk costing 43 pence per pint, two loaves of bread costing 78 pence each and 500 grams of cheese costing £1.10
How much change will she receive from a £10 note? (3)

5.10 The information on a caramel bar is

mass per 100 g	
protein	6 g
fat	20 g
carbohydrate	54 g

(a) What fraction of the bar is fat? (2)

(b) What percentage of the bar is carbohydrate? (1)

A caramel bar has a mass of 55 grams.

(c) What will be the mass of fat in a bar? (2)

5.11 The 16 pupils in a class make biscuits in a cookery lesson.
Here is the recipe which each pupil uses to make 12 biscuits:

plain flour	180 g
cornflour	45 g
butter	215 g
icing sugar	80 g

(a) How many biscuits will the class make altogether? (2)

(b) (i) How much icing sugar will be needed altogether? (2)

(ii) The teacher opens a 2 kg packet of icing sugar. How many grams of icing sugar will be left at the end? (2)

(c) What is the total mass of ingredients used by each pupil? (2)

(d) The biscuits lose 15% of their mass during the cooking process. What will be the mass of one pupil's cooked biscuits? (2)

(e) The cost of the ingredients for each pupil is 72 pence. What is the cost of each biscuit? (1)

(f) Half of the children sell their biscuits for 5 pence each at a school charity event. How much money will they raise altogether? (2)

S Summary

You should be able to do the following:

1. Develop your own strategies for solving problems and use these strategies. **4**

2. Look for patterns and relationships. **4**

3. Search for a solution by trying out ideas of your own. **4**

4. Present information and results in a clear and organised way. **4**

5. Check that your results are reasonable. **4**

6. Use your knowledge, understanding and skills, often in several areas of mathematics, to tackle everyday problems.

Use the glossary at the back of the book for definitions of key words.

TY Test yourself

Before moving on to the next chapter, make sure you can answer the following questions.

The answers are at the back of the book.

1. Find the area of your hand.

2. Rhona has thought of a number and has given these clues.

   The number:

   ● is larger than 10 but smaller than 60
   ● has a units digit which is one less than the tens digit
   ● is prime.

   What is Rhona's number?

3. Jo has the three tiles shown below.

She arranges the tiles edge to edge to make the following shape.

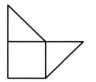

See how many different shapes you can make using all three tiles.

Note that non-exact edge fits and congruent shapes as shown below don't count.

   non-exact edge fit   congruent shapes

4. The best six runners took part in the school cross-country challenge. The table below shows their times.

Angus	51 minutes 2 seconds
Brenda	48 minutes 43 seconds
Clare	50 minutes 27 seconds
David	48 minutes 58 seconds
Ed	49 minutes 4 seconds
Flora	49 minutes 11 seconds

(a) (i) Who won?
    (ii) Who finished last?

(b) What was the difference between the first and last runners' times?

Unfortunately Flora fell in the stream and she lost 20 seconds scrambling out.

(c) Had Flora not fallen in the stream, in what position would she have finished?

5. Janet had a good idea for raising money for charity. She bought 200 plastic balls of different colours. The balls were identical apart from the colour.

The table shows the numbers of the balls of each colour.

The number of orange balls was the same as the number of purple balls.

The number of green balls was three times the number of orange balls.

Colour	Number of balls
Red	40
Blue	25
Yellow	35
Green	
Orange	
Purple	

(a) How many green balls were there?

Janet paid £20 for the balls and sold all of them at 15p each.

(b) (i) How much was the cost of each ball?

(ii) How much profit did Janet make altogether?

The purchasers wrote their names on the balls and then the balls were dropped at the same time from a bridge over the narrow river. Everyone ran to the next bridge 100 metres downstream and Janet stood ready to fish the winning ball from the water.

(c) Which colour ball was most likely to win?

Gail bought one ball of each colour and Stephanie bought six green balls.

(d) Who was the most likely to have the winning ball, Gail or Stephanie?

Chapter 6: 13+ Problem solving

Note: The material in this chapter is not detailed in the ISEB syllabus but it is included here to help with learning and practising important skills needed in examinations.

6.1 Decision making

Generalising and testing

Generalising and testing usually involves forming a 'rule' and then testing it before using it to solve the problem.

We will look again at the 'steps' problem from page 67 in Chapter 5.

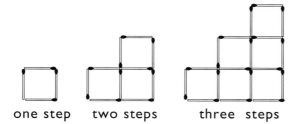

one step   two steps   three steps

How many matches would be needed for 100 steps?

We could simply follow the pattern described in Chapter 5 but clearly this would take a long time!

We can draw up a table, where the number of steps is n, as follows:

n	1	2	3	4	5	6
n^2	1	4	9	16	25	36
$3n$	3	6	9	12	15	18
$n^2 + 3n$	4	10	18	28	40	54

The expression $n^2 + 3n$ gives us the numbers of matches in the different steps.

This gives us the formula (rule) $m = n^2 + 3n$, where n is the number of steps and m is the number of matches.

We can test the formula by applying it to 7 steps. If it doesn't work, we need to think again!

We can then use the formula to find the solution to the problem. This is much quicker! When n is 100, $n^2 + 3n$ is 10 300

You will find more information about this on page 88.

Try these sample questions for yourself. The answers are given at the back of the book. The sample questions in this chapter are not necessarily reflective of typical examination questions as the material in this chapter is more concerned with practising important skills.

Some of the questions involve ideas met in earlier work which may not be covered by the notes in this chapter.

6.1 Decide which strategy you would use to solve each of the following problems. You do not need to solve the problems!

● Make an organised list

● Try a practical approach (such as drawing a diagram)

● Guess and check

● Try a simpler example first

● Look for a pattern

● Find a formula and then test it before using it

(a) How many diagonals does a regular nonagon have?   (1)

(b) What is the most likely score you could get by adding together the numbers when these two spinners are used together?   (1)

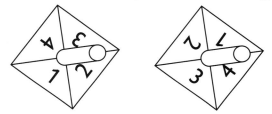

(c) **Without using a calculator**, find the square root, to 1 decimal place, of thirty. (1)

(d) Find the next two terms of this sequence.   (1)

1   6   16   36   ...

(e) How many different routes are there through this maze?   (1)

(f) Find the hundredth term of this sequence.   (1)

3   8   13   18   ...

6.2 Reasoning about numbers or shapes

Triangular numbers

At the start of a game of snooker there are 15 reds in the triangle.

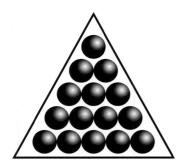

Which other numbers of balls could be arranged in a triangle this way?

The answer is a sequence of numbers which we call the triangular numbers.

They come up a lot in mathematics.

Here are the first ten triangular numbers:

n	T_n
1	1
2	3
3	6
4	10
5	15
6	21
7	28
8	36
9	45
10	55

In the table, T_n simply means the *nth triangular number*.

Notice how they go up:

+2, +3, +4, +5 etc. added on to the one before.

Also notice that any two consecutive **triangular** numbers give a sum which is a **square** number, e.g. 21 + 28 = 49

In general though, we can jump to any triangular number we want simply by using this formula:

$T_n = \frac{1}{2}n(n+1)$

The sum of two consecutive triangular numbers is a square number.

3 + 6 = 9

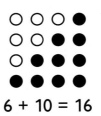

6 + 10 = 16

Try these sample questions for yourself. The answers are given at the back of the book.

Some of the questions involve ideas met in earlier work which may not be covered by the notes in this chapter.

6.2   A plant produces three flowers in its first year. Every year after that, it produces two more flowers than in the previous year, as shown in the diagram below.

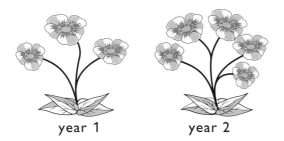

year 1   year 2

(a)   Complete the table below to show the number of flowers in each year.   (2)

Year	Number of flowers
1	3
2	5
3	7
4	
5	

(b)   How many flowers will the plant have in its seventh year?   (2)

(c)   Assuming that the plant continues to grow at the same rate, during which year will the plant produce more than 30 flowers for the first time?   (2)

6.3   The diagram shows a cuboid made up of small cubes.

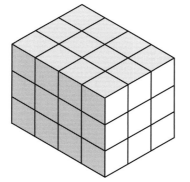

(a)   How many small cubes have been used to make the cuboid?   (2)

The whole outer surface of the cuboid is painted blue.

(b) How many of the small cubes have

    (i)   only one face painted blue   (2)

    (ii) only two faces painted blue   (2)

    (iii) three faces painted blue   (2)

    (iv) no faces painted blue?   (1)

6.4   Answer the following puzzles:

(a) I am a multiple of 7

     I am less than ten squared.

     The sum of my digits is 10

     What number am I?   (2)

(b) I am a four-sided two-dimensional shape.

     My diagonals cross at right-angles.

     My sides are of two different lengths.

    (i)   Draw me.   (2)

    (ii) What is my name?   (1)

    (iii) How many lines of symmetry do I have?   (1)

6.5   Here are the first three patterns in a sequence, using 1 cm lines drawn on dotted paper.

pattern 1   pattern 2   pattern 3

(a) Draw the next pattern in the sequence.   (2)

(b) Extend the following table of values for pattern numbers 3 to 5   (6)

Pattern Number	Number of squares	Total number of dots	Perimeter (cm)
1	1	4	4
2	3	8	8

(c) By considering the sequence of numbers in each column of the table from part (b), extend the table to include values for pattern number 8   (3)

6.3 Real-life mathematics

An examination question can cover a number of syllabus areas and require a wide range of strategies.

Many questions are concerned to some extent with money or with fractions, decimals and percentages.

The real-life situations may include:

- Shopping – money, discounts
- Cooking and baking – recipes
- Eating and diets – calories
- Medicines and health – measures
- Growth – measurement, line graphs
- Exercise and sports – times, speeds, scores
- Holidays and travel – driving, exchange rates
- Planning events – hiring equipment, fundraising
- Gardening – weed killing, filling a pond
- DIY tasks – building a shed, decorating a room
- Business and banking – VAT, profit and loss, interest rates
- Design – tessellations, symmetry
- Exploring – maps, scales
- Model-making – scales, nets
- Puzzles

Use these general hints to help you solve a problem:

- Since questions can be rather 'wordy', read each question very carefully to make sure that you understand what is required. Remember that the little word 'not' changes the meaning considerably!

- It may help to draw a sketch. For example, if a scale drawing is required, drawing a sketch first will help you make sure your drawing fits into the available space.

- Plan your strategy before putting pen to paper, particularly if the question is not already structured into stages.

- Write what you are doing rather than simply jotting down calculations.

- If the use of a calculator is permitted, then write down the full calculator display for each calculation before correcting it to 3 significant figures for a final answer. When several calculations are needed, always use the full value in your calculator for later calculations.

- Pay attention to units throughout and always check that your final answer is in the correct units.

● When you have finished, ask yourself: 'Can the marker follow through this and see exactly what I have done?' In the event that your answer (for whatever reason) is incorrect, then the marker will still be able to award marks for the written evidence of your thinking.

Sample questions

Try these sample questions for yourself. The answers are given at the back of the book.

Some of the questions involve ideas met in earlier work which may not be covered by the notes in this chapter.

6.6 (a) **Estimate** the cost of 49.8 litres of petrol at 101.1 pence per litre.
Give your answer to the nearest pound. (2)

(b) On a journey of 450 miles, my car uses 1 litre of petrol every 9.1 miles.
Estimate the number of litres of petrol which my car uses on the journey. (2)

6.7 (a) Alice went to the shop and bought seven DVDs costing £5.99 each.
How much did Alice spend on the DVDs? (2)

(b) (i) Max bought five books, three costing £6.99 each and the other two costing £3.49 each.
What was the total amount that Max spent? (2)

(ii) How much change should Max receive from a £50 note? (2)

(c) Mr Lester purchased 28 identically priced theatre tickets for a school trip, at a total cost of £474.60
What was the cost of each ticket? (2)

6.8 Flora intends to bake 18 small cakes for her party. She looks up a recipe in an old cookery book and finds that to make a dozen cakes she needs the following ingredients:

flour	8 ounces
margarine	6 ounces
sugar	4 ounces

(a) Write down the amount of each ingredient that Flora needs to bake the 18 cakes. (3)

Flora finds that she has only 10 ounces of flour, but plenty of the other ingredients.

(b) What is the largest number of cakes she can bake? (2)

S | Summary

Remember that you should be familiar with all of the ideas in Chapter 5.

You should also now be able to do the following:

1.	Show understanding of situations by describing them mathematically using symbols, words and diagrams.	**5**
2.	Draw simple conclusions of your own and explain your reasoning.	**5**
3.	Check your working and results, considering whether they are sensible.	**5**
4.	Carry out substantial tasks and solve quite complex problems by breaking them down into smaller, more manageable tasks.	**6**
5.	Give mathematical justifications, making connections between the current situation and situations you have met before.	**6**
6.	Use your knowledge, understanding and skills, often in several areas of mathematics, to tackle everyday problems.	

Use the glossary at the back of the book for definitions of key words.

TY | Test yourself

Before moving on to the next chapter, make sure you can answer the following questions. The answers are at the back of the book.

1. How many diagonals does a regular nonagon have?

2. What is the most likely score you could get by adding together the numbers when these two spinners are used together?

3. **Without using a calculator**, find the square root, to 1 decimal place, of thirty.

4. Find the next two terms of this sequence.
   1   6   16   36   ....

5. How many different routes are there through this maze?

6. Find the hundredth term of this sequence.

   3   8   13   18   ...

7. Aunt Jane has divided her bear collection between her three nieces as follows:

   Gail has $\frac{1}{3}$ of the total.

   Hilda has $\frac{1}{4}$ of the total.

   Isla has the rest.

   (a) What fraction of the total does Isla have?

   Gail divides her share equally between her twin brothers, Jack and Kane.

   (b) What fraction of the total does Jack have?

   (c) If Kane now has four of Aunt Jane's bears, how many bears were there in Aunt Jane's collection?

8. George stacks shelves at the supermarket.

   He earns £7 per hour for the first 32 hours he works in a week.

   (a) How much is he paid for a 32-hour working week?

   George is paid £8.50 per hour for every extra hour he works over 32 hours.

   (b) One week he worked for a total of 40 hours.
        How much did he earn in that week?

   (c) Another week he earned £334.50
        How many hours did he work that week?

■■□ 9. A shallow tray is made from a rectangular sheet of card.
       Small squares of side 2 cm are removed from the corners, as shown, to make the net.

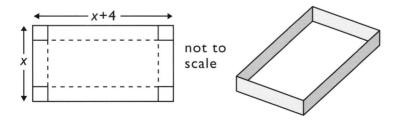

   The card is folded along the dotted lines to make the tray.

   (a) What is the height of the tray?

   (b) Write down, in terms of x, expressions for:

        (i)   the length of the tray

        (ii) the width of the tray

        (iii) the surface area of the inside of the tray.

(c) If I start with a sheet of card measuring 24 cm by 20 cm, find

    (i) the surface area of the inside of the tray

    (ii) the volume of the tray.

10. A useful indicator of appropriate human body mass (and therefore weight) is the Body Mass Index (BMI).

BMI can be found using the formula: $\text{BMI} = \dfrac{\text{mass}}{\text{height}^2}$, where the mass is in kilograms and the height is in metres.

For example, if a man is 1.80 metres tall and weighs 72 kg, his BMI is $\dfrac{72}{1.8^2}$ = 22.22 to 2 decimal places.

(a) Calculate the BMI of the following people. Give your answers to 2 decimal places:

    (i) Angus is 1.65 m tall and weighs 67 kg

    (ii) Beatrice is 1.78 m tall and weighs 83 kg

    (iii) Colin is 1.59 m tall and weighs 66 kg

The range of BMI values **for adults** covers various categories, including:

Category	underweight	normal	overweight
BMI	18.5	25	

If a person's BMI is greater than 25, then he/she is considered to be overweight.

(b) Who is overweight in part (a)?

(c) If a man is 1.85 metres tall, calculate his maximum mass (to 2 d.p.) before he is considered to be overweight.

Chapter 7: 11+ Algebra

7.1 Equations and formulae

Word formulae and function machines

● You need to be able to form and use simple formulae expressed in words or as a picture.

How many months old are you?

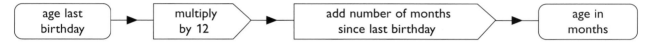

This is an example of a word formula, in this case to change years and months into just months.

A word formula is a set of instructions telling you how to change one number into another.

Here's another type of word formula, written as a puzzle:

> I think of a number, double it, add 11 and the answer is 99
>
> What was my number?

And now a word formula which converts degrees Celsius into degrees Fahrenheit:

> multiply by 9, divide by 5, then add 32

Example

What are these temperatures in Fahrenheit?

(a) 0 °C $\dfrac{0 \times 9}{5} + 32 = 32$ °F

(b) 40 °C $\dfrac{40 \times 9}{5} + 32 = 104$ °F

(c) 100 °C $\dfrac{100 \times 9}{5} + 32 = 212$ °F

Diagrams like the one above are very useful.

Two more follow on the next page.

1. Function machine

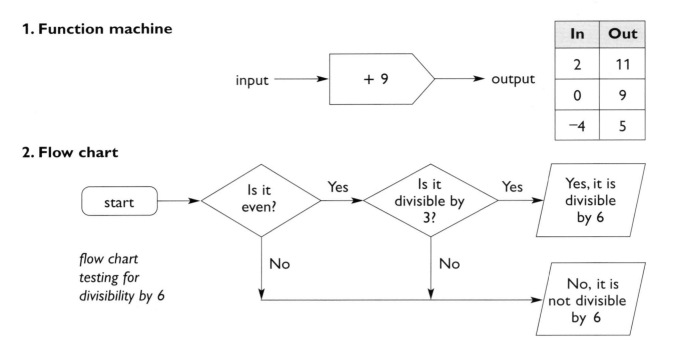

In	Out
2	11
0	9
−4	5

2. Flow chart

flow chart testing for divisibility by 6

Sample questions

Try these sample questions for yourself. The answers are given at the back of the book.

Some of the questions involve ideas met in earlier work which may not be covered by the notes in this chapter.

7.1　Find the numbers represented by the symbols in these equations.

    (a)　6 + ▲ = 12 (1)

    (b)　■ − 4 = 19 (1)

    (c)　6 × □ = 18 (1)

    (d)　3 × ☆ × 5 = 15 (1)

    (e)　24 + 21 = ▲ × 5 (2)

7.2　Find the unknown number in each case.

    (a)　Mike is three years older than Emma. He is 12

        12 − 3 = ⊙

        How old is Emma? (1)

    (b)　A regular pentagon has a perimeter of 30 cm.

        5 × ☆ = 30

        What is the length of a side of the pentagon? (1)

7.3 Amy has made a machine which subtracts 4 from every input number.

input → | −4 | → output
5   1

(a) What will be the output if Amy puts 7 into the machine? (1)

(b) What will be the output if Amy puts 3 into the machine? (2)

(c) If 6 comes out of the machine, which number did Amy put in? (1)

7.4 (a) Sally has thought of a number. When she adds 4 she gets 13
What is Sally's number? (1)

(b) Fred has thought of a number. When he subtracts 6 he gets 17
What is Fred's number? (1)

(c) Alice has thought of a number. When she multiplies it by 7 she gets 42
What is Alice's number? (1)

(d) Graham has thought of a number. When he divides it by 9 he gets 6
What is Graham's number? (1)

7.5 Jenny has made a machine.

input → | ×3 | → | −5 | → output
7   21   16

Her machine multiplies by 3 and then subtracts 5

(a) What will be the output if Jenny puts in 4? (1)

(b) What will be the output if she puts in 1? (2)

(c) If 1 comes out, which number did Jenny put in? (2)

7.6 (a) Bella has thought of a number. When she adds 4 and then multiplies by 3
she gets 18
What is Bella's number? (2)

(b) Colin has thought of a number. When he multiplies by 3 and then subtracts 4
he gets 11
What is Colin's number? (2)

7.2 Sequences and functions

Exploring and describing number patterns

● You need to be able to spot, explore and describe patterns in a series of numbers.

Look at these arrangements made with match sticks:

arrangement 1	arrangement 2	arrangement 3
4 sticks	7 sticks	10 sticks

Can you see a pattern here?

How many sticks are there in arrangement 4 and arrangement 5?

One of the best ways to explore number patterns is to look at the difference between each number and the next, as in this diagram:

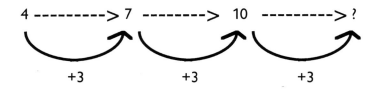

We can then say: 'It's going up in threes' and predict that the next number will be 13

Let's see if we were right.

arrangement 4

13 sticks

Yes, 13 is correct.

Now, can you predict the number of sticks needed for arrangement 10?

88

Sample questions

Try these sample questions for yourself. The answers are given at the back of the book.

Some of the questions involve ideas met in earlier work which may not be covered by the notes in this chapter.

7.7 Clare has started to thread beads onto a string in a pattern.

Continue the pattern for the next eight beads. (2)

7.8 Write the next two numbers in each of these sequences.

(a) 2   4   6   8   10   ... (1)

(b) 2   6   10   14   18   ... (2)

(c) 30   25   20   15   10   ... (2)

(d) $\frac{1}{4}$ $\frac{1}{2}$ $\frac{3}{4}$ 1 $1\frac{1}{4}$ ... (2)

7.9 Write the next two numbers in each of these sequences.

(a) 2   6   4   8   6   ... (2)

(b) 1   2   4   7   11   ... (2)

7.10 (a) Which multiplication function machine could produce all these outputs?

5   10   45   60   95   1005 (2)

(b) Which multiplication function machine could produce all these outputs?

12   24   30   45   102   3000 (2)

7.3 Graphs

First quadrant co-ordinates

● You should be able to read and plot co-ordinates using positive whole numbers.

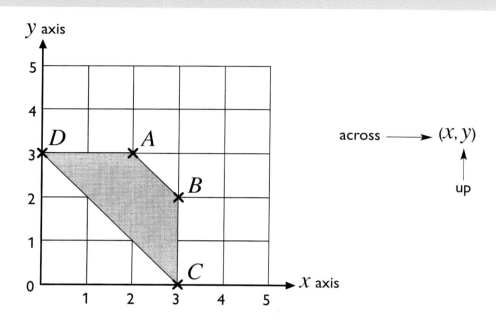

The point $(0, 0)$ is the reference point for all co-ordinates. It is called the **origin**.

The point A is at $(2, 3)$: 2 across, 3 up

The point B is at $(3, 2)$: 3 across, 2 up

The point C is at $(3, 0)$: 3 across, 0 up   (It stays on the x-axis.)

The point D is at $(0, 3)$: 0 across, 3 up   (It stays on the y-axis.)

If we were to slide the shape across or up (or both), we could redraw it anywhere else on the grid. This sliding move is called **translation**. Although the shape would look the same, its co-ordinates would change.

You also need to be able to answer questions about the shapes on graphs.

Example

What shape is $ABCD$?

Answer: Isosceles trapezium

Sample questions

Try these sample questions for yourself. The answers are given at the back of the book.

Some of the questions involve ideas met in earlier work which may not be covered by the notes in this chapter.

7.11 (a) Complete the table of outputs for this function machine. (2)

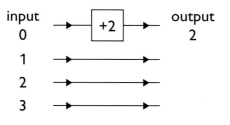

(b) Plot points representing the pairs of input and output numbers on this grid. (2)

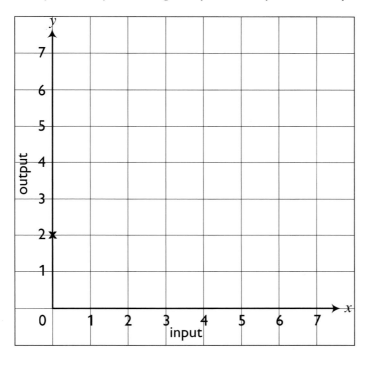

7.12 A function machine has produced the input/output pairs of numbers plotted on this grid.

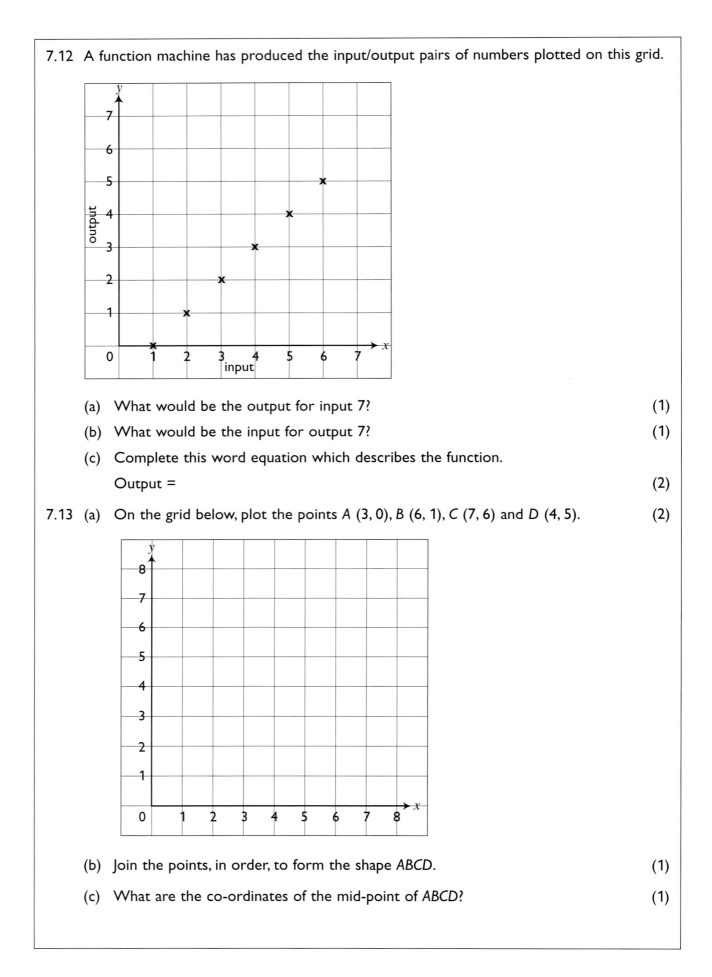

(a) What would be the output for input 7? (1)

(b) What would be the input for output 7? (1)

(c) Complete this word equation which describes the function.

Output = (2)

7.13 (a) On the grid below, plot the points A (3, 0), B (6, 1), C (7, 6) and D (4, 5). (2)

(b) Join the points, in order, to form the shape ABCD. (1)

(c) What are the co-ordinates of the mid-point of ABCD? (1)

Summary

You should be able to do the following:

1.   Use simple formulae expressed in words.   **4**

2.   Continue sequences and understand simple function machines.

3.   Use and interpret co-ordinates in the first quadrant.   **4**

Use the glossary at the back of the book for definitions of key words.

S

Test yourself

TY

Before moving on to the next chapter, make sure you can answer the following questions. The answers are at the back of the book.

1.   Find the numbers represented by symbols in the following equations.

   (a)   4 + 13 = 10 + ☆

   (b)   23 – 9 = ▲ – 14

   (c)   6 × ▲ = 16 × 3

   (d)   35 ÷ 5 = 28 ÷ ⊙

2.   Will and Gina have each thought of a positive whole number less than 9
      The sum of their numbers is 12
      We could write this as $w + g = 12$, where w is Will's number and g is Gina's number.

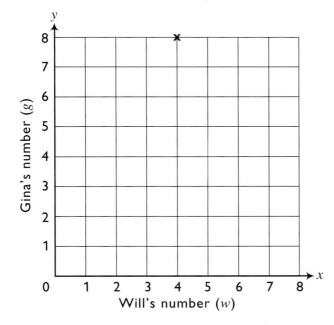

On the diagram, one possibility is shown by a cross.
Complete the diagram to show all of the other possibilities.

3. (a) Tommy has thought of a number. When he multiplies it by 3, he gets exactly the same result as he would by adding 8 to his number. What is his number?

    (b) Nancy has thought of a number. When she subtracts 3 from twice her number, the result is $1\frac{1}{2}$ times her number. What is her number?

4. Look at these arrangements of matches.

arrangement 1   arrangement 2   arrangement 3

    (a) Sketch arrangements 4 and 5

    (b) (i)   How many matches would be needed for arrangement 6?

        (ii) How many matches would be needed for arrangement 10?

    (c) Gloria suggests that it is easy to find the number of matches needed. She says you simply multiply the number of triangles by 2 and then add 1

        (i)   Does Gloria's idea give the correct number of matches for arrangement 6 and arrangement 10?

        (ii) Use Gloria's idea to find how many matches would be needed for arrangement 100

5. Here is an unusual arrangement of counting numbers up to 53

0	1	2	3	4	5	6	7	8
9	10	11	12	13	14	15	16	17
18	19	20	21	22	23	24	25	26
27	28	29	30	31	32	33	34	35
36	37	38	39	40	41	42	43	44
45	46	47	48	49	50	51	52	53

    (a) Circle all the numbers which would be produced by a ×3 machine.

    (b) Shade all the numbers which would be produced by a ×5 machine.

6. (a) (i) On the grid below, plot the points A (3, 4), B (5, 6), C (3, 8) and D (1, 6).

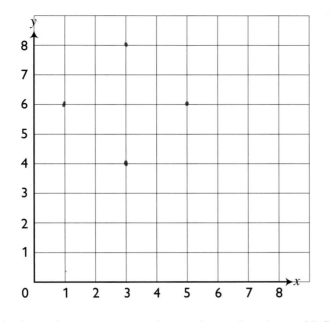

(ii) Join the points in order to form the shape ABCD and name ABCD.

(b) In a space on the grid, plot three points P, Q and R which when joined make an isosceles triangle. Write down the co-ordinates of P, Q and R.

Chapter 8: 13+ Algebra

8.1 Equations and formulae

Simple symbolic formulae

- You need to know about simple symbolic formulae (one or two step).

A quick review of the basics

1. We do not use × (times) or ÷ (division) signs

Example	ab means a times b	$\dfrac{a}{b}$ means a divided by b

2. Like terms

Like terms have exactly the same letter part. The following pairs are like terms:

Example	$3a$ and $7a$	$5b$ and $-2b$	$6ab$ and ab	$3a^2$ and $8a^2$

3. Collecting like terms

Example	a + $5b$ − $3ab$ + $3a$ + $4ab$ − b = $4a + 4b + ab$

4. Multiplying out brackets

Remember to multiply the number outside by everything in the brackets. And watch the plus and minus signs!

Example	$3(2a + 5b) = 6a + 15b$	$a(b - 2c) = ab - 2ac$

5. Factorising into brackets

Example	$4a + 4b = 4(a + b)$	$15p^2 - 10pq = 5p(3p - 2q)$

6. Equivalent fractions

The numerator and denominator must always be divided (or multiplied) by the same number.

Example	$\dfrac{4}{12} \to \dfrac{2}{6} \to \dfrac{1}{3} \to \dfrac{10}{30} \to$ ... (etc.)

7. Simplifying powers

When multiplying, you **add** the powers; when dividing you **subtract** the powers.

Example	$aa = a^2$	$a(a + a^2) = a^2 + a^3$	$\dfrac{12a^3}{4a^2} \to \dfrac{3a^3}{a^2} \to 3a$

BODMAS and algebraic substitution

- You need to be able to substitute numbers into simple formulae using BODMAS correctly, with or without a calculator.

Armed with the knowledge of everything on the previous page, we can now tackle a wide variety of questions involving algebraic substitution. But first we must find out – who or what is BODMAS?

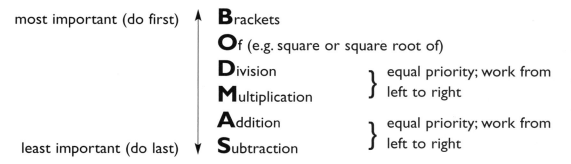

most important (do first) ↑ **B**rackets

Of (e.g. square or square root of)

Division } equal priority; work from

Multiplication } left to right

Addition } equal priority; work from

least important (do last) ↓ **S**ubtraction } left to right

BODMAS means that there is now no doubt about the answer to ambiguous questions:
$3 + 4 \times 5 = 23$ (not 35) because we work out the 4×5 first.

Your calculator may be a BODMAS calculator. Type in the above question to check! There are two types of calculator: LTR and MDF. Type in $10 - 2 \times 3$ and then press equals. LTR (Left To Right) gives the answer 24, while MDF (Multiplication and Division First) gives 4. MDF knows BODMAS. Does yours?

Algebraic examples

(a) Given that $p = 2q + 3(q + r)$, find p when $q = 3, r = 4$
$p = 6 + 3 \times 7$ [since $q + r = 7$]
$p = 27$ [since $3 \times 7 = 21$]

(b) Given that $E = mc^2$, find E when $m = 10$ and $c = 5$
$E = 10 \times 5^2$
$E = 10 \times 25$
$E = 250$

Algebraic fractions

Level 1 and Level 2 papers may include examples such as $\dfrac{3x}{15}$

Level 3 papers may include examples where the variable
appears in both the numerator and the denominator, for example $\dfrac{4x}{x}$

Solving simple linear equations

- You need to be able to solve simple linear equations.

Many people find it helpful to think of equations as a set of balance scales, with the = sign as the pivot. At every stage of your working, be careful not to upset the balance!

How to solve equations: some guidelines

1. At every stage apply the same working to both sides of the equation.

2. Think about the order in which the equation was written (BODMAS may help you), and work backwards to the unknown variable by *undoing* each step in reverse order.

3. Try to collect letter terms on one side and number terms on the other.

4. Don't be put off if the answer is negative or a fraction.

Example 1

Solve the equation $4x + 5 = 26 - 3x$

equation	do this to both sides
$4x + 5 = 26 - 3x$	subtract 5
$4x = 21 - 3x$	add $3x$
$7x = 21$	divide by 7
$x = 3$	**check original equation**
(check **LHS**) $4(3) + 5 = 17$	
(check **RHS**) $26 - 3(3) = 17$	**It's the right answer!**

Example 2

Solve the equation $5(19 - x) = 3(3x - 1)$

equation	do this to both sides
$5(19 - x) = 3(3x - 1)$	multiply out the brackets
$95 - 5x = 9x - 3$	add 3
$98 - 5x = 9x$	add $5x$
$98 = 14x$	divide by 14
$7 = x$	**check original equation**
(check **LHS**) $5(19 - 7) = 60$	
(check **RHS**) $3(21 - 1) = 60$	**It's the right answer!**

Linear equations

Level 1 papers may include examples such as:

$x - 4 = 10$ $4x = 20$ $2x + 3 = 9$

Level 2 papers may, in addition, include examples such as:

$6 = 2x - 2$ $2x + 5 = 11 - x$ $2(x + 3) = 12$ $\frac{1}{2}x = 3$

Level 3 papers may, in addition, include examples such as:

$6 - 4x = 3$ $\frac{1}{2}x + 3 = 5$ $\frac{2}{3}(2x - 3) = 12$

Forming and solving linear equations

● You need to be able to form and solve linear equations when solving problems.

Here is a puzzle that can be solved by setting up a simple equation.

> I have x sweets. You have three fewer than twice the number I have.
> One third of your sweets is five fewer than the number I have.
> How many do we each have?

We make the equation up step by step:

I have x sweets.

You have three fewer than twice the number I have.

So you have three fewer than twice x.

You have $2x - 3$ sweets.

One third of your sweets is five fewer than my number of sweets.

So one third of $(2x - 3)$ is $x - 5$

So the equation is $\frac{1}{3}(2x - 3) = x - 5$

Now we can solve it.

$\frac{1}{3}(2x - 3) = x - 5$	Multiply both sides by 3
$2x - 3 = 3x - 15$	Add 15 to both sides
$2x + 12 = 3x$	Subtract $2x$ from both sides
$12 = x$	So I had 12 sweets ...
$2(12) - 3 = 21$	... and you had 21

■■■ Solving quadratic equations using trial and improvement methods

● You need to be able to solve quadratic equations using trial and improvement methods.

A **root** of an equation is a value of x which will make the value of that equation equal to zero. Quadratic equations can have two different roots.

Trial and improvement helps you to zoom in on one of those roots. You are usually told where to start looking and then each subsequent trial improves your answer. An example follows on the next page.

Example

The equation $x^2 - 3x + 1 = 0$ has a root (solution) between $x = 2$ and $x = 3$

Find this value of x to 2 decimal places.

x	$x^2 - 3x + 1$	**Verdict**
2	−1	too small
3	1	too big
2.5	−0.25	too small
2.7	0.19	too big
2.6	−0.04	too small
2.65	0.0725	too big
2.62	0.0044	too big
2.61	−0.0179	too small
2.615	−0.006 775	too small

We always choose our next x value to be somewhere between the most recent *too small* and *too big* values.

Our conclusion at this stage is that x must be between 2.615 and 2.62

Both of these, when expressed to 2 decimal places, give 2.62

In order to give an answer to 2 decimal places, we must calculate to 3 decimal places.

If x is between two numbers which both round to 2.62 to 2 decimal places, then x must also round to 2.62 to 2 decimal places.

■■■ Solving inequalities and finding integer solution sets

● You need to be able to solve simple inequalities and find integer solution sets.

Inequalities

Consider the inequality: $5 + \frac{1}{2}x > 4$

Subtract 5 from both sides $\frac{1}{2}x > -1$

Multiply by 2 $x > -2$

So x could be −1, 0, 1, 2, 3, 4, 5, ...

Any of these would make $(5 + \frac{1}{2}x)$ more than 4

We could show the solution on a number line, by shading out the part that we don't want:

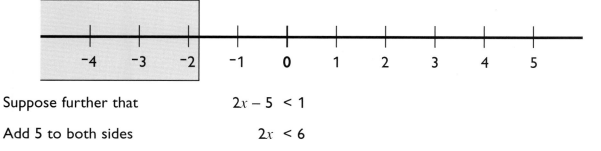

Suppose further that $2x - 5 < 1$

Add 5 to both sides $2x < 6$

Divide through by 2 $x < 3$

Represented on the number line as:

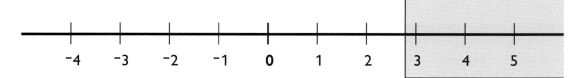

Then the set of integers which satisfies both inequalities at the same time (the integer solution set) is shown by the combination diagram below:

■■■ Algebraic formulae*

Multiplying out brackets

This section is included for interest at Level 3 and Scholarship, and is unlikely to be tested in a Common Entrance examination.

$a(x + y) = ax + ay$

$a(x - y) = ax - ay$

$(a + b)(x + y) = ax + ay + bx + by$

$(a + b)(x - y) = ax - ay + bx - by$

$(a - b)(x + y) = ax + ay - bx - by$

$(a - b)(x - y) = ax - ay - bx + by$

Be careful with the signs!

*note that Level 3 applies to all the sub-sections in this section.

Squaring a bracket

$$(a + b)^2 = a^2 + 2ab + b^2$$

$$(a - b)^2 = a^2 - 2ab + b^2$$

$$(a + b + c)^2 = a^2 + ab + ac + ab + b^2 + bc + ac + bc + c^2$$

$$= a^2 + b^2 + c^2 + 2ab + 2ac + 2bc$$

Difference of two squares/cubes

$$a^2 - b^2 = (a - b)(a + b)$$

$$a^3 - b^3 = (a - b)(a^2 + ab + b^2)$$

Alphabetical order of letters

When we write algebraic formulae, it is conventional to write the letters in alphabetical order, with numbers first. This helps us to spot like terms more easily.

So cad is written as acd, and $f \times 3 \times d^2$ is written as $3d^2f$

Pythagoras' Theorem

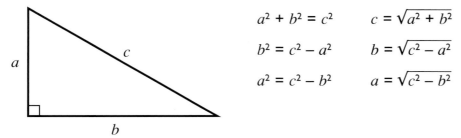

$$a^2 + b^2 = c^2 \qquad c = \sqrt{a^2 + b^2}$$

$$b^2 = c^2 - a^2 \qquad b = \sqrt{c^2 - a^2}$$

$$a^2 = c^2 - b^2 \qquad a = \sqrt{c^2 - b^2}$$

Examples of Pythagorean Triples (triangles with integer side lengths):

(3, 4, 5)   (5, 12, 13)   (6, 8, 10)   (9, 12, 15)   (10, 24, 26) etc.

Sample questions

Try these sample questions for yourself. The answers are given at the back of the book.

Some of the questions involve ideas met in earlier work which may not be covered by the notes in this chapter.

8.1 Simplify the following expressions:

(a) $5c - 3c + 6c$ (1)

(b) $4d^2 + 2d^2 - 5d^2$ (2)

(c) $5e^2 \times 3e$ (2)

(d) $\dfrac{9f}{3}$ (2)

(e) $\dfrac{9b + 3b}{6b}$ (2)

8.2 Factorise completely:

(a) $3h - 12$ (2)

(b) $20e - 15f$ (2)

(c) $2e^2 + 4e$ (2)

(d) $4p^2 - 8pq$ (2)

8.3 Multiply out the brackets and simplify:

(a) $4(a + 3b)$ (1)

(b) $2(3q + 3r) - 2r$ (2)

(c) $3(m + 2n) - (m + 3n)$ (3)

8.4 Given that $d = 4$, $e = 6$ and $f = 5$, find the value of:

(a) $d - e$ (2)

(b) def (2)

(c) $\dfrac{d + e}{f}$ (2)

(d) $d^2 - f^2$ (3)

8.5 If $m = 3$, $n = -2$ and $p = 4$, find the value of each of the following expressions:

(a) $m + n$ (1)

(b) np (1)

(c) $m(n - p)$ (2)

(d) mn^2 (2)

8.6 Tom has thought of a number which he has called t.
Write an expression for:

(a) the number which is 3 more than Tom's number (1)

(b) the number which is 4 times Tom's number (1)

(c) the number which is 5 less than Tom's number (1)

(d) the number which is half of Tom's number (1)

(e) the square of Tom's number. (1)

8.7 In a game of numbers, Rosie chooses a number b.
Ellie chooses a number which is two more than Rosie's number.

(a) Write down an expression, in terms of b, for Ellie's number. (1)

Kori chooses a number which is three times Rosie's number.

(b) Write down an expression, in terms of b, for Kori's number. (1)

(c) Write down an expression, in terms of b, for the sum of the three numbers.
Simplify your answer. (2)

The sum of the three numbers is 22

(d) Form an equation and solve it to find the number which Rosie chose. (2)

8.8 A pork pie costs x pence.

(a) Write down, in terms of x, the cost of five pork pies. (1)

A cup of tea costs 3 pence more than a pork pie.

(b) Write down, in terms of x, the cost of a cup of tea. (1)

(c) Write down, in terms of x, the cost of seven cups of tea. (2)

(d) Write down, in terms of x, the cost of three pork pies and four cups of tea.
Simplify your answer. (2)

Mandy buys three pork pies and four cups of tea for £4.67

(e) Form an equation, in terms of x, and solve it. (3)

(f) If Mandy had bought only two pork pies and two cups of tea, how much change should she have received from a £10 note? (2)

8.9 Solve the following equations:

(a) $q + 8 = 12$ (1)

(b) $3p = 12$ (1)

(c) $4n - 3 = 9$ (2)

(d) $3y + 7 = 13$ (2)

(e) $6x + 5 = 4x - 10$ (3)

8.10 Solve the following equations:

(a) $4s = s + 12$ (2)

(b) $4a - 5 = {}^-3$ (2)

(c) $5 - 2r = 2$ (2)

(d) $5(y + 3) - 4(y - 5) = 50$ (3)

(e) $\frac{1}{2}m = 13$ (2)

(f) $3(s - 4) = 16 - s$ (3)

8.11 Solve the following equations:

(a) $21 - 2a = 7$ (2)

(b) $3(u - 2) = 4(2 - u)$ (3)

(c) $4 - 2(3v + 5) = 0$ (3)

(d) $\frac{1}{2}c - 6 = 8$ (2)

(e) $\frac{3}{4}(v + 4) = 5$ (3)

8.12 For the function $y = x^2 - 2x$ find, by 'trial and improvement', the value of x when y is 30. Complete a table like the one below, giving your answers to 3 significant figures. (5)

x	x^2	$2x$	$x^2 - 2x$

■ ■ ■ | 8.13 (a) (i) Solve the inequality $4 + 5x < 15$ (2)

(ii) List the positive integers which satisfy the inequality in part (i). (1)

(b) (i) Solve the inequality $6 - \frac{1}{2}n \geq 3$ (3)

(ii) Write down the largest value n can take in part (b)(i). (1)

8.2 Sequences and functions

Describing in words the next term of a sequence

● You need to be able to describe in words the next term of a sequence.

As a warm-up to this page, write down the next two terms of each of the following sequences:

a)   3, 5, 7, 9, 11, 13 ..., ...   15, 17

b)   27, 23, 19, 15, 11, 7, ..., ...   3, −1

c)   2, 3, 5, 8, 12, 17, ..., ...   23, 30

d)   32, 16, 8, 4, 2, 1, ..., ...   0.5, 0.25

'Describing in words' is when you explain what the sequence is doing. From above:

a)   adding 2 each time

b)   subtracting 4 each time

c)   adding one more than the previous time

d)   dividing by 2 each time.

Remind yourself again of the method described on page 88.

This method (The Difference Method) will show up almost every hidden pattern.

■ ■ □ Describing in words the nth term of a sequence

● You need to be able to describe in words the nth term of a sequence where the rule is linear.

It's all very well being able to find the next term in a sequence, but could you find the 10th term, the 100th term, without plodding through all the other terms along the way?

If a sequence is going up or down by the same amount each time, then that number becomes your multiplying number.

Example

Find the 100th term of the sequence: 2, 5, 8, 11, 14, ...

Note that this is going up each time by 3

first term:	2	$1 \times 3 = 3$
second term:	5	$2 \times 3 = 6$
third term:	8	$3 \times 3 = 9$
fourth term:	11	$4 \times 3 = 12$

Look at the last column: 3, 6, 9, 12 – it is always one more than the number we want (2, 5, 8, 11).

Multiplying by 3 is therefore not enough. We then have to subtract 1

Fifth term should be: 14

Find it by calculation. $5 \times 3 = 15$

$15 - 1 = 14$ Yes! It works!

Now we can find the 100th term easily.

Hundredth term: $100 \times 3 = 300$

$300 - 1 = 299$

■■■ Describing the *n*th term of a linear sequence algebraically

- You need to be able to describe algebraically the *n*th term of a sequence where the rule is linear.

This follows on very simply and neatly from the last section. We just need to learn a bit of special notation for sequences.

n The number of the term indicates the **position** in the sequence:
$n = 1$ for the first term in the sequence
$n = 2$ for the second term and so on.

T_n As for the *n*th term itself, T stands for *term*, and *n* can be any number (see above).
Thus we have:
T_1 for the first term
T_2 for the second term and so on.

An example follows on the next page.

Example

Find the nth term of the sequence 2, 7, 12, 17, ...

We start by making a table:

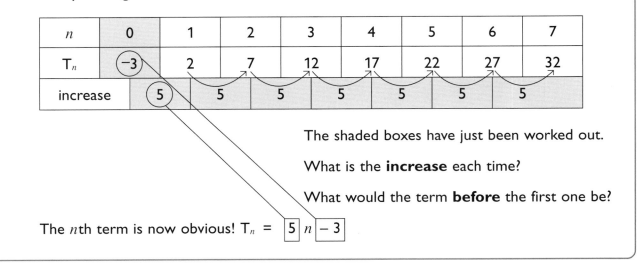

n	0	1	2	3	4	5	6	7
T_n	−3	2	7	12	17	22	27	32
increase	5	5	5	5	5	5	5	

The shaded boxes have just been worked out.

What is the **increase** each time?

What would the term **before** the first one be?

The nth term is now obvious! $T_n = \boxed{5}\,n\,\boxed{-3}$

■■■ Quadratic sequences: the nth term and substitution

● You need to be familiar with nth terms and substitution into a quadratic rule.

Can you find the next two terms of this sequence: 4, 7, 12, 19, 28, ...

We can make a table similar to the one above.

n	1	2	3	4	5	6	7
T_n	4	7	12	19	28	39	52
increase		3	5	7	9	11	13
increase			2	2	2	2	2

As you can see, for quadratic rules we need **two** rows of differences in the table. It turns out (you wouldn't be expected to find it for yourself at Common Entrance or Key Stage 3) that the quadratic rule for the above sequence is

$$T_n = n^2 + 3$$

It is much easier if you are told the rule at the start. To find each term, you just substitute $n = 1, 2, 3, ...$ into the formula.

108

Example

Give the first three terms of the sequence $T_n = 2n^2 - 1$

Substituting in $\quad n = 1,\quad$ we obtain $\quad 2 \times 1 - 1 = 1$

$\qquad\qquad\qquad n = 2,\qquad\qquad\qquad 2 \times 4 - 1 = 7$

$\qquad\qquad\qquad n = 3,\qquad\qquad\qquad 2 \times 9 - 1 = 17$

Sample questions

Try these sample questions for yourself. The answers are given at the back of the book.

Some of the questions involve ideas met in earlier work which may not be covered by the notes in this chapter.

8.14 Write down the next two **terms** in each of the following **sequences**:

(a) 47   43   39   35   ...   (2)

(b) 1   3   7   13   ...   (2)

(c) 800   400   200   100   ...   (2)

(d) 3   8   13   18   ...   (2)

(e) 1   4   16   64   ...   (2)

(f) 31   15   7   3   ...   (2)

8.15 (a) A sequence starts with 1
          Using the rule 'multiply by 2 and then add 4', write down the next four terms
          of the sequence.   (2)

     (b) Write a simple **rule** for finding the next term in this sequence.   (1)

          1   4   7   10   13   ...

8.16 Ann has been studying this sequence.

     2   5   8   11   14   ...

     She has written the formula $T_n = 3n - 1$ for finding the nth term of the sequence.

     (a) Use Ann's formula to find the 100th term of the sequence.   (1)

     (b) Find the smallest value of n for which T_n is more than 1000   (2)

8.17 For the **linear function** $y = x + 4$, complete this table of input (x) and output (y) values. (2)

x	−1	0	1	2	3	4
y	3	4				

8.18 For the **quadratic function** $y = x^2$, complete this table of x and y values. (2)

x	−2	−1	0	1	2	3
y	4				4	

8.3 Graphs

Four-quadrant co-ordinates

- You should be familiar with co-ordinates in all four quadrants and know about graph mappings.

The four quadrants are the four regions on the graph formed by extending both the x and y axes into the negative numbers.

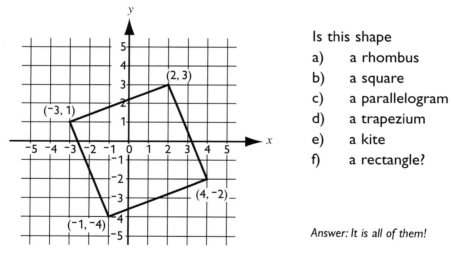

Is this shape
a) a rhombus
b) a square
c) a parallelogram
d) a trapezium
e) a kite
f) a rectangle?

Answer: It is all of them!

Mappings

Graph mappings, or line equations, are usually given in one of the following forms:

	type 1	type 2	type 3	type 4
form	$x = k$	$y = k$	$y = mx$	$y = mx + c$
example	$x = 5$	$y = -3$	$y = 2x$	$y = 2x + 5$

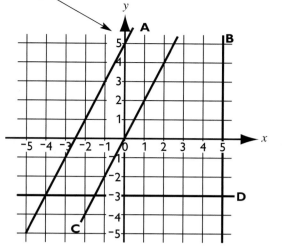

intercept

type 1
These are always vertical lines.

type 2
These are always horizontal lines.

type 3
These are always sloping lines going through the origin.

type 4
These are the rest. They slope up or down and cross both axes.

Can you match each of the lines **A**, **B**, **C** and **D** with the correct equation from the examples in the box on page 110?

Answer: **A** *is type 4,* **B** *is type 1,* **C** *is type 3 and* **D** *is type 2*

Level 1 papers will test only types 1 and 2, for example $x = 4$ and $y = -2$

Level 2 papers will also test types 3 and 4, for example $y = 3x$ and $y = 2x - 1$

Level 3 papers may, in addition, involve mappings of quadratic functions, for example $y = x^2 - 4$

■■■ Solving simultaneous equations graphically and algebraically

● You need to be able to solve simultaneous equations graphically and algebraically.

Any pair of simultaneous equations may be solved using algebra or by drawing a graph. Consider the following pair of simultaneous equations:

$$2x - 3y = 4 \quad \text{①}$$
$$3x + 2y = 19 \quad \text{②}$$

These equations will be solved both ways to show and compare the two methods on the next page.

Algebraic method

We note that equations ① and ② have opposite signs in the middle. We will therefore want to add them. (If the signs were the same, then we would subtract.) To do this, first make the y coefficients the same:

① × 2 is $4x - 6y = 8$ ③ | Substitute $x = 5$ into ② :

② × 3 is $9x + 6y = 57$ ④ | $15 + 2y = 19$

Add ③ and ④ $13x = 65$ | $2y = 4$

                        $\boxed{x = 5}$ | $\boxed{y = 2}$

                                                Check

                                                ① $10 - 6 = 4$ OK!

                                                ② $15 + 4 = 19$ OK!

Graphical method

We can make a table for each equation so that we can draw them both as straight line graphs.

① becomes $3y = 2x - 4$

x	2	5	8
$2x - 4$	0	6	12
y	0	2	4

② becomes $2y = 19 - 3x$

x	1	3	5
$19 - 3x$	16	10	4
y	8	5	2

which we then plot and draw, as has been done below:

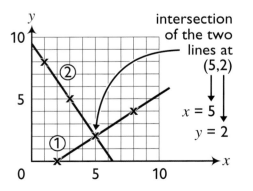

intersection
of the two
lines at
(5,2)

$x = 5$
$y = 2$

Thus we are able to read off from the graph that the solution to our simultaneous equations is $x = 5, y = 2$

Sample questions

Try these sample questions for yourself. The answers are given at the back of the book.

Some of the questions involve ideas met in earlier work which may not be covered by the notes in this chapter.

8.19 Prepare a co-ordinate grid with axes numbered -5 to 5. On the grid, draw and label lines representing these functions:

   (a) $x = 4$ (1)

   (b) $y = 5$ (1)

   (c) $x = -3$ (1)

8.20 (a) Tom has prepared this table of x and y values for the function $y = 2x + 3$

x	-1	0	1	2	3	4
y	1	3	5	7	9	11

        Plot several of the **co-ordinate pairs** (x, y) on a suitable co-ordinate grid and draw the graph of $y = 2x + 3$ (2)

   (b) On the same grid, draw and label the graph of the function $y = x - 4$ (2)

8.21 Sarah has prepared this table of x and y values for the function $y = x^2 - 2$

x	-3	-2	-1	0	1	2	3
y	7	2	-1	-2	-1	2	7

Prepare a co-ordinate grid with the x-axis numbered from -3 to 3 and the y-axis numbered from -3 to 8

Plot the co-ordinate pairs (x, y) on the grid and draw the graph of $y = x^2 - 2$ (2)

8.22 (a) Complete the table of values for the graph of $y = x^2 + 2x$ (3)

x	-4	-3	-2	-1	0	1	2
x^2	16		4	1	0		
$2x$	-8			-2	0		4
y	8			-1	0		

   (b) Draw the graph of $y = x^2 + 2x$ on a suitable co-ordinate grid.   (3)

   (c) Use your graph to find the values of x where the graph crosses the line $y = 4$ (2)

   (d) Write down the value of x when y takes its lowest value on the graph.   (1)

■■■ 8.23 The graphs of two functions, $y = x + 2$ and $y = 6 - x$, are drawn on the grid below.

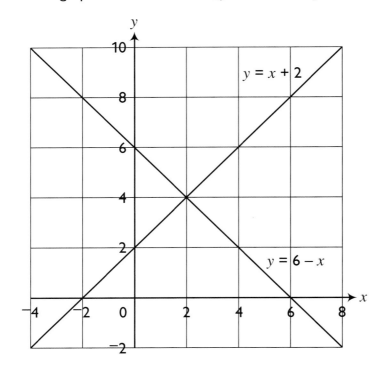

(a) What are the co-ordinates of the point of intersection of the two graphs? (1)

(b) By substitution, check that the co-ordinate pair satisfies both equations. (2)

■■■ 8.24 Consider this pair of **simultaneous equations**.

$y = 2x - 3$

$y = x + 1$

(a) **Substitute** y to combine this pair of equations into a single equation in x. (1)

(b) Solve the equation to find x. (2)

(c) Substitute the value of x in one original equation to find the value of y. (1)

(d) Check your answers by substitution in the second equation. (1)

■■■ 8.25 Consider this pair of simultaneous equations.

$3y = x + 5$

$y = {}^-x + 3$

(a) **Eliminate** x by adding the two equations, thus forming an equation in y. (1)

(b) Solve the equation to find y. (1)

(c) Substitute the value of y in one original equation to find the value of x. (2)

■■■ 8.26 Apples cost x pence each and pears cost y pence each.

    (a) Three apples and two pears cost £1.10
        Write this information as an equation in terms of x and y.   (1)

    (b) Five apples cost the same as four pears.
        Write this information as an equation in terms of x and y.   (1)

    (c) Use your answers to parts (a) and (b) to find the values of x and y.   (4)

    (d) Tamara spends exactly £2.25 when buying a selection of apples and pears for her friends.
        Write down all the different combinations of apples and pears which she could buy.   (3)

Summary

S

Remember that you should be familiar with all of the material in Chapter 7.

You should also now be able to do the following:

1.	Construct, express in symbolic form, and use simple formulae involving one or two operations.	**5**
✳ 2.	Use brackets appropriately.	**5**
✳ 3.	Formulate and solve linear equations with whole-number coefficients and simple fractional coefficients.	**6**
■■■ 4.	Solve equations, using trial-and-improvement methods.	**6**
■■■ 5.	Solve simple inequalities.	**7**
■■■ 6.	Multiply two expressions of the form $(x + n)$ and simplify the corresponding quadratic expression.	**7**
✳ 7.	Find and describe in words the rule for the next term or the nth term of a sequence where the rule is linear, when exploring number sequences.	**6**

✳ **Footnotes**

2. ISEB Level 1 requires candidates to be familiar with examples such as: $2(x - 3)$ and $3(b - c)$.
   ISEB Level 2 requires candidates to be familiar with examples such as: $2(3x - 5)$. ISEB Level 3 requires candidates to be familiar with examples such as: $x(x + 4)$.
3. ISEB Level 1 requires candidates to be familiar with examples such as: $x + 7 = 15$; $4x = 20$; $2x - 3 = 5$
   ISEB Level 2 requires candidates to be familiar with examples such as: $5 = 2x - 3$; $2x + 3 = 5 - 2x$; $\frac{1}{4}x = 5$
   ISEB Level 3 requires candidates to be familiar with examples such as: $6 - 2x = 4$; $\frac{1}{4}x - 3 = 9$; $\frac{2}{3}(2x + 5) = 8$
7. ISEB Level 1 candidates may be expected to give the next two terms of a sequence and could reasonably be asked to give an explanation such as 'Add 3 to get the next number.'
   ISEB Level 2 requires candidates to give an explanation as to how to give the next term of a sequence such as 'Multiply by 2 and add 1.'
   ISEB Level 3 requires candidates to give the nth term, or provide an expression for the nth term.

■■■ 8.   Describe the rule for a linear sequence algebraically.   **6+**

■■■ 9.   Find and describe in symbols the next term or the nth term of a sequence where
         the rule is quadratic.   **7**

    10. Use and interpret co-ordinates in all four quadrants.   **5**

 11.   Represent mappings expressed algebraically, and use Cartesian co-ordinates for
         graphical representation, interpreting general features.   **6**

■■■ 12. Represent mappings including quadratic functions.   **6+**

■■■ 13. Use algebraic and graphical methods to solve simultaneous linear equations in
         two variables.   **7**

Use the glossary at the back of the book for definitions of key words.

TY Test yourself

Before moving on to the next chapter, make sure you can answer the following questions.
The answers are at the back of the book.

1.   Simplify:

     (a) $3k + 3k$

     (b) $5k - 2k + 3k$

     (c) $k \times 3k$

     (d) $(3k)^2$

     (e) $6c^3 + 3c^3$

     (f) $4t^3 \times 5t^3$

2.   Multiply out the brackets and simplify, where possible:

     (a) $4(a - 2)$

     (b) $3(2a + 5)$

     (c) $2(3a - 4) + 5a - 2$

     (d) $5(2t + 3u) - 2v$

     (e) $5e - 2(2e + 3f)$

✳ **Footnote**

11. ISEB Level 1 requires candidates to represent mappings such as: $x = 3$; $y = {}^-5$.

   ISEB Level 2 requires candidates to represent mappings such as: $y = 2x$; $y = x - 2$.

   ISEB Level 3 requires candidates to represent mappings such as: $y = 2x^2 - 3x$; $y = 5 - x^2$ (see also Summary point 12.)

■■□ 3. Simplify:

(a) $5rs + r^2 - 3rs + 4r^2$

(b) $(2b)^2 - 4b^2$

(c) $4(5b + 2) - 5(3b - 3)$

■■■ (d) $4d^3 \div 5cd^3$

■■■ (e) $\dfrac{9b^2 + 6b^2}{3b}$

■■■ (f) $\dfrac{4n^2 + (2n)^2}{n}$

4. Factorise completely:

(a) $3a + 6$

(b) $4b - 10$

(c) $2a + 4b - 8$

■■■ (d) $a^2 + 2a$

■■■ (e) $6r^3 - 3r^2$

5. When $a = 5$, $b = ^-2$ and $c = 6$, find the value of:

(a) $2a - b$

(b) $2b^2$

(c) $c(a + b)$

(d) $\dfrac{2ac}{b}$

6. Sam is four years older than Jack, who is c years old.

(a) How old, in terms of c, is Sam?

Six years ago, Sam was twice as old as Jack was.

(b) Form an equation and solve it to find the value of c

(c) How old will Sam be in three years' time?

7. y is an integer.

(a) Write down, in terms of y, the integer which is

(i) four less than y

(ii) three times y.

(b) Calculate, in terms of y, the mean of the three integers.

(c) The mean is 22; form an equation in y and solve it.

(d) Use your answer to part (c) to write down the three integers.

8. Solve the following equations:

(a) $d - 7 = 12$

(b) $4w + 3 = 15$

(c) $4 + 4c = 16$

(d) $5a + 6 = 1$

(e) $5e + 3 = 2e + 9$

(f) $b - 9 = {}^-3$

■■□ 9. Solve the following equations:

(a) $\frac{1}{4}d = 3$

(b) $\frac{3}{4}r = 15$

(c) $2y + 4 = 4y - 12$

■■■ (d) $5 - 4x = 11$

■■■ (e) $\frac{1}{4}x - 8 = {}^-2$

■■■ (f) $\frac{1}{4}(x - 8) = {}^-2$

■■■ 10. The function $y = 12x - x^2$ can be written in the form $y = x(12 - x)$.

(a) By **trial and improvement** find, correct to 3 significant figures, the value of x when y is 30

Complete a table like the one below.

x	$12 - x$	$x(12 - x)$

When y is 32, there are two possible values for x:

x could be 8 since $8(12 - 8) = 32$

x could be 4 since $4(12 - 4) = 32$

(b) Find a second value for x when y is 30

(c) Find two values for x when y is 20

118

11. Write down the next two terms in each of the following sequences:

(a) 21   18   15   12   ...

(b) 2560   640   160   40   ...

(c) 1   3   4   7   11   ...

12. Find the 6th term and the 8th term of each of the following sequences:

(a) 3   6   9   12   15   ...

(b) 1   4   9   16   25   ...

(c) 1   2   5   10   17   ...

13. (a) Apply the rule 'multiply by 3 and then subtract 2' to write down the next four terms of the sequence beginning 2, 4, ...

(b) Apply the rule 'subtract 2 and then multiply by 3' to write down the next four terms of the sequence beginning 4, 6, ...

14. (a) The rule 'multiply by 2 and then add 1', starting with 1, produces this sequence:

1   3   7   15   31   ....

Suggest a similar rule which will give this sequence:

2   3   5   9   17   ...

■■□ (b) Suggest a formula of the form $T_n = ...$ which represents this sequence:

3   7   11   15   19   23   ....

■■■ 15. (a) (i) Write down the first term (T_1) and 100th term (T_{100}) of the sequence which can be written as $T_n = n^2 - 2$

(ii) Find the smallest value of n for which $T_n > 400$

(b) (i) Write down the first and 100th terms of the sequence which can be represented by $T_n = \dfrac{2n - 1}{3n + 1}$

(ii) What happens to T_n as n gets very large?

■■■ 16. (a) Complete the table of values for the function $y = 2x^2 + x - 2$

x	−3	−2	−1	0	1	2	3
x^2	9						
$2x^2$	18						
y	13						

(b) On a suitable co-ordinate grid, plot the (x, y) pairs and sketch the curve for $-3 \le x \le 3$

119

■■■ 17. Molly is m years old and her younger sister Natascha is n years old.

(a) Write down expressions, in terms of m and n, for

(i) the sum of their ages

(ii) the difference between their ages.

They calculate that the sum of their ages is 20 years.

(b) Write down an equation, in terms of m and n, to show this information.

Molly is 6 years older than Natascha.

(c) Use this information and your answer to part (b) to find Natascha's age.

Chapter 9: 11+ Shape, space and measures

9.1 Measures

Reading scales

● You should be familiar with all the common scales used for measuring and know how to read them.

In this first example, we can see that the scale is going up in tens, using intervals of two. This arrow is therefore pointing to **134**

This one goes up in fifties, so each division is worth 10. The arrow here therefore points to **70**

Attention! This one is going down not up! The scale is marked in tens and divided into twos, so the arrow here is pointing to **166**

This scale is simply going up in fives, with each division representing one. The arrow here is therefore pointing to **142**

Finally a decimal scale: each unit is divided into 5 divisions, so each one represents 0.2 units (1 ÷ 5). The arrow here is pointing to **148.4**

The metric system

● You need to know about common metric units and how to convert between them.

The metric system is based on powers of 10; that means 10, 100, 1000 and so on, as well as 0.1, 0.01, 0.001 etc. The scale goes outwards both ways.

Using a simple system of prefixes or 'multipliers', we can talk about any position on this scale. The actual unit of measurement is the same each time!

For	**length** we use	**metres** and the abbreviation	**m**
For	**mass**	**grams**	**g**
For	**time**	**seconds**	**s**
For	**capacity**	**litres**	**l**

and there are a few others which scientists use. (Can you find any other examples?)

So what are the prefixes?

Effect	Put this in front	Say this
× 1	(nothing)	(nothing)
× 1 000	k	kilo
× 1 000 000	M	mega
× 1 000 000 000	G	giga
× 1 000 000 000 000	T	tera
÷ 10	d	deci
÷ 100	c	centi
÷ 1 000	m	milli
÷ 1 000 000	μ	micro
÷ 1 000 000 000	n	nano

Now let's try it out!

250 cm is the same as (250 ÷ 100) m = 2.5 m
5.75 kg is the same as (5.75 × 1000) g = 5750 g

Write 4.8 cm in mm like this: (4.8 ÷ 100) is the same as (48 ÷ 1000) so it's 48 mm. Or just remember that 10 mm makes 1 cm and go from there.

This is silly but it helps! You have to say it out loud to make it work:

'One thousand metres in a kilometre, one thousand grams in a kilogram and one thousand whales in a killer whale ...'

Common units

● You need to be familiar with metric and imperial units in common use, and know how to estimate the answer to complicated calculations.

It is a very useful skill to be able to make reasonable estimates, both of measurements and calculations. The guidance on this page should improve your reliability!

To estimate...	think of...
millimetre	window glass 3 mm thick
centimetre	width of little finger
inch	two fingers
foot	adult foot
yard	child's arm span
metre	doorway 2 m high
mile	15-minute walk
kilometre	3-minute bike ride
millilitre	medicine spoon, 5 ml
pint	pint of milk
litre	carton of orange juice
gram	milk bottle top, 3 g
ounce	egg, 2 oz
pound	three or four apples
kilogram	bag of sugar
stone	two house bricks
hundredweight	older child's weight
metric tonne	small car
ton	Range Rover, 3 tons
square cm	postage stamp, 5 sq cm
square yard	floor carpet, 20 sq yd
square metre	4 paving slabs

Metric and Imperial unit conversions

The system of measurement in use in Britain now is almost completely metric, but many examples of imperial measurements still exist (especially miles, feet, inches, pints, stone and tons), and you should be aware of them.

You do not need to learn these conversions but it is useful to know a selection such as miles → km; lbs → kg; inches → cm etc.

metric	imperial	
to convert	to	multiply by
millimetres	inches	0.0394
centimetres	inches	0.3937
centimetres	feet	0.0328
metres	inches	39.37
metres	feet	3.281
metres	yards	1.094
kilometres	yards	1094
kilometres	miles	0.621
grams	ounces	0.035
grams	pounds	0.0022
kilograms	pounds	2.205
kilograms	stone	0.158
kilograms	hundredweight	0.01968
kilograms	tons	0.00098
tonnes	tons	0.9842
square cm	square inches	0.155
square m	square yards	1.196
square m	acres	0.00025
hectares	acres	2.471
square km	square miles	0.386
cubic cm (ml)	fluid ounces	0.0352
litres	pints	1.76
litres	gallons	0.22
km per hour	miles per hour	0.625
m per second	miles per hour	2.2374

imperial	metric	
to convert	to	multiply by
inches	millimetres	25.4
inches	centimetres	2.54
feet	centimetres	30.48
inches	metres	0.0254
feet	metres	0.3048
yards	metres	0.914
yards	kilometres	0.0009
miles	kilometres	1.609
ounces	grams	28.35
pounds	grams	453.6
pounds	kilograms	0.4536
stone	kilograms	6.35
hundredweight	kilograms	50.8
tons	kilograms	1016
tons	tonnes	1.016
square inches	square cm	6.45
square yards	square m	0.8361
acres	square m	4047
acres	hectares	0.4047
square miles	square km	2.59
fluid ounces	cubic cm (ml)	28.41
pints	litres	0.568
gallons	litres	4.546
miles per hour	km per hour	1.6
miles per hour	m per second	0.4469

To convert degrees Fahrenheit to degrees Celsius: $C = \frac{5}{9}(F - 32)$

To convert degrees Celsius to degrees Fahrenheit: $F = \frac{9}{5}C + 32$

Perimeter, area and volume

● You need to know the difference between these three words, and be able to determine them in simple cases.

Perimeter – units of length, e.g. cm, m

Perimeter is the distance around the edge of a shape. Think of a fly walking all the way around it. How far would the fly walk?

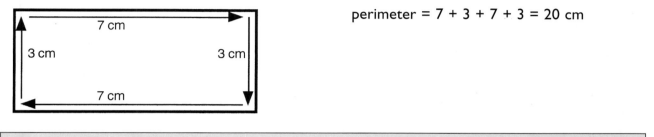

perimeter = 7 + 3 + 7 + 3 = 20 cm

'**Perim**eter' contains the word 'rim'!

Area

Area means counting squares inside the shape. If each square is 1 cm wide we say 'square cm'. We usually measure in units of square cm, square m or square km.

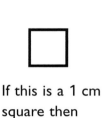

If this is a 1 cm square then

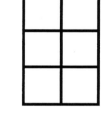

6 squares
6 sq. cm
(6 cm²)

12 squares
12 sq. cm
(12 cm²)

There is a formula that we can use to help us calculate the area of a rectangle.

Study these drawings of two rectangles.

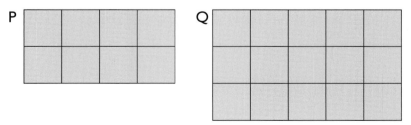

The area of rectangle P is 8 cm² (2 rows of 4 centimetre squares).

The area of rectangle Q is 15 cm² (3 rows of 5 centimetre squares).

You will notice that 2 × 4 = 8, and 3 × 5 = 15

We can write the formula for the area of a rectangle as $A = L \times W$ where A is the area, L is the length and W is the width of the rectangle.

125

Volume

Volume can be thought of as cubes inside a solid shape. We often count in cubic centimetres (a cube 1 cm each way), but cubic metres are also useful.

Each cube in this cuboid box is one cubic centimetre.

It has two layers each of 12 cubes (4 × 3).

So the volume of the box is:

2 × 12 = 24 cubic cm (24 cm³)

The 24-hour clock

Note that all you have to do is add 12 to the normal numbers on the clock to find the 24-hr clock equivalents.

Use am (morning) and pm (afternoon) only when using the 12-hr clock.

When using the 24-hr clock always write the time using four digits.

The time shown on this clock depends on whether it is morning or afternoon.

morning	1.55 am (12-hr clock)	0155 (24-hr clock)
afternoon	1.55 pm (12-hr clock)	1355 (24-hr clock)

Sample questions

Try these sample questions for yourself. The answers are given at the back of the book.

Some of the questions involve ideas met in earlier work which may not be covered by the notes in this chapter.

9.1　What are the readings on these scales?

(a)　　10　　　20　　　30　　　40　　　　　　　　(2)

(b)　　50　60　70　80　90　100　110　　　　　(2)

9.2 The diagram below shows two measuring beakers containing water.

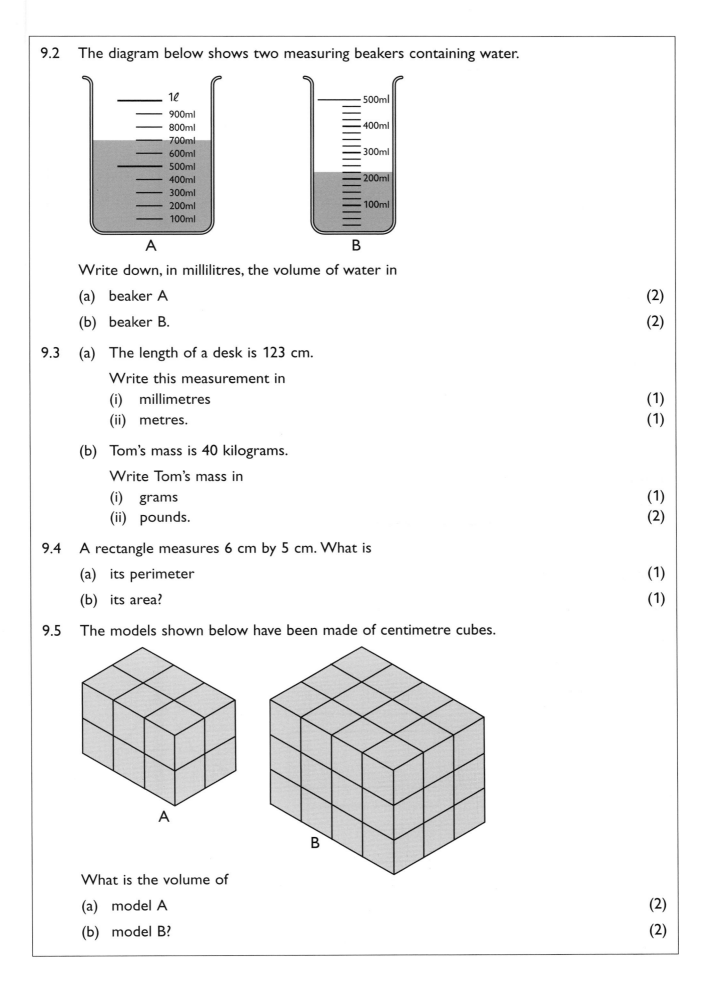

Write down, in millilitres, the volume of water in

(a) beaker A (2)

(b) beaker B. (2)

9.3 (a) The length of a desk is 123 cm.

Write this measurement in
(i) millimetres (1)
(ii) metres. (1)

(b) Tom's mass is 40 kilograms.

Write Tom's mass in
(i) grams (1)
(ii) pounds. (2)

9.4 A rectangle measures 6 cm by 5 cm. What is

(a) its perimeter (1)

(b) its area? (1)

9.5 The models shown below have been made of centimetre cubes.

What is the volume of

(a) model A (2)

(b) model B? (2)

9.2 Shape

Drawing solids and nets

● You need to be able to draw 3-D objects on paper and construct the nets of simple solids.

How to draw a cuboid

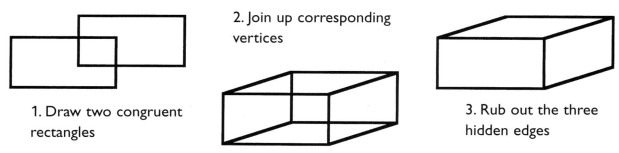

1. Draw two congruent rectangles

2. Join up corresponding vertices

3. Rub out the three hidden edges

The most important rule is to make sure lines are parallel. In the middle diagram above there are three sets of parallel lines.

Nets

A net is a cardboard cut-out which can be folded up to make a solid shape. Here are three common examples:

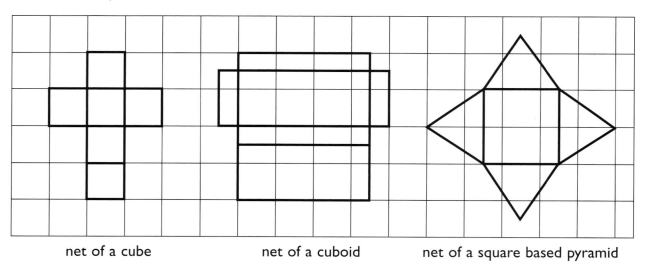

net of a cube   net of a cuboid   net of a square based pyramid

Symmetry and congruence

● You need to understand the difference between reflection and rotation symmetry and know the meaning of the phrase **congruent shapes**.

Reflection (reflective) symmetry

This happy face has only one line of reflection symmetry (one mirror line).

You could place a mirror down the middle and see the hidden half of the picture in the reflection.

This would **not** work if you placed the mirror any other way.

Rotation (rotational) symmetry

These four strange birds are arranged in a pattern which has rotation symmetry. Here the symmetry is **four-fold** or **order 4** because there are four right ways up with this picture.

Another way of thinking of this is to see that the pattern fits exactly onto itself in four ways.

This triangle has **no** mirror lines, but it does have three-fold rotation symmetry. The mirror lines don't work because of the way the triangle is shaded.

Congruence

Two shapes are described as congruent if one is an exact copy of the other. It doesn't matter if one is rotated or reflected, provided the size and shape of both are identical. (If only the sizes are different, we say that the shapes are *similar*.)

congruent shapes

Types of triangle, types of quadrilateral

Triangles and quadrilaterals are so common that we sort them into different categories according to their properties.

Triangles

1. **Equilateral** triangles have all the angles the same (each 60°) and all sides equal length.

2. **Isosceles** triangles have two equal angles and two equal sides.

3. **Right-angled** triangles have one angle of 90°.

4. **Scalene** triangles are those which are not included in the above list.

| equilateral | isosceles | right-angled | scalene |

Quadrilaterals

1. A **square** has four equal sides and four equal angles (each 90°). Opposite sides are parallel.

2. A **rectangle** (oblong) also has four equal (right) angles, but only opposite sides are equal length. Opposite sides are parallel.

3. A **rhombus** (diamond) has four equal sides, but only opposite angles are equal. Opposite sides are parallel.

4. A **parallelogram** has two pairs of parallel sides. Opposite sides are not only parallel but also equal in length. Opposite angles are equal.

5. A **kite** has two pairs of adjacent equal sides and two equal angles (including delta).

6. A **trapezium** has one pair of parallel sides. In an isosceles trapezium the non-parallel sides are also equal in length.

| square | rectangle | rhombus | parallelogram |

| kite | delta (arrowhead) | trapezium | isosceles |

Sample questions

Try these sample questions for yourself. The answers are given at the back of the book.

Some of the questions involve ideas met in earlier work which may not be covered by the notes in this chapter.

9.7 The cuboid represented by the drawing below has been made from cardboard marked with centimetre squares.

(a) Draw an accurate net for the cuboid. (3)

(b) What area of cardboard is needed to make the cuboid? (Edges are glued together without any 'tabs'.) (3)

9.8 Two quadrilaterals are drawn below.

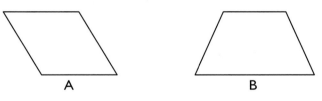

A   B

(a) Name the shapes. (2)

(b) Draw all lines of symmetry on the shapes. (3)

(c) Describe the rotational symmetry of the shapes. (2)

9.9 Look carefully at the shapes drawn on this grid.

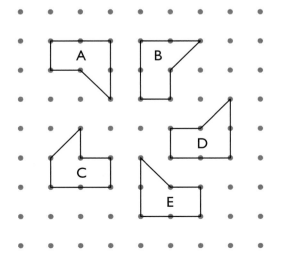

List the letters of the shapes which are congruent to shape A. (4)

9.3 Space

Triangle construction

● You need to be able to draw accurate scale diagrams (to within one millimetre and one degree) and to be able to construct triangles using just the information given.

Three sides

Example

Draw a triangle of side lengths 3 cm, 5 cm and 7 cm.

First draw the longest side at the bottom of the page. Place the point of a pair of compasses at one end of this line and draw an arc whose radius is one of the other two lengths. Repeat for the other side. The point where the two arcs cross is the apex of the triangle.

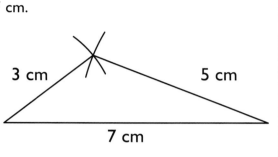

Two sides and the angle between them

Example

Draw a triangle in which two of the sides measure 7 cm and 5 cm. The angle between them is 35°.

Draw the longer of the two sides horizontally on the page and measure out the given angle at one end. Extend this second side a little further than you think you will need. Now measure along this second side for the correct distance before closing up the triangle.

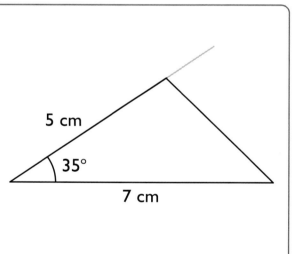

One side and the angle at each end

Example

Draw a triangle with base 4 cm and base angles 60° and 30°.

This is rather like the situation above, but with two angles drawn rather than one. Here, however, only one length has to be measured.

Draw the given side horizontally on the page and construct the desired angle at each end. Continue these two new lines until they cross – the intersection point is the apex of the triangle.

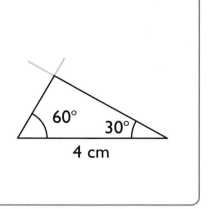

Types of angle

Angles can be any size from 0° to 360°. They are given special names according to their size.

size of angle (degrees)	name
less than 90	acute
90	right
90 to 180	obtuse
180	straight
180 to 360	reflex

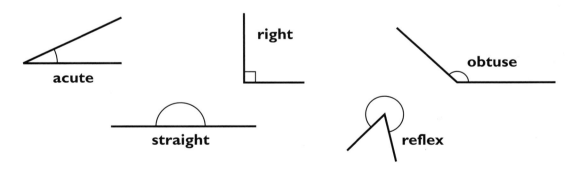

Think of a mnemonic for remembering the order of these names: e.g. Always Run Over Stupid Robots!

Knowing the approximate size of each type of angle helps with estimation, especially in bearings questions. It is good practice to sketch out a scale diagram in rough before you draw it accurately with the exact angles, to make sure you don't run out of paper!

133

The eight-point compass

● You need to be able to describe the position of something using distance and one of the eight compass directions.

How do you remember the points of the compass? People have suggested *Naughty Elephants Squirt Water* or even *Nice Easy School Work*! Perhaps the best is simply to remember *North East South West*.

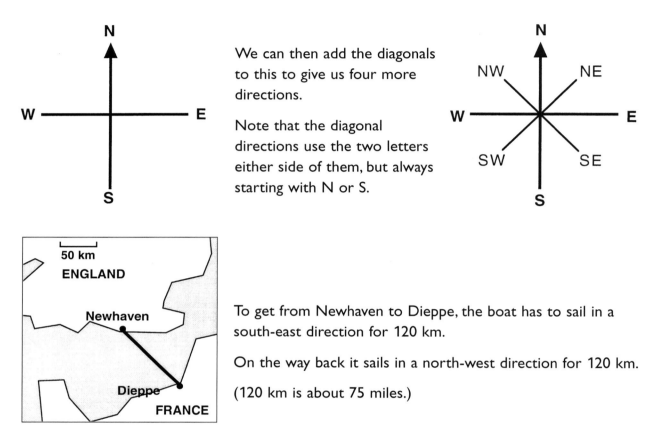

We can then add the diagonals to this to give us four more directions.

Note that the diagonal directions use the two letters either side of them, but always starting with N or S.

To get from Newhaven to Dieppe, the boat has to sail in a south-east direction for 120 km.

On the way back it sails in a north-west direction for 120 km.

(120 km is about 75 miles.)

Compass points

Bearings are always given clockwise from north, and are always given as a three-digit number.

Try to get used to estimating angles before drawing or measuring them, in order to prevent the mistake of reading the wrong scale on your angle measurer or protractor.

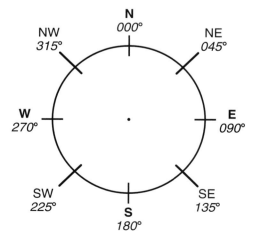

Reflections on diagonal lines

● You need to be able to complete reflections in diagonal lines, sloping either up or down (45°).

Our eyes are good at looking at symmetry which is lateral (left-right) but we find it much harder if it goes up or down (vertical). Symmetry on a diagonal is even harder.

To make it easier, just turn the paper through 45° and the symmetry line is now vertical! If the symmetry line is now horizontal then you turned it the wrong way. Go back and turn it in the other direction!

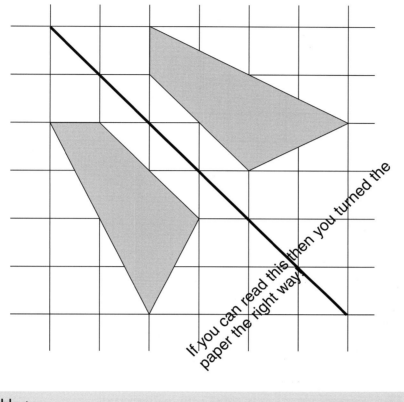

You need to be able to:

● see when a shape or pattern has a diagonal line of symmetry

● complete a shape or pattern so that it has diagonal symmetry.

In both cases, turning the page makes it all very straightforward.

Three transformations: reflection, rotation and translation

- There are **three** types of transformation which move a shape around without changing its size. You need to be familiar with all three.

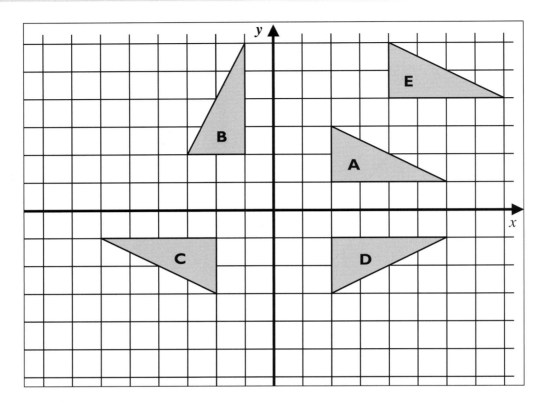

The three transformations used above were reflection, rotation and translation:

To map **A** on to **B** the transformation is rotation 90° anti-clockwise about (0, 0).

To map **A** on to **C** the transformation is rotation 180° about (0, 0).

To map **A** on to **D** the transformation is reflection in the x-axis.

To map **A** on to **E** the transformation is translation two units right and three units up.

Sample questions

Try these sample questions for yourself. The answers are given at the back of the book.

Some of the questions involve ideas met in earlier work which may not be covered by the notes in this chapter.

9.10 (a) Construct triangle *ABC* where *AB* is 6 cm, *BC* is 5 cm and *AC* is 4 cm. (3)

(b) Measure, to the nearest degree, angle *BAC*. (1)

9.11 Triangle *PQR* is drawn below.

(a) What type of angle is
  (i) angle *PQR*   (1)
  (ii) angle *PRQ*?   (1)

(b) What name is given to this type of triangle?   (1)

9.12 The diagram below shows four pupils standing on a patio.

Using the eight points of the compass, describe the direction of

(a) Ben from Amy   (1)

(b) Amy from Ben   (1)

(c) Clara from Amy   (1)

(d) Diane from Ben.   (1)

9.13 Reflect the shape in the line.   (3)

9.14 On the grid below:

(a) rotate shape *A* through 90° clockwise about the large dot (2)

(b) translate the shape *A* two units right and three units down. (2)

S Summary

Remember that you should be familiar with all of the material in National Curriculum Key Stage 1, for example, knowledge of plane and solid shapes.

You should also now be able to do the following:

1.	Choose and use appropriate units and instruments, interpreting, with accuracy, numbers on a range of measuring instruments.	**4**
2.	Make 3-D mathematical models by linking given faces or edges; draw common 2-D shapes in different orientations on grids.	**4**
3.	Find perimeters of simple shapes and find areas.	**4**
4.	Find volumes by counting cubes.	**4+**
5.	Know the rough metric equivalents of imperial units still in daily use and convert one metric unit to another.	**5**
6.	Understand and use the formula for the area of a rectangle.	**5**
7.	Reflect simple shapes in a mirror line.	**4**
8.	Specify location by means of angle and distance.	**4+**
9.	Understand and use the transformations rotation and translation; identify congruent shapes and orders of rotational symmetry.	**4+**
10.	Measure and draw angles to the nearest degree, when drawing or using shapes, and use language associated with angle.	**5**

Use the glossary at the back of the book for definitions of key words.

Test yourself

Before moving on to the next chapter, make sure you can answer the following questions. The answers are at the back of the book.

1. What are the readings on these scales?

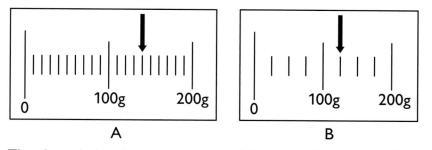

A   B

2. The shape below has a perimeter of 14 cm and an area of 6 cm².

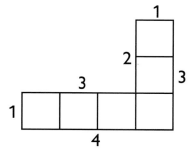

(a) Draw a shape which has perimeter 10 cm and area 6 cm².

(b) Draw a shape which has perimeter 14 cm and area 10 cm².

3. This model has been made from interlocking centimetre cubes.

(a) What is its volume?

(b) On isometric paper, draw a different view of the model.

4. (a) Construct triangle ABC where AB is 10 cm, angle BAC is 30° and angle ABC is 40°.

(b) Measure and write down
   (i) angle ACB
   (ii) AC

5. Five congruent shapes are drawn on the grid below.

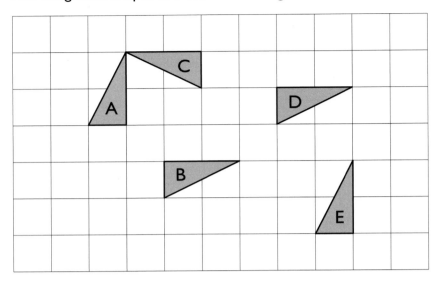

(a) What does *congruent* mean?

(b) Which shape could be reached from shape A by:
  (i)   reflection
  (i)   rotation
  (iii) translation?

6. The square below has area 16 cm², 4 lines of symmetry and rotational symmetry of order 4

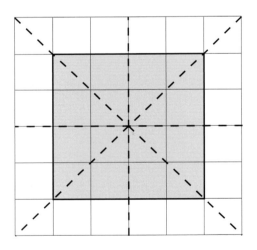

On squared paper, draw three shapes, A, B and C, all with area 16 cm², and with the following extra features:

Shape A   one line of symmetry only

Shape B   two lines of symmetry

Shape C   rotational symmetry of order 4 but no lines of symmetry

Hint: start with a square each time and modify it.

Chapter 10: 13+ Shape, space and measures

10.1 Measures

● You should be able to make sensible estimates of a range of measures in relation to everyday situations. It would be a good idea to remind yourself of the information on pages 123–124 in Chapter 9.

■■□ Parts of a circle and the value of pi

The **circumference** of the circle is the same as its perimeter – it is the distance all the way around the edge.

The **diameter** is any straight line which goes from one side of the circle to the other, through the centre. The diameter divides the circle into two equal halves.

The **radius** is any straight line which runs from the centre of the circle to the circumference.

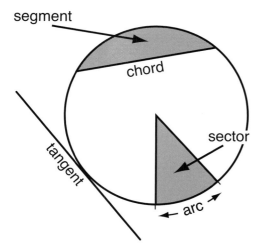

A **chord** is a straight line joining any two points on the circumference.

A **segment** is part of a circle cut off by a chord.

A **sector** is part of a circle cut off by two radii.

An **arc** is a section of the circumference.

A **tangent** is a straight line which just touches the circumference.

A **semicircle** is half a circle, cut at the diameter.

Pi

Pi is the famous number which is calculated by dividing the circumference of any circle by its diameter. Its approximate value is 3.14 or $\frac{22}{7}$ or $\frac{355}{113}$ or even $\frac{312\ 689}{99\ 532}$!

Let's give it a few more decimal places. How about the first fifty?

π = 3.141 592 653 589 793 238 462 643 383 279 502 884 197 169 399 375 10 ...

■■□ Areas of circles

● You need to know the formulae for circles, and apply them to circumference, area and volume calculations.

Start by reminding yourself of the words used to describe the parts of a circle on page 141.

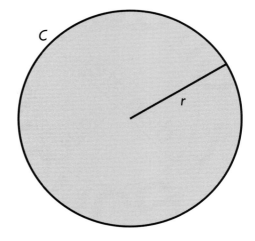

abbreviation	meaning
r	radius
d	diameter
C	circumference
A	area
h	height (of a cylinder for example)

(Note that we use capital letters for C and A)

You need to learn these formulae:

$$d = 2r \qquad C = \pi d \qquad C = 2\pi r \qquad A = \pi r^2 \qquad \text{volume of cylinder} = \pi r^2 h$$

If there is no π (pi) on your calculator, then you can use 3.14 instead.

Example

How far along the ground will a wheel of radius 30 cm travel if it turns 1000 times?

The radius is 30 cm (0.3 m).

So the circumference (one turn of the wheel) is 2 × π × 0.3 which comes to 1.884 96 m.

Thus after 1000 turns, the wheel has travelled 1884.96 m or about 1.9 km.

Area and volume formulae

Level 1 candidates will be given a sheet of formulae for Common Entrance. Other candidates need to learn the formulae.

Area formulae

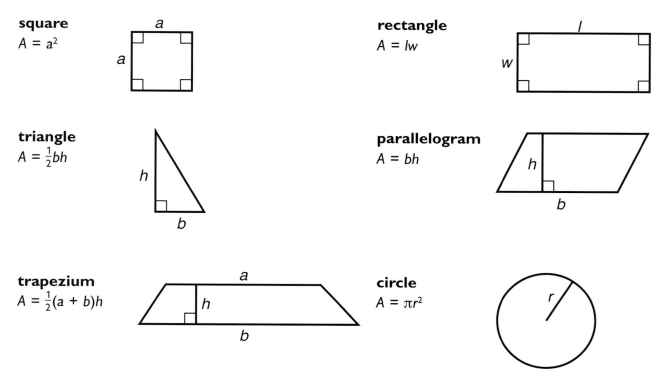

square
$A = a^2$

rectangle
$A = lw$

triangle
$A = \frac{1}{2}bh$

parallelogram
$A = bh$

trapezium
$A = \frac{1}{2}(a + b)h$

circle
$A = \pi r^2$

Volume formulae

cube $V = a^3$
(edge-length cubed)

cuboid $V = lwh$
(length × width × height)

prism volume = cross section area × height (length). This includes cylinders!

pyramid $\frac{1}{3}$ × base area × height. This includes cones!

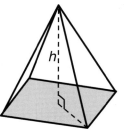

Level 1 questions may involve calculating:

● the areas of triangles and parallelograms

● the volumes of cuboids.

■■□ Calculating areas of fractional and composite shapes

- You need to be able to calculate the area of any shape, including fractional and composite ones.

Fractional shapes are those which are ordinary shapes such as rectangles and circles, but with holes cut out or pieces missing. You calculate the area of a fractional shape using subtraction.

Composite shapes are those which are made by sticking together simpler shapes such as squares and triangles. You calculate the area of a composite shape using addition.

The path around this small garden is 1 m wide. The area of the path is found by subtracting the area of the garden from the area of the surrounding rectangle.

area of garden = 4 × 6
= 24 m²

area of surrounding rectangle =
(1 + 4 + 1) × (1 + 6 + 1) = 48 m²

so area of path = 48 − 24
= 24 m²

With composite shapes, it is usually up to you to work out the best way of dividing the area up into simpler shapes.

Of course, it doesn't actually matter which way you do it – they all give the same answer!

This archway looks complicated but it is really just made up of simpler shapes, as the second diagram clearly shows.

When working out its area, we would subtract the area of the small circle from the area of the large circle and then halve the answer to find the area of the curved part of the arch. To this we would add the area of the two rectangular feet and obtain the final answer.

■■□ Calculating the volumes of fractional and composite shapes

- You need to be able to calculate the volume of any solid, including prisms.

Check that you are familiar with the standard volume formulae on page 143, especially of the prism. Here is one more:

sphere volume = $\frac{4}{3}\pi r^3$

Example 1

A cake in the shape of a cylinder (height 7 cm, radius 12 cm)
is cut into sectors of 60 degrees each. Find the volume of each piece.

$360° \div 60° = 6$, so each piece is $\frac{1}{6}$ of the cake

volume of whole cake (cylinder) = $\pi r^2 h$

so volume of cake is $\pi \times 12^2 \times 7 = 3166.725$ cm³

thus volume of piece $\frac{3166.725}{6} = 527.8$ cm³

12 cm

60°

7 cm

12 cm

Example 2

The base of this toy is a hemisphere (half a sphere).

To find the volume of the toy we add up the volumes
of the upper cone and the lower hemisphere:

volume of hemisphere = $\frac{1}{2} \times \frac{4}{3} \times \pi \times 2^3$

$= 16.76$ cm³

volume of cone = $\frac{1}{3} \times (\pi \times 2^2) \times 5$

$= 20.94$ cm³

so volume of toy = 37.7 cm³

5 cm

2 cm

Distance, speed and time

● You need to be able to solve problems involving distance, speed and time calculations.

If you learn the 'magic triangle' below, then you will surely become a wizard at working out
these problems!

distance

speed ✕ *time*

Simply put your finger over the one you want to find and the
magic triangle tells you what calculation to do with the other
two. For example, to find *speed* you have to do *distance ÷ time*.

An example follows on the next page.

Example

How long does it take to travel 80 miles if you are travelling at 50 miles per hour?

time = distance ÷ speed

= 80 ÷ 50

= 1.6 hours

(OK, but what does the 0.6 hours mean?)

0.6 hours = 0.6 × 60 minutes

= 36 minutes

So the journey takes 1 hour 36 minutes.

Speed is an example of a compound measure. Other compound measures, density and pressure, may be met in your science studies.

Mathematics papers at all levels will test only speed. Level 3 questions may involve average speeds of multi-stage journeys.

Sample questions

Try these sample questions for yourself. The answers are given at the back of the book.

Some of the questions involve ideas met in earlier work which may not be covered by the notes in this chapter.

10.1 (a) The **length** of Tom's pencil is 13 cm.
  (i) Write this length in millimetres. (1)
  (ii) Write this length in metres. (1)
  (iii) What is this length, approximately, in inches? (1)

 (b) Mr Smith is 6 feet tall.
  What is his approximate height in metres? (1)

 (c) 5 miles is approximately the same as 8 kilometres.
  The road distance between John O'Groats and Land's End is about 600 miles.
  What is this distance in kilometres? (2)

10.2 (a) A field has an **area** of 50 000 square metres.
  What is this in **hectares** (ha)? (1)

 (b) A cube has edges of length 10 cm.
  (i) What is the **area** of one face in square centimetres (cm²)? (1)
  (ii) What is the **volume** of the cube in cubic centimetres (cm³)? (1)

10.3 (a) A beetle crawled 36 centimetres in 3 minutes.
  (i) What was its **average speed** in centimetres per minute? (1)
  (ii) What was the average speed in cm/s? (1)
  (iii) How far, at this average speed, could the beetle crawl in an hour? (1)

  (b) Mr Williams drives at an average speed of 63 mph (miles/h) on a motorway.

  (i) How many miles does he travel in 10 minutes? (2)

  He passes the Yummy Snack service station at 0900

  (ii) At what time will he pass the Last Chance service station which is 21 miles away from the Yummy Snack? (2)

10.4 (a) (i) Construct triangle ABC with AB = 9 cm, BC = 7.5 cm and AC = 8 cm. (4)
  (ii) Measure and write down the shortest distance from C to AB. (2)

  (b) A square has **diagonals** of length 10 centimetres.

  (i) Make an accurate drawing of the square. (3)
  (ii) By taking suitable measurements, find the perimeter of the square. (2)

10.5 (a) On an isometric grid, draw a representation of a cuboid measuring 7 cm by 5 cm by 4 cm. (2)

  (b) Calculate the volume of the cuboid. (2)

  (c) Calculate the total surface area of the cuboid. (4)

10.6 Felix is making a scale model of a battleship, using a scale of 1 : 250

  (a) If the length of the battleship is 90 metres, what will be the length, in centimetres, of the model? (3)

  Felix then makes a model sailor to stand on the deck.

  (b) What is the approximate height of the model sailor? (1)

10.7 A circle has radius 5 cm. Taking π to be 3, estimate:

  (a) the circumference of the circle (2)

  (b) the area of the circle. (2)

10.8 A circle has radius 6 cm.

  Giving your answers to three significant figures, and using either $\pi = 3.142$ or the π value in your calculator, calculate:

  (a) the circumference of the circle (2)

  (b) the area of the circle. (3)

■■□ 10.9 The diagram below shows a design made up of a square and four semicircles.

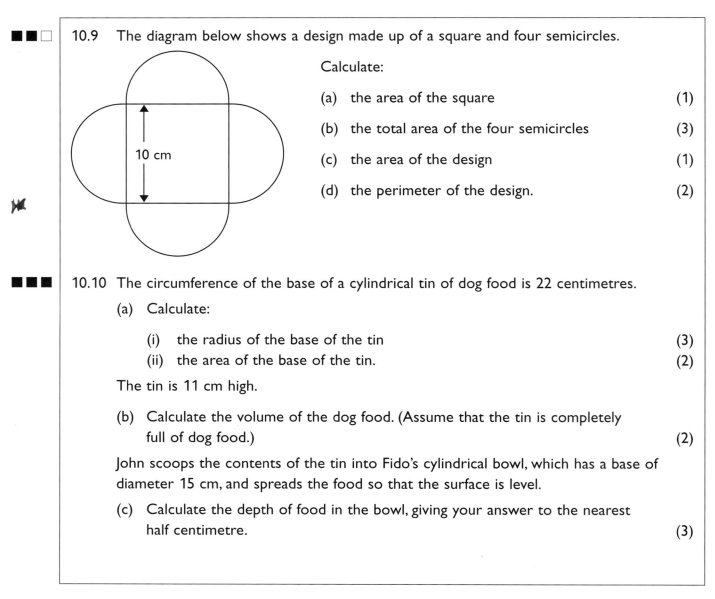

Calculate:

(a) the area of the square (1)

(b) the total area of the four semicircles (3)

(c) the area of the design (1)

(d) the perimeter of the design. (2)

10 cm

■■■ 10.10 The circumference of the base of a cylindrical tin of dog food is 22 centimetres.

(a) Calculate:

(i) the radius of the base of the tin (3)
(ii) the area of the base of the tin. (2)

The tin is 11 cm high.

(b) Calculate the volume of the dog food. (Assume that the tin is completely full of dog food.) (2)

John scoops the contents of the tin into Fido's cylindrical bowl, which has a base of diameter 15 cm, and spreads the food so that the surface is level.

(c) Calculate the depth of food in the bowl, giving your answer to the nearest half centimetre. (3)

10.2 Shape

Reflection symmetry in plane shapes

● You need to understand reflection symmetry in two-dimensional shapes.

Lines of symmetry, or mirror lines, always go through the centre of a shape. This may help you decide where they are. A shape can have any number of mirror lines.

Only one of the signs above does **not** have any reflection symmetry. Which one is it? (Answer on the next page).

Don't forget that mirror lines can go diagonally as well as across or up (think of a square). However, many people think that rectangles and parallelograms have diagonal mirror lines too – don't be caught out!

Rectangles

Rectangles have two lines of symmetry.

This is what you get if you try to reflect them diagonally! (A kite.)

Parallelograms

Parallelograms do not have **any** lines of symmetry.

This is what you get if you try to reflect them diagonally. (A kite again!)

Answer: the second sign has rotation symmetry but not reflection symmetry.

Rotation symmetry in plane shapes

● You need to understand rotation symmetry in two-dimensional shapes.

If you can picture in your mind how many right-ways up a picture has, then you know its order of rotational symmetry. Don't worry if you find this difficult to do in your head. It's a very good idea to trace the shape and then turn the tracing paper round to see if the tracing will fit over the original as it turns.

Order of rotation

If a shape has *rotation symmetry order 2*, then it simply means that the shape looks the same in two positions as it is turned around. *Order 3* means it looks the same in three positions and so on.

order 2

order 3

order 4

A shape with *order 1 rotation symmetry* has *no* rotation symmetry.

Centre of rotation

The *centre of rotation* is the name given to the point on a picture where you would put a pin if you wanted to spin it round. See if you can find the centre of rotation for each of the three pictures on page 149.

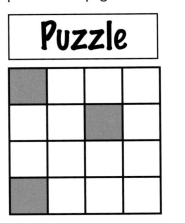

Puzzle

What is the smallest number of squares you have to shade in order to give the pattern rotation symmetry of order 4?

Answer: 5

■■□ Properties of quadrilaterals

● You need to know the types and properties of the different quadrilaterals.

diagram of shape	lines of symmetry	order of rotation	notes
square	4	4	The only regular quadrilateral: four equal sides and four equal angles. Diagonals bisect each other at right angles.
rectangle	2	2	Includes squares (that is, a square is a special type of rectangle). Non-square ones are called 'oblongs'. Diagonals bisect each other.
rhombus	2	2	Diamond – includes squares. Opposite angles are equal. Diagonals bisect each other at right angles.

diagram of shape	lines of symmetry	order of rotation	notes
parallelogram	0	2	Includes rhombus, rectangle and square. Opposite angles are equal. Diagonals bisect each other.
arrow head (delta)	1	1	The only concave quadrilateral: one diagonal is external. A special type of kite. Diagonals do not intersect.
kite	1	1	Includes rhombus, square and arrowhead. One pair of opposite equal angles. Diagonals intersect at right angles.
(isosceles) trapezium	1 or 0	1	Includes rectangle, parallelogram, and square. The isosceles trapezium has two equal sides and two equal angles.

■■□ Polygons

Names of the polygons

A polygon is a shape with straight sides. In fact, the word is just the Greek for *many angles* (literally *many knees*). Polygons can have any number of sides from three upwards and each polygon has a corresponding special name. Here are the first ten names:

Number of sides	Polygon name	Number of sides	Polygon name
3	triangle	8	octagon
4	quadrilateral	9	nonagon
5	pentagon	10	decagon
6	hexagon	11	hendecagon
7	heptagon	12	dodecagon

Regular polygon angles

A regular polygon is one in which all the sides are the same length and all the angles are equal. These are made by drawing the required number of points at equal intervals around the circumference of a circle.

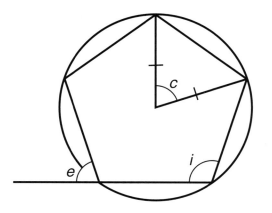

This is a regular pentagon, but the following rules work for any regular polygon.

Let's assume that the polygon has n sides.

(Here $n = 5$)

Then the angle at the centre is given by $c = \dfrac{360°}{n}$.

The triangle made by joining the centre of the circle to any two vertices is always isosceles. From this fact it is easy to show that the interior angle formula is:

$i = 180° - c$

$\quad = 180° - \dfrac{360°}{n}$

Imagine making the polygon out of a straight length of wire. The exterior angle is the angle through which you would bend the wire at each corner.

$e = 180° - i$

$\quad = \dfrac{360°}{n} = c$

Finally for any polygon, the sum of all the interior angles is given by $180(n - 2)°$

■■□ Drawings of 3-D objects on isometric paper

● You need to be able to draw 3-D objects in 2-D, using isometric paper.

Tips

1. Hold the paper the right way up. You need straight vertical lines, not straight horizontal lines.

2. Use the lines on the paper to guide your drawing.

3. Look at the way right angles are drawn – they are not 90 degrees!

4. Use your ruler carefully. Check especially that you are drawing parallel lines of equal length on corresponding edges.

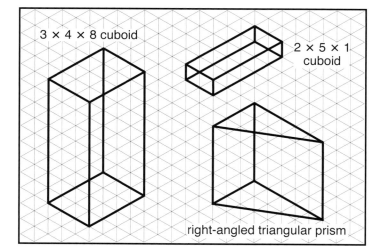

Sample questions

Try these sample questions for yourself. The answers are given at the back of the book.

Some of the questions involve ideas met in earlier work which may not be covered by the notes in this chapter.

10.11 (a) Name these plane shapes. (3)

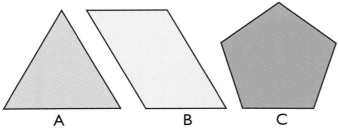

A   B   C

(b) Sketch the following shapes, clearly marking all equal angles and lengths and parallel sides:
   (i)   rhombus   (1)
   (ii) kite   (1)
   (iii) isosceles trapezium   (1)

(c) Sketch the following shapes and draw all lines of symmetry:
   (i)   square   (1)
   (ii) kite   (1)
   (iii) regular hexagon   (1)

10.12 Describe fully the reflection and/or rotation symmetry of the following plane shapes:
   (a) regular hexagon   (2)
   (b) parallelogram   (1)
   (c) isosceles triangle   (1)

10.13 (a) Name these solid shapes. (3)

(b) Sketch a **net** for the triangular prism shown below. (1)

2 cm

2 cm

2 cm

3 cm

2 cm

10.14 Choose your answers from the following list of quadrilaterals.

square   rectangle   rhombus   parallelogram   kite   isosceles trapezium

Note: A quadrilateral may appear more than once in your answers.

List the quadrilaterals which have:

(a) all sides the same length (2)

(b) all pairs of opposite angles equal (2)

(c) diagonals intersecting at right angles (2)

(d) diagonals which are equal (2)

(e) no reflection symmetry (2)

(f) no rotation symmetry. (2)

10.15 (a) The exterior angle of a regular hexagon is 60°.

What is the **interior angle** of a regular hexagon? (1)

(b) Bella has drawn a regular **polygon** which has 15 sides.

What size is
(i) the exterior angle (1)
(ii) the interior angle (1)
(iii) the sum of the interior angles? (2)

10.16 On isometric paper, draw representations of the solids which are sketched below:

(a) a cuboid (1)

1 cm
2 cm   3 cm

(b) a step structure (3)

3 cm
2 cm   3 cm

(c) a triangular prism. (3)

4 cm   4 cm

4 cm

10.3 Space

Angle laws for straight lines

● You need to know and apply the angle laws of straight lines and understand the symmetry of polygons.

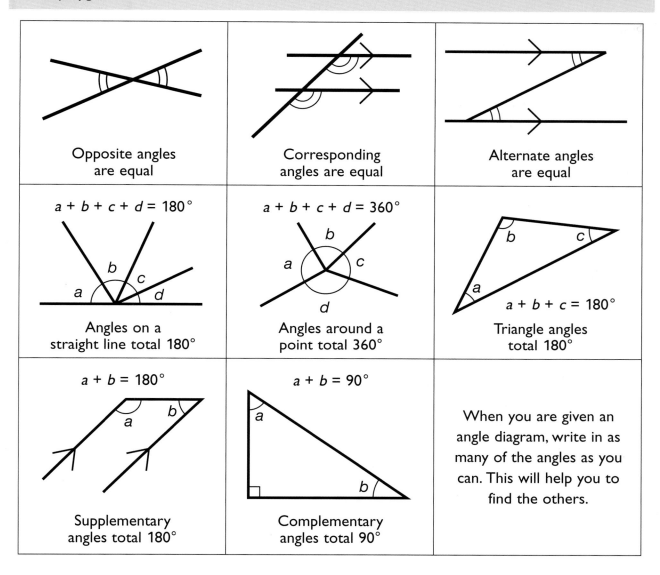

Opposite angles are equal	Corresponding angles are equal	Alternate angles are equal
$a + b + c + d = 180°$ Angles on a straight line total 180°	$a + b + c + d = 360°$ Angles around a point total 360°	$a + b + c = 180°$ Triangle angles total 180°
$a + b = 180°$ Supplementary angles total 180°	$a + b = 90°$ Complementary angles total 90°	When you are given an angle diagram, write in as many of the angles as you can. This will help you to find the others.

■■□ Angle laws for polygons

Most of what you need to know about angles in regular polygons is on page 152. Look out for isosceles triangles! The fact that they have two equal sides and two equal angles can often provide you with lots of clues. All regular polygons (including the equilateral triangle) have both rotation and reflection symmetry. This is always the same as the number of sides. For example, a regular octagon has 8 mirror lines and rotation symmetry of order 8

Level 1 questions will be restricted to solving problems using the angle properties of intersecting and parallel lines.

■■□ Enlargement and linear scale factor

- You need to understand the importance of **scale factor** and **centre of enlargement** when making enlargement constructions.

Constructing an enlargement

Step 1   Draw a line from the centre of enlargement to each corner of the shape **and keep going**.

Step 2   For each corner of the shape, measure the distance from the centre of enlargement and multiply this by the scale factor. Mark a new point along the same line of this new distance from the centre of enlargement.

Step 3   Join up all the points made in Step 2.

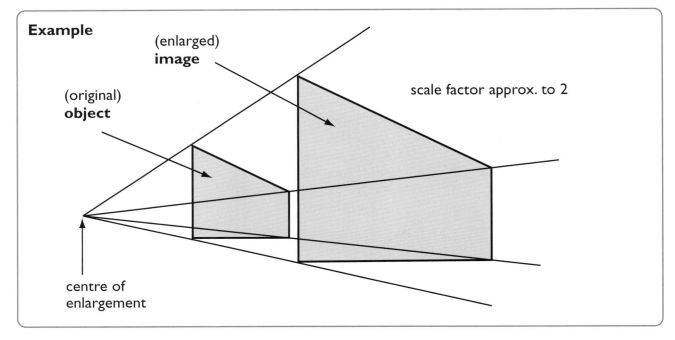

Example

(enlarged) **image**

(original) **object**

scale factor approx. to 2

centre of enlargement

When one shape is an enlargement of the other we call them *similar*.

Finding the centre of enlargement and the scale factor

If the construction has already been made, draw lines from each corner of the image to its corresponding corner on the object **and keep going**. The point where these lines intersect is the centre of enlargement. To find the scale factor, just choose any two corresponding edges: the scale factor is the length of the image edge divided by the length of the object edge.

■■□ Area scale factor

● You need to understand the importance of the area factor when making enlargement constructions.

Recall from the previous page that the scale factor was the number by which all lengths were multiplied to make the enlargement (so a scale factor of 2 produced a ×2 enlargement).

Area factor is similar. It is the number by which the original area is multiplied to obtain the area of the enlargement. The clever part of it is that there is an easy link between the two.

To find the area factor you just square the scale factor.

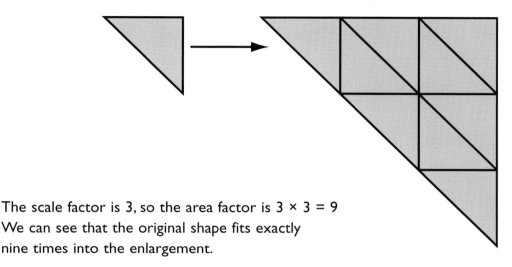

The scale factor is 3, so the area factor is 3 × 3 = 9
We can see that the original shape fits exactly
nine times into the enlargement.

Similarly for this enlargement
(scale factor 2)

 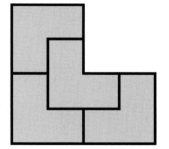

It's true for every shape!

■■□ Three-figure bearings and scale drawings

● You need to be able to use three-figure bearings in measuring and constructions.

Bearings

Follow these tips to find three-figure bearings:

● Always measure **clockwise** from **north**.

● Try to measure to the nearest degree.

● Make sure you have read the direction the right way round. *The bearing of X from Y* means put a north line through Y, then measure round from the north line as far as the line joining Y to X.

Examples

Find the bearing of:

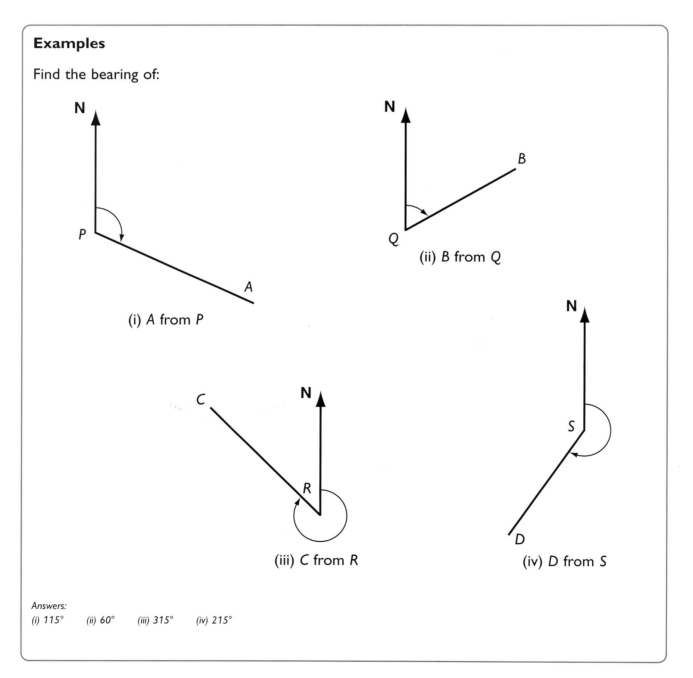

(i) A from P

(ii) B from Q

(iii) C from R

(iv) D from S

Answers:
(i) 115°   (ii) 60°   (iii) 315°   (iv) 215°

Scale drawings

We can use scale drawings to find the answers to problems by measuring.

Example

An amateur pilot leaves the airfield in his plane and flies towards an island which is 10 km away on a bearing of 095°. However, after he has flown 10 km, he notices he has been flying on a bearing of 085° by mistake. How far is he from the island?

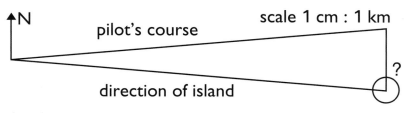

Careful measuring gives the length of the line as 1.7 cm, and so the pilot is 1.7 km or 1700 m off course!

■■■ Pythagoras' theorem

● You need to know and apply Pythagoras' theorem in two dimensions.

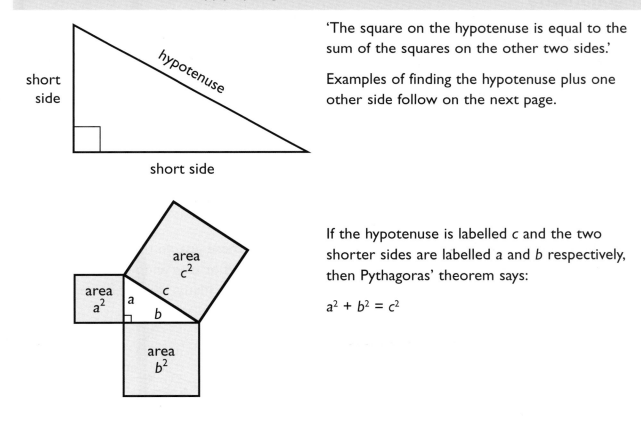

'The square on the hypotenuse is equal to the sum of the squares on the other two sides.'

Examples of finding the hypotenuse plus one other side follow on the next page.

If the hypotenuse is labelled c and the two shorter sides are labelled a and b respectively, then Pythagoras' theorem says:

$$a^2 + b^2 = c^2$$

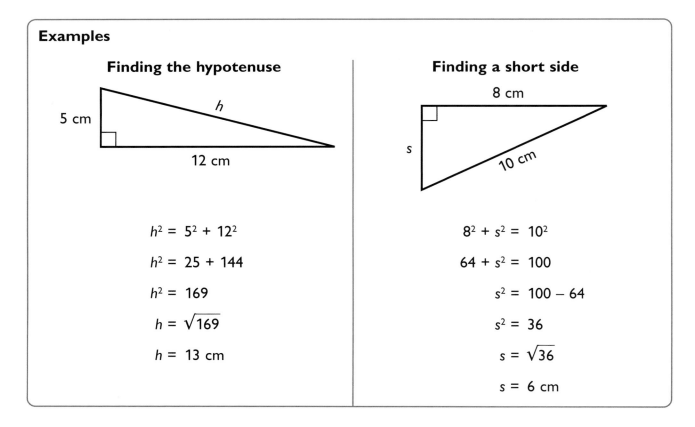

Examples

Finding the hypotenuse

5 cm
12 cm
h

$h^2 = 5^2 + 12^2$

$h^2 = 25 + 144$

$h^2 = 169$

$h = \sqrt{169}$

$h = 13$ cm

Finding a short side

8 cm
s
10 cm

$8^2 + s^2 = 10^2$

$64 + s^2 = 100$

$s^2 = 100 - 64$

$s^2 = 36$

$s = \sqrt{36}$

$s = 6$ cm

■■■ Trigonometry

● This topic is not included in the ISEB Common Entrance syllabus, but it is in KS3. Some of you may start to study trigonometry as an extension topic, so brief notes are included here.

When we know the length of two sides of a right-angled triangle, we can use Pythagoras' theorem to find the length of the third side (page 159).

When we know the length of only one side, but we also know the size of one of the acute angles, we can use trigonometry.

Trigonometry uses sine, cosine and tangent. Your calculator should have three buttons labelled $\boxed{\text{sin}}$, $\boxed{\text{cos}}$ and $\boxed{\text{tan}}$.

Above these buttons you usually see $\sin^{-1}$, $\cos^{-1}$ and $\tan^{-1}$, and these just do the opposite or inverse function. You also need to check your calculator shows **d** or **deg** and not **r** (**radians**) or **g** (**grads**) so that it works out the angles in degrees. (See your Maths teacher if you need to change this – it usually involves pressing MODE or something similar.)

Triangle anatomy

You need to learn the special names of the parts of the triangle.

hypotenuse

acute angle

adjacent side

right angle

opposite side

- The **hypotenuse** (hyp) is always the longest side, and always opposite the right angle.
- The **opposite side** (opp) is always opposite the acute angle you are studying (imagine a torch shining on the *opposite* wall).
- The **adjacent side** (adj) is always between the acute angle and the right angle, adjacent to (next to) the acute angle.

Finding an angle

Use the two sides you are given in the diagram on page 160, divide one by the other as shown below and then use the appropriate inverse function to find the angle.

$$\sin x = \text{opp} \div \text{hyp} \qquad \cos x = \text{adj} \div \text{hyp} \qquad \tan x = \text{opp} \div \text{adj}$$

You can remember this by saying '**sohcahtoa**'!

Finding a side

Label your triangle as above, based on the angle you are given. You only need to know one other side. Then use **sohcahtoa** to find the missing side.

For example, if you are given an angle of 42° and a hypotenuse of 12 cm, and you have to find the adjacent, then you need cos since this is the only one with adj and hyp.

Write $\cos 42° = ? \div 12$ and find adj by working out $12 \times \cos 42° = 8.92$ cm.

Sample questions

Try these sample questions for yourself. The answers are given at the back of the book.

Some of the questions involve ideas met in earlier work which may not be covered by the notes in this chapter.

10.17　(a)　Name these angles.　　　　　　　　　　　　　　　　　(3)

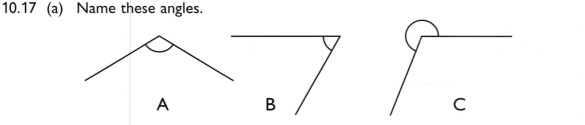

A　　　　　　　　　B　　　　　　　　　C

(b)　On these diagrams, clearly mark all angles which are the same as those indicated with stars.　　　　　　　　　　　　　　　　　(3)

10.18 Look at this diagram.

(a) Name an angle which is **alternate** to angle a. (1)

(b) Name an angle which is **vertically opposite** to angle b. (1)

(c) Name an angle which is **corresponding** to angle c. (1)

10.19 Look at this diagram.

not to scale

(a) Calculate the angles marked a and b. (2)

(b) Calculate the angles marked c and d. (4)

10.20 Look at this diagram.

regular octagon
and square

not to
scale

(a) Calculate the angles marked p and q. (2)

(b) Calculate the angles marked r and s. (4)

10.21 (a) **Enlarge** triangle A using (1, 1) as the **centre of enlargement** and
scale factor 2 (2)

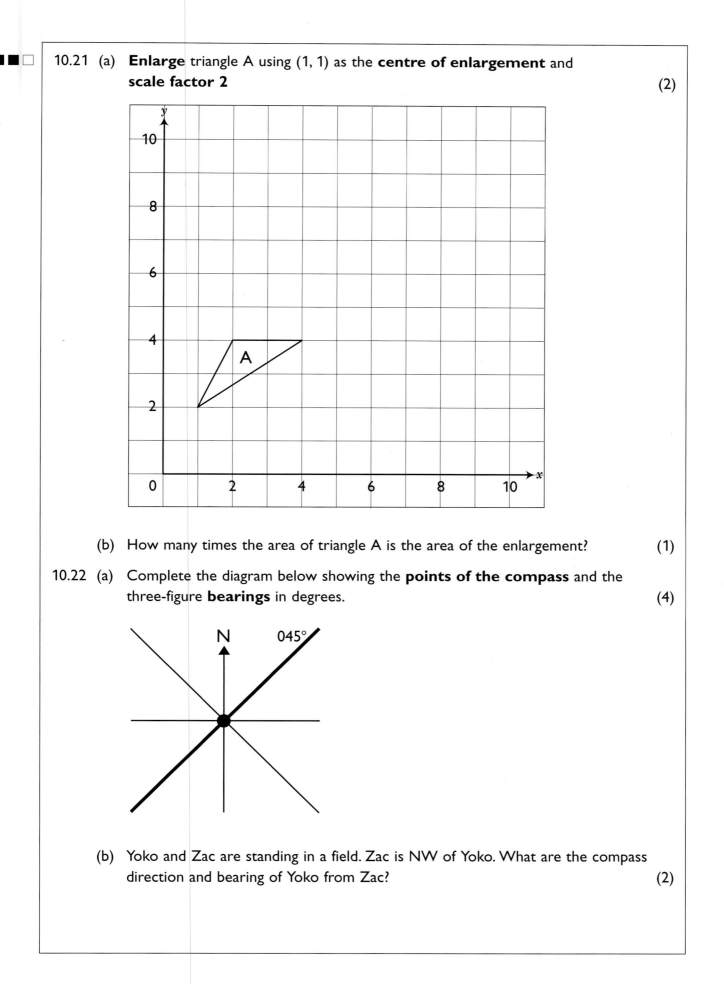

(b) How many times the area of triangle A is the area of the enlargement? (1)

10.22 (a) Complete the diagram below showing the **points of the compass** and the
three-figure **bearings** in degrees. (4)

(b) Yoko and Zac are standing in a field. Zac is NW of Yoko. What are the compass
direction and bearing of Yoko from Zac? (2)

■■□   10.23   Alan is standing in the middle of a playing field. Beatrice is 20 metres north of Alan and Chris is 15 metres east of Beatrice.

      (a)   Using a scale of 1 cm to 2 m, make a scale drawing showing the positions of the three friends.   (3)

      (b)   Measure and write down:
         (i)   the bearing of Chris from Alan   (1)
         (ii)   the bearing of Alan from Chris   (2)
         (iii)   the distance of Alan from Chris.   (2)

■■■   10.24   (a)   Using **Pythagoras' theorem**, calculate the length of the third side of this right-angled triangle.   (2)

      (b)   Calculate the length of the diagonal of a rectangle measuring 6 cm by 4 cm.   (2)

      (c)   The diagonals of a square are 8 cm long. What is the length of a side of the square?   (3)

S   Summary

Remember that you should be familiar with all of the material in Chapter 9.

You should also now be able to do the following:

1.   Make sensible estimates of a range of measures in relation to everyday situations.   **5**

✳ 2.   Understand and use appropriate formulae for finding circumferences and areas of circles, areas of plane rectilinear figures and volumes of cuboids when solving problems.   **6**

■■■ 3.   Calculate lengths, areas and volumes in plane shapes and right prisms.   **7**

✳ 4.   Understand and use compound measures, such as speed.   **7**

✳ **Footnotes**

2. ISEB Level 1 requires candidates to find the volume of a cuboid and the areas of triangles and parallelograms. The necessary formulae will be given.
ISEB Level 2 requires candidates to find the volume of a cuboid, the areas of triangles, parallelograms and circles, and the circumference of a circle.
ISEB Level 3 requires candidates to find the volume of a cuboid, the areas of triangles, parallelograms and circles, the circumference of a circle, and the radius of a circle, given the circumference or area.

4. Only speed will be tested. ISEB Level 1 candidates might be expected to answer a question such as: 'If Jane takes 2h 30m to cycle 40 km, how far does she cycle in one hour?'
ISEB Level 2 candidates might be expected to answer a question such as: 'How far will Tom travel if he cycles for three quarters of an hour at a speed of sixteen kilometres per hour?'
ISEB Level 3 candidates might be expected to calculate the average speeds of multi-stage journeys.

5. Identify all the symmetries of 2-D shapes. **5**

■■□ 6. Know and use the properties of quadrilaterals in classifying different types of quadrilateral. **6**

■■□ 7. Recognise and use common 2-D representations of 3-D objects. **6**

8. Know the angle sum of a triangle and the sum of angles at a point. **5**

■■□ 9. Enlarge shapes by a positive whole-number scale factor. **6**

■■□ 10. Understand and use three-figure bearings to define direction. **6+**

11. Solve problems using angle properties of intersecting and parallel lines, and explain these properties. **6**

■■□ 12. Solve problems using angle and symmetry properties of polygons and explain these properties. **6**

■■■ 13. Understand and apply Pythagoras' theorem when solving problems in two dimensions. **7**

Use the glossary at the back of the book for definitions of key words.

Test yourself

TY

Before moving on to the next chapter, make sure you can answer the following questions.

The answers are at the back of the book.

1. (a) Estimate the diameter of
    (i)   a hockey ball
    (ii) a table-tennis ball
    (iii) a basketball.

    (b) Estimate the mass of
    (i)   a hockey ball
    (ii) a table-tennis ball
    (iii) a banana.

    (c) Estimate the capacity of
    (i)   an ordinary mug
    (ii) a standard bath.

□■■ 2. The diagram shows a Chinese cash coin which is circular with a square hole in the middle. The diameter of the coin is 29 mm and the square hole has side 6 mm.

    (a) Calculate the area of one side of the coin.

    The thickness of the coin is 2 mm.

    (b) Calculate the volume of the metal in the coin.

not to scale

3. In a school swimming competition, the individual swimmers' times in the 4 × 200 metre freestyle relay are:

swimmer A	2 minutes 5 seconds
swimmer B	1 minutes 59 seconds
swimmer C	2 minutes 11 seconds
swimmer D	2 minutes 9 seconds

(a) What was the total time for the team?

(b) What was the mean (average) time for a swimmer?

(c) By how many seconds did the fastest swimmer beat the mean time?

4. Describe in full the symmetries of shapes A and B below.

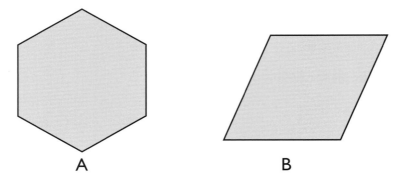

A   B

5. Calculate the angles a, b, c, d and e.

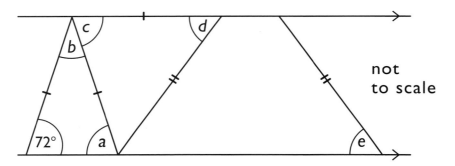

not to scale

6. Prepare a co-ordinate grid with axes numbered from 0 to 10

(a) Plot the points (1, 1), (2, 1) and (2, 3) and join the points to form triangle A.

(b) **Reflect** triangle A in the line x = 3 and label the image B.

(c) **Rotate** triangle A through 90° clockwise about (2, 3) and label the image C.

(d) **Translate** triangle A six units to the right and three units up. Label the image D.

(e) (i) **Enlarge** triangle A, with (0, 0) as the centre of enlargement and scale factor 3, to form triangle E.

   (ii) How many triangles congruent to triangle A could fit into triangle E?

7. The diagram shows a solid made from interlocking centimetre cubes, drawn on an isometric dotted grid..

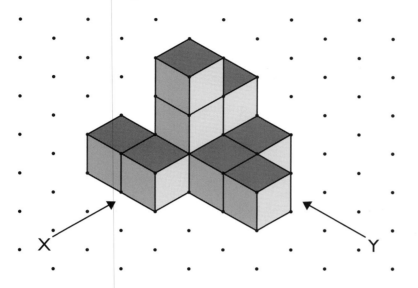

Draw views of the solid seen from positions X and Y.

8. Fiona, Grant and Henrietta are standing on a hockey pitch. Fiona is 20 m due west of Grant. Henrietta is 35 m south east of Fiona.

    (a) Make a scale drawing to show the relative positions of the three children. It is always a good idea to make a sketch first.

    (b) Use your scale drawing to find
        (i)   the bearing of Grant from Henrietta
        (ii) the distance of Grant from Henrietta.

■■■ 9. The diagonals of a rhombus are of lengths 16 cm and 12 cm.

    (a) Use Pythagoras' theorem to find the length of a side of the rhombus.

    The rhombus is cut along its diagonals to form four congruent triangles. These four triangles are rearranged to form a rectangle.

    (b) Draw labelled sketches to show the two different shaped rectangles which could be formed.

    (c) What is the length of a diagonal of the rectangle with the larger perimeter?

Chapter 11: 11+ Handling data

11.1 Data handling

Sorting shapes; Venn and Carroll diagrams

On this page we use a flow chart to sort six different quadrilaterals (can you name them all?) and then we sort them, in a different way, using a Carroll Diagram.

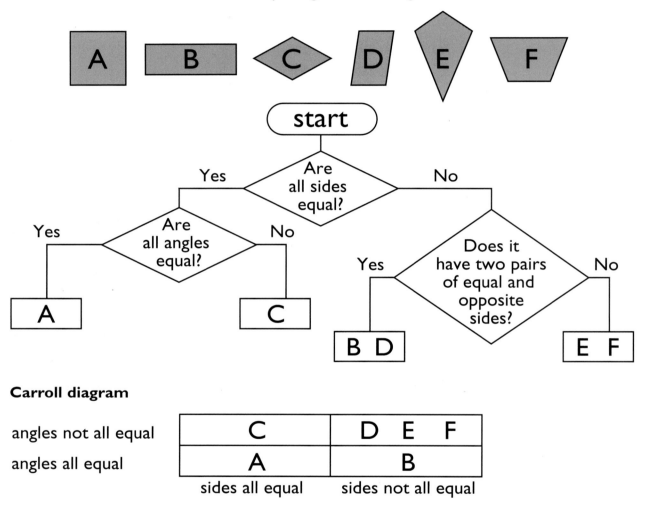

Carroll diagram

	sides all equal	sides not all equal
angles not all equal	C	D E F
angles all equal	A	B

Finally we use a Venn diagram to sort the shapes. Which way do you prefer to sort the quadrilaterals?

Venn diagram

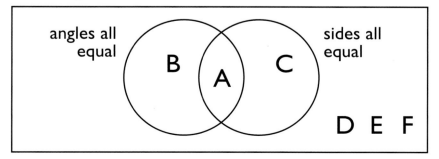

Frequency tables using discrete data

● You should be able to collect discrete data and organise them using a frequency table.

Discrete data are the sort of data you can count or sort into easy categories. For example, we could ask:

'How many children are in your family?' or 'What is your favourite colour?'

A frequency table is a good way of collecting and organising discrete data. In this example, we look at the work of a pupil carrying out a survey on favourite breakfast cereals:

Cereal	Tally	Frequency
corn flakes	JHT I	
wheat flakes	III	
bran flakes	I	
oat flakes	IIII	

At this stage she had only asked 14 people. Eventually, however, it looked like this:

Cereal	Tally	Frequency
corn flakes	JHT JHT II	12
wheat flakes	JHT JHT	10
bran flakes	IIII	4
oat flakes	JHT IIII	9
	total	35

The pupil has now filled in the frequencies (row totals) and found the overall total. The table is complete.

Finding the mode, median and range

● You need to know how to find the mode, median and range of a set of data, and be able to understand their use.

When we have lots of data (information), usually the result of a survey, we need a way of understanding them more clearly. Maths to the rescue! The branch of mathematics which we use for this job is called *statistics*; it is a very useful topic to study.

The **mode** is the category in the survey which came up most often, i.e. the one with the greatest frequency. The mode is the most common, or most popular choice.

The **median** means *middle value*. If we sort our numerical data into order, the median is the value in the middle, or halfway between the middle two, if the number of items of data is even.

The **range** tells us how spread out numerical results are. It is simply the difference between the smallest and largest values in the data.

eye colour of class 6F

Example

I put the question 'How many children are in your family?' to 41 different families, and received these answers (sorted into increasing order of size):

1, 1, 1, 1, 1, 1, 1, 1, 2, 2, 2, 2, 2, 2, 2, 2, 2, 2, 2, 2, 3, 3, 3, 3, 3, 3, 3, 3, 3, 3, 4, 4, 4, 4, 4, 4, 4, 5, 5, 5, 6

                                           — half-way point

So the mode is 2 (most common), the median is 3 (half way through the list), and the range is 5 (since 6 − 1 = 5).

Calculating the mean; comparing two distributions

● You need to be able to calculate the mean of discrete data, and to use your knowledge of averages to compare two distributions.

How to find the mean

This is one of the simplest calculations in statistics. All you do is add up your data and divide by the number of items in the list.

Example

Find the mean of the following pupil masses (all in kg):

42, 37, 39, 40, 45, 37, 35, 49, 36, 43

Add them up.

42 + 37 + 39 + 40 + 45 + 37 + 35 + 49 + 36 + 43 = 403

There are ten pupils in this set of data so we divide by 10

403 ÷ 10 = 40.3

Thus the mean pupil mass is 40.3 kg.

Comparing two distributions

When comparing two distributions, we should take the mean, mode, median and range into consideration.

Example

A cricket team needs 25 runs in order to win. A choice has to be made between two players whose past run totals look like this:

Arthur: 19, 24, 30, 27, 23, 24, 29, 21, 31, 25
mean 25.3   median 24.5   range 12

Daley: 8, 48, 22, 32, 19, 42, 7, 59, 0, 18
mean 25.5   median 20.5   range 59

Note: for Arthur, the median is halfway between 24 and 25; for Daley, the median is halfway between 19 and 22

So whom should they choose? Daley certainly has a greater mean, but he is very inconsistent (large range) and the median tells us that over half his previous games fell short of the desired 25 runs. Arthur, on the other hand, although he has a lower mean, is a much more consistent player (small range), and the median shows us that he had as many results above 25 as below it.

Whom would **you** choose?

Grouped data and equal class intervals

- You should understand the importance of using equal class intervals when organising data into groups for making a frequency diagram.

Using grouped data

Junior Splash Swimming Club recently asked its 55 members how many lengths they swam last weekend. The raw data results were as follows, and an easy way to group the data is on the next page:

14	31	54	40	22	45	57	26	33	56	52
34	24	37	33	36	27	36	34	23	60	29
47	47	57	21	17	37	22	11	32	23	44
32	25	41	42	38	29	44	25	38	39	23
43	46	50	36	38	26	44	33	33	52	34

To make it easier to follow, we group the data:

Number of lengths	Tally		Frequency
0 to 9			0
10 to 19	III		3
20 to 29	︱︱︱︱ ︱︱︱︱ IIII		14
30 to 39	︱︱︱︱ ︱︱︱︱ ︱︱︱︱ IIII		19
40 to 49	︱︱︱︱ ︱︱︱︱ I		11
50 to 59	︱︱︱︱ II		7
60 to 69	I		1
		total	55

Note the equal class intervals (10 lengths each). It is now much clearer that the modal class is 30 to 39 lengths.

From the original data, the range is 49 (60 − 11) lengths. We cannot find the median of grouped data, but we can see that it will be somewhere in the 30 to 39 lengths group. In this case, there are 17 who swam fewer than 30 lengths and 19 who swam more than 39 lengths. If we wanted to find it more accurately, we would have to sort the original data.

Line graphs and conversion graphs

- You need to be able to interpret data presented as a line graph, and be able to read values from it.

Temperature and other time graphs

One type of line graph consists of short line segments joined up to show how something is changing over a period of time. Here is a temperature graph:

The temperature was measured and plotted every hour, on the hour. The line segments joining these points are really only guesses at the intermediate values – the real change is likely to

172

have been a smooth **curve** throughout the day, but the graph is still a useful way of displaying the collected information.

Conversion graphs

Another type of graph is the conversion graph. The one on the right converts between pounds (£) and dollars ($). Check that £5 = $8

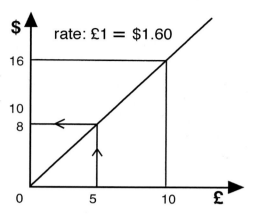

rate: £1 = $1.60

When drawing conversion graphs, it is important to choose a suitable scale. Choose one that is big enough to read accurately, but do use the squares on the graph paper sensibly.

And don't forget to label the axes!

Sample questions

Try these sample questions for yourself. The answers are given at the back of the book.

Some of the questions involve ideas met in earlier work which may not be covered by the notes in this chapter.

11.1   The first nine counting numbers are:

1   2   3   4   5   6   7   8   9

(a) Write each of the above numbers in the correct region of this Carroll diagram.   (4)

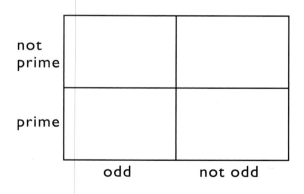

(b) Write each number in the correct region of this Venn diagram.   (4)

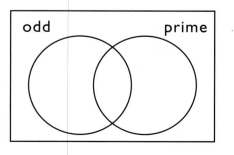

11.2 The pictogram below shows the number of Valentine's Day cards received by five friends.

Amy	♥ ♥ ♥ ♥ ♥
Ben	♥ ♥ ♥ ♥ ♥ ♥ ♥
Clare	♥ ♥ ♥ ♥ ♥ ♥ ♥ ♥ ♥
Dan	♥ ♥ ♥ ♥ ♥ ♥
Enid	♥ ♥ ♥ ♥ ♥ ♥ ♥ ♥

Key: ♥ represents 1 card

(a) How many cards did Ben receive? (1)

(b) What is the total number of cards received by the friends? (2)

11.3 Alison has drawn this graph to show where the children in her school spent their holiday.

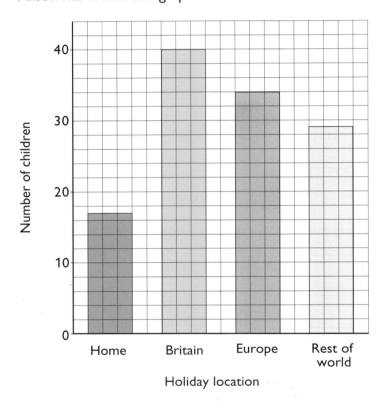

(a) How many children stayed at home? (1)

(b) How many children took part in Alison's survey? (3)

(c) How many more children went to Europe than went to the rest of the world? (1)

(d) What fraction of the children went away from home on holiday in Britain? (2)

174

11.4 Here are the numbers of books read in a week by five children.

Fay	Gill	Hal	Ian	Jon
1	2	7	1	4

For these numbers, what is

(a) the range   (1)

(b) the median   (1)

(c) the mode   (1)

(d) the mean?   (2)

11.5 The masses of five children in a family are 40 kg, 38 kg, 32 kg, 41 kg and 39 kg.
      What is the mean mass of the children?   (3)

11.6 The children in Miss de Cova's class have made this list of their heights in metres:

1.41	1.52	1.28	1.43	1.49
1.48	1.37	1.52	1.39	1.47
1.30	1.51	1.40	1.48	1.57
1.45	1.33	1.42	1.44	1.45

(a) Complete the table below.   (4)

Height (m)	Tally marks	Frequency
1.25 to 1.29		
1.30 to 1.34		
1.35 to 1.39		
1.40 to 1.44		
1.45 to 1.49		
1.50 to 1.54		
1.55 to 1.59		
	Total	

(b) Use the table to draw a frequency diagram.   (4)

(c) Which group of heights is the mode?   (1)

11.7 The line graph below shows the amount of fuel in the fuel tank of Mr McPhee's car.

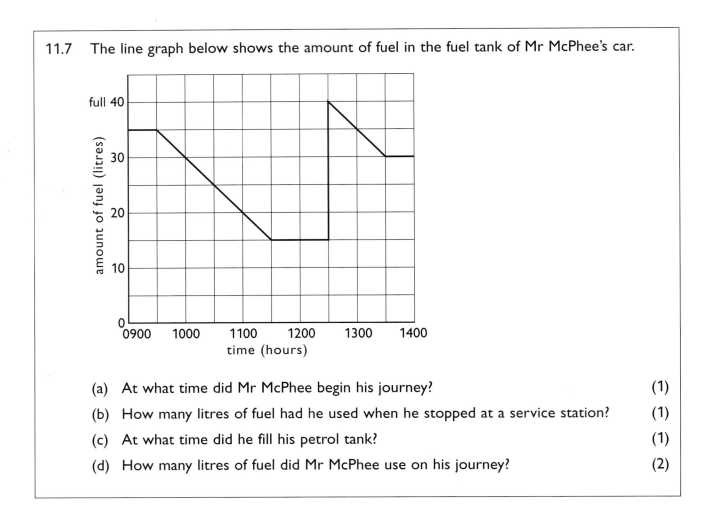

(a) At what time did Mr McPhee begin his journey? (1)

(b) How many litres of fuel had he used when he stopped at a service station? (1)

(c) At what time did he fill his petrol tank? (1)

(d) How many litres of fuel did Mr McPhee use on his journey? (2)

11.2 Probability

Words to describe probability

● When describing and comparing the likelihood of future events you need to be able to use the common words associated with probability.

How likely?

How likely is it that the sun will rise tomorrow morning?
Certain.

How likely is it that your pet stick insect will grow into a tree?
Impossible!

In-between questions are more difficult.
How likely is it that it will rain tomorrow? Difficult to say, even if you have had rain every day so far this week. The weather could improve!

Even so, we can use this word scale to describe and compare the probabilities (chance or likelihood) of things happening.

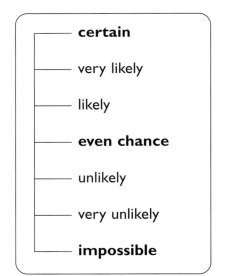

- **certain**
- very likely
- likely
- **even chance**
- unlikely
- very unlikely
- **impossible**

Sample questions

Try these sample questions for yourself. The answers are given at the back of the book.

Some of the questions involve ideas met in earlier work which may not be covered by the notes in this chapter.

11.8   Jamie has an ordinary coin and a triangular spinner.

 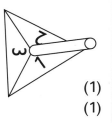

    (a)   How many possible outcomes are there when Jamie
        (i)   tosses the coin   (1)
        (ii)   spins the spinner?   (1)

    (b)   Jamie tosses the coin and spins the spinner at the same time.

        One possible outcome is H (heads) and 2

        List all the possible outcomes.   (3)

11.9   Sally has two ordinary dice; one red and one blue.

    (a)   Describe all the ways it is possible for her to score a total of
        (i)   5   (2)
        (ii)   8   (2)

    Use the tables below to help you.

Score 5	
Red	**Blue**
4	1

Score 8	
Red	**Blue**

Sally and Minnie play a game with the two dice. To start, the player must roll two sixes. Minnie says it would be easier to roll two ones.

    (b)   Do you think Minnie is right? Explain your answer.   (1)

11.10 Tina is using this spinner in a game.
Choose your answers from the following:

impossible   unlikely   even chance
        ikely   certain

Which of the above words best describes the
probability of scoring:

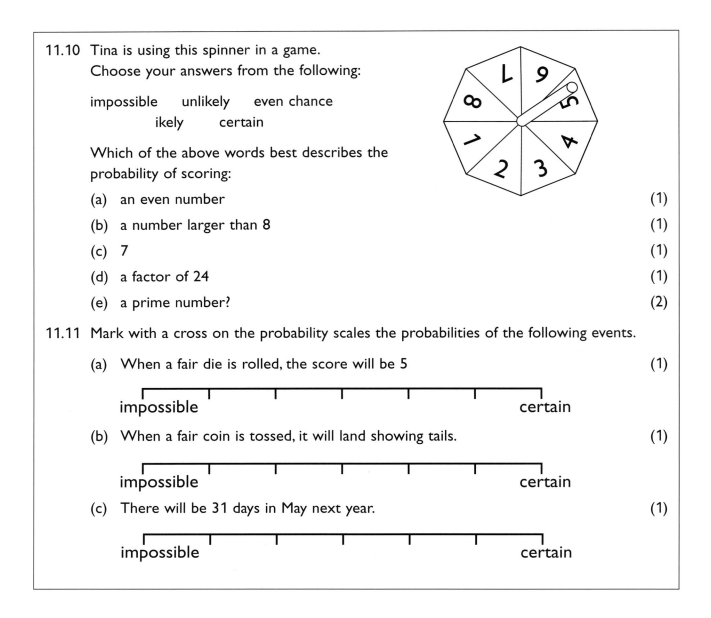

(a) an even number   (1)

(b) a number larger than 8   (1)

(c) 7   (1)

(d) a factor of 24   (1)

(e) a prime number?   (2)

11.11 Mark with a cross on the probability scales the probabilities of the following events.

(a) When a fair die is rolled, the score will be 5   (1)

impossible   certain

(b) When a fair coin is tossed, it will land showing tails.   (1)

impossible   certain

(c) There will be 31 days in May next year.   (1)

impossible   certain

S Summary

Remember that you should be familiar with all of the material in National Curriculum Key
Stage 1, for example, Venn diagrams and Carroll diagrams.

You should also now be able to do the following:

1.   Collect discrete data and record them using a frequency table.   **4**

2.   Understand and use the mode and range to describe sets of data.   **4**

3.   Group data, where appropriate, in equal class intervals, represent collected data in
      frequency diagrams and interpret such diagrams.   **4**

4.   Construct and interpret simple line graphs.   **4**

5.   Understand and use the mean of discrete data.   **5**

6. Understand and use the median of a set of data. **5+**

7. Understand and use simple vocabulary associated with probability, including **fair**, **certain** and **likely**. **4+**

Use the glossary at the back of the book for definitions of key words.

Test yourself

Before moving on to the next chapter, make sure you can answer the following questions.

The answers are at the back of the book.

1. The scores below were achieved by 20 pupils in a mathematics quiz.

| 11 | 14 | 8 | 17 | 14 | 17 | 13 | 9 | 20 | 10 |
| 12 | 10 | 16 | 15 | 19 | 12 | 16 | 17 | 7 | 13 |

(a) For this set of marks, what is
  (i) the range
  (ii) the mode
  (iii) the median?

The pupils were awarded grades as indicated in the table below.

Grade	Scores	Tally	Frequency
A	17–20		
B	13–16		
C	9–12		
D	5–8		
E	1–4		

(b) Complete the table.

(c) Draw a frequency diagram to show the numbers of pupils awarded each grade.

(d) What is the mean of the top five scores?

2. The line graph below shows Paula's cycle ride to visit Jayne.

(a) At what time did Paula leave home?

Paula had a puncture and spent half an hour repairing it.

(b) How far from her home did Paula have the puncture?

(c) At what time did Paula reach Jayne's house?

(d) How long did Paula stay at Jayne's house before heading home?

(e) How far did Paula cycle altogether?

(f) For how long was Paula away from her home?

3. Jasmine has drawn this conversion graph to help her compare distances in miles and kilometres.

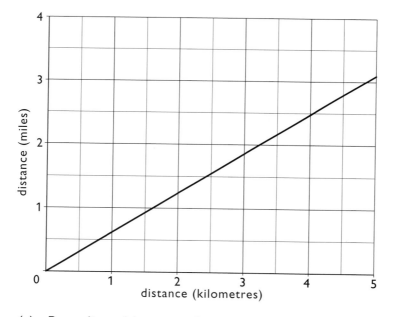

(a) Peter lives 4 km away from Jasmine. What is this distance in miles?

(b) Jasmine sets off to run a mile. What is this distance in metres?

4. Give an example of an event which

   (a) is impossible

   (b) is **very** unlikely

   (c) is unlikely

   (d) has an even chance of happening

   (e) is likely

   (f) is **very** likely

   (g) is certain to happen.

5. At a funfair there was a stall where people could roll a die.

   ROLL THE DIE
   £1 to enter
   Choose your own die
   Roll a 6 and win £6

   Tim thought about this and decided to have six tries, knowing that he'd spend £6, and thinking that he'd be bound to win £6 on one of his six rolls, so he couldn't lose! Since blue is his favourite colour, he chose a blue die and rolled it six times.

   He was dismayed to discover that he didn't roll a single six. The numbers he rolled were: 5, 2, 3, 1, 2, 4

   Tim claimed that the die must be biased!

   (a) (i) What do you think about Tim's strategy?
       (ii) Do you think the die was biased?

   The stallholder told Tim to choose another die and try again, free of charge. This time Tim chose a large gold coloured die and rolled 1 six times!

   (b) Do you think that this second die is fair?

   (c) Describe a sensible way of finding out if a die is biased.

   (d) Suggest a way in which the stallholder can be fairly certain that he will make money.

Chapter 12: 13+ Handling data

12.1 Data handling

Drawing conclusions from graphs, charts and diagrams

- You need to be able to draw valid conclusions from a variety of graphs, charts and diagrams.

Whatever the type of graph, it is important to look at the whole picture before you try to conclude anything. Many graphs are deliberately misleading because they have something to hide – the newspapers are full of examples – don't be deceived!

Example

Which country below has more rain?

At a first quick glance, you might be forgiven for thinking that it was Anglea because of its tall bars. However, it is in fact Basen, because it has fewer days of low rain (0–5 mm) and more days of high rain (20–25 mm) than Anglea.

Frequency diagrams (bar charts) using discrete data

- You need to be able to construct and interpret frequency diagrams using discrete data.

Example

The first 20 draws of the UK National Lottery produced these numbers (7 each week) in the order given. Bonus numbers are printed in **bold type**.

30	3	5	44	14	22	**10**	16	6	44	31	12
15	**37**	21	11	17	30	29	40	**31**	26	47	49
43	35	38	**28**	13	3	38	5	14	9	**30**	27
29	39	3	44	2	**6**	17	44	36	32	9	42
16	21	32	2	5	25	22	**46**	23	38	17	7
32	42	**48**	47	6	16	31	30	20	**4**	31	16
25	43	4	26	**21**	46	42	1	38	7	37	**20**
48	38	15	29	18	35	**5**	45	16	36	19	21
29	**43**	18	33	8	31	5	10	**28**	17	36	11
12	42	26	**13**	2	22	13	46	29	27	**36**	41
19	31	18	9	24	**21**	4	49	41	44	42	17
24	43	41	22	25	30	32	**29**				

To make a frequency chart of these numbers, we first draw up a frequency table.

Note that we have had to make the first group (1 to 9), only 9 numbers instead of 10, because there is no zero ball.

Numbers drawn	Frequency
1 to 9	24
10 to 19	28
20 to 29	30
30 to 39	30
40 to 49	28

Well, it seems fair. That first bar is a bit shorter than the others because, of course, it is counting only 9 balls not 10, as mentioned above.

Mathematical pause for thought: every time somebody becomes a lottery millionaire, it means that between them the others have lost over a million pounds.

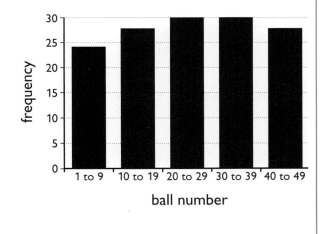

Pie charts

- You need to be able to construct and interpret simple pie charts, using degrees or percentages.

Example

Twenty children were asked about their favourite ice cream. The replies were as follows:

chocolate: 9; vanilla: 6; strawberry: 4; toffee: 1; total: 20

Display the results of the ice cream survey using a pie chart.

For a pie chart measured in degrees, this total of 20 must be made into 360°. For a pie chart measured in percentages, it must be made into 100%. We shall work through both calculations here.

Degrees version 360° ÷ 20 = 18°, so each child is represented by 18°

Flavour	Frequency	Factor		Angle of sector
chocolate	9	× 18°	=	162°
vanilla	6	× 18°	=	108°
strawberry	4	× 18°	=	72°
toffee	1	× 18°	=	18°
total	20		total	360°

Percentage version 100% ÷ 20 = 5%, so each child is represented by 5%

Flavour	Frequency	Factor		Angle of sector
chocolate	9	× 5%	=	45%
vanilla	6	× 5%	=	30%
strawberry	4	× 5%	=	20%
toffee	1	× 5%	=	5%
total	20		total	100%

Results of ice cream survey

toffee 18° (5%)
strawberry 72° (20%)
chocolate 162° (45%)
vanilla 108° (30%)

Scattergraphs and correlation

● You need to be able to construct and interpret scattergraphs and correlation diagrams.

Sometimes the data we collect comes in pairs of numbers. We might ask people for their height and mass, for example, or we might measure oxygen levels at different altitudes. To keep each data item as a pair, we plot them as Cartesian (x, y) co-ordinates:

(x, y) = (height, mass) or

(x, y) = (altitude, oxygen level) and so on.

When we have plotted several points, we end up with a graph called a **scattergraph**.

Examples

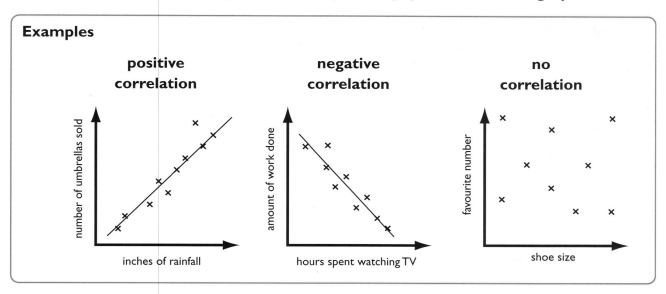

Note that when there is either positive or negative correlation, we can draw a line showing the approximate direction of the trend in the points.

This line, drawn by eye, is called the **line of best fit**.

When there is correlation (positive or negative), it means that the pairs of numbers are related in some way.

Sets and Venn diagrams

● You need to be able to understand set notation, and construct and interpret Venn diagrams.

Sets

Sets are simply collections of things, all of which have something in common. For example, we might talk about the set of odd numbers less than 20, or the set of prime numbers between 10 and 30

With Venn diagrams we can show things which are in more than one set at the same time.

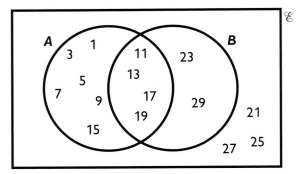

$\mathcal{E}$ = {odd numbers less than 30}

A = {odd numbers less than 20}

B = {prime numbers between 10 and 30}

Set notation

A list of signs and symbols used in describing sets:

$\in$	is a member (element) of
$\notin$	is not a member of
$\cup$	union: elements in either one set or the other (or both) are included
$\cap$	intersection: only elements in **both** sets are included
$\subset$	is a subset of
$\supset$	contains
$\varnothing$	the empty set (contains no elements)
A'	complement: those items **not** in set A
$\mathcal{E}$	the universal set: this set contains all elements under consideration

We list the elements in a set within curly brackets, e.g. A = {a, e, i, o, u}.

We count the number of elements in a set using $n(\ )$, as in $n(A) = 5$ for the set A above.

Sets and Venn diagrams

These Venn diagrams show how the signs and symbols listed above can be represented visually. In the first six diagrams, the notation below the diagram describes the shaded area.

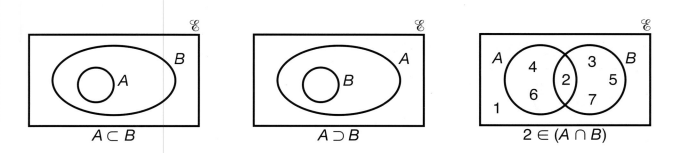

$A \subset B$ $A \supset B$ $2 \in (A \cap B)$

You need to be able to answer questions using set notation.

Example

Look again at the Venn diagram showing the odd numbers less than 30 (page 186).

(i) List the members of the set $A \cap B$.

(ii) Find $n(A')$

(iii) How would you describe the numbers in the set $(A \cup B)'$?

Answers:

(i) 11, 13, 17, 19

(ii) 5

(iii) Numbers between 20 and 30 which are odd but not prime.

Sample questions

Try these sample questions for yourself. The answers are given at the back of the book.

Some of the questions involve ideas met in earlier work which may not be covered by the notes in this chapter.

12.1 The 38 boys in Year 8 were asked which sports teams they played in. The results are shown in the **Venn diagram** below.

(a) Record the same results on the **Carroll diagram** on the right   (2)

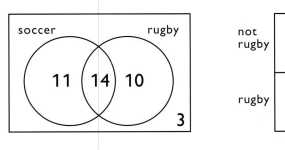

	soccer	not soccer
not rugby		
rugby		

(b) How many boys in Year 8 play in just one team?   (1)

12.2 This fraction diagram shows the proportion of 3 metals in an alloy.

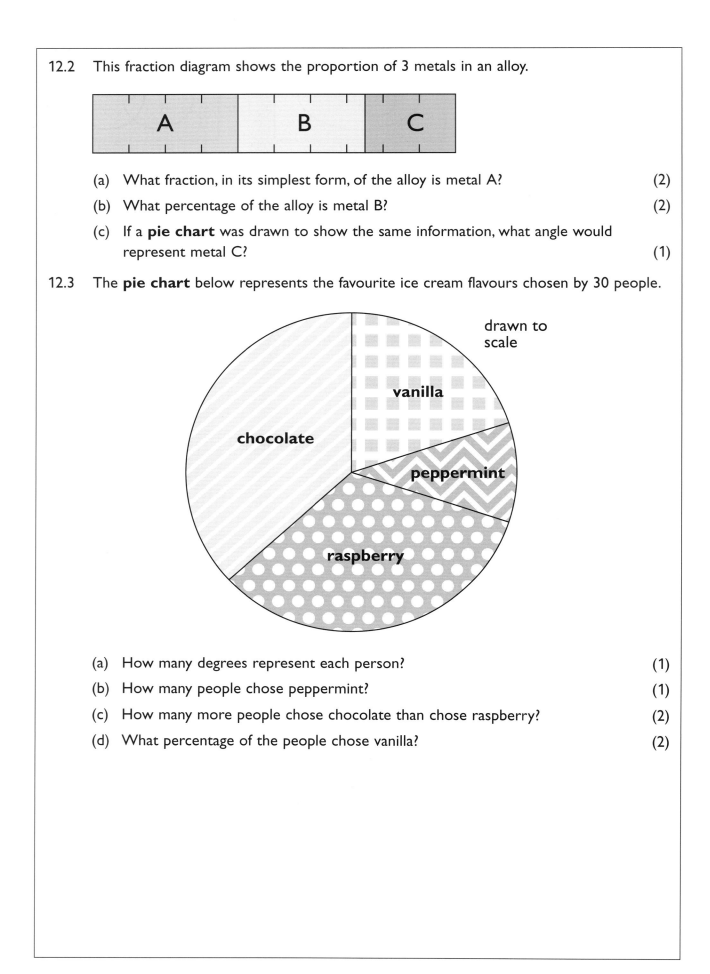

(a) What fraction, in its simplest form, of the alloy is metal A? (2)

(b) What percentage of the alloy is metal B? (2)

(c) If a **pie chart** was drawn to show the same information, what angle would represent metal C? (1)

12.3 The **pie chart** below represents the favourite ice cream flavours chosen by 30 people.

(a) How many degrees represent each person? (1)

(b) How many people chose peppermint? (1)

(c) How many more people chose chocolate than chose raspberry? (2)

(d) What percentage of the people chose vanilla? (2)

12.4 The **frequency diagram** below shows the scores in a school quiz.

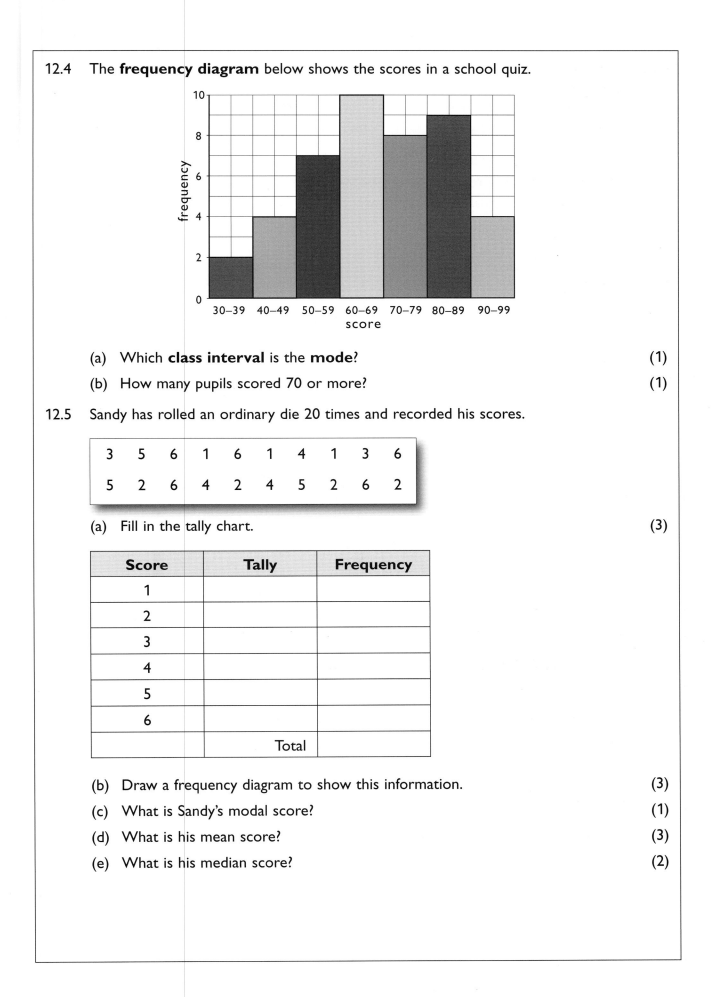

(a) Which **class interval** is the **mode**? (1)

(b) How many pupils scored 70 or more? (1)

12.5 Sandy has rolled an ordinary die 20 times and recorded his scores.

3	5	6	1	6	1	4	1	3	6
5	2	6	4	2	4	5	2	6	2

(a) Fill in the tally chart. (3)

Score	Tally	Frequency
1		
2		
3		
4		
5		
6		
	Total	

(b) Draw a frequency diagram to show this information. (3)

(c) What is Sandy's modal score? (1)

(d) What is his mean score? (3)

(e) What is his median score? (2)

12.6 Each girl in a class of 18 girls counted how many peas she had on her plate. The results were as follows:

27	25	30	26	28	20	24	26	25
25	22	27	25	29	31	26	28	21

(a) What is the modal number of peas?   (1)

(b) Complete the tally chart below.   (3)

Number of peas	Tally	Frequency
20–22		
23–25		
26–28		
29–31		
	Total	

(c) What is the modal class?   (1)

12.7 Two football teams, Rovers and Wanderers, have played each other 12 times. The numbers of goals scored per match are shown in the frequency diagrams below.

(a) (i)   What is the range of the number of goals scored per match by Rovers?   (1)
     (ii) What is the modal number of goals scored per match by Wanderers?   (1)
     (iii) What is the median number of goals scored per match by Rovers?   (2)

(b) Compare the performance of the two teams, making use of the frequency diagrams and any additional calculations you have made.   (2)

12.8 The mean mass of ten children is 36.2 kg.

(a) What is the total mass of the children? (2)

When two of the children leave, the mean mass of the eight remaining children falls to 35 kg.

(b) What is the total mass of the eight remaining children? (1)

(c) What is the mean mass of the two children who left the class? (2)

12.9 Some children were asked to state their favourite breakfast cereal. The results, recorded below, are to be represented on a pie chart.

puffs	30%
crispies	15%
flakes	20%
muesli	the rest

(a) Draw a pie chart, naming each sector clearly and giving the angles. (4)

(b) If 60 children took part in the survey:
   (i) How many children chose crispies as their favourite cereal? (2)
   (ii) How many children chose muesli as their favourite cereal? (2)

12.10 Below is a graph which could be used for converting British pounds (£) into US dollars ($) one day in June 2009

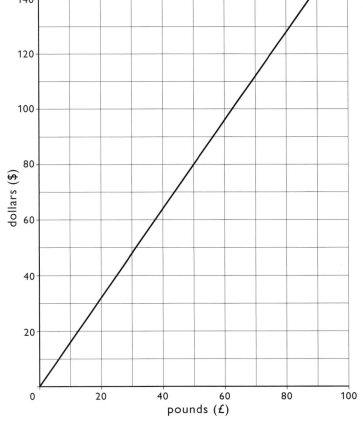

(a) Use the graph to find:
  (i) how many dollars were equivalent to £35 (2)
  (ii) how many pounds were equivalent to $80 (2)

(b) On a flight to New York, a duty free watch was priced at £65

   In the airport duty free shop, the same item was priced at $80
  (i) Which price was the better value? (2)
  (ii) What was the difference in the prices? Give your answer in GBP to the
       nearest 1 pound. (2)

12.11 The masses and heights of ten girls are recorded in the table below.

Mass (kg)	30	40	50	42	56	38	35	36	39	33
Height (cm)	165	140	145	148	144	135	142	150	152	148

(a) Plot points representing this information as a scattergraph. (3)

(b) Draw, **if appropriate**, the line of best fit. If this is not possible, then
    explain why not. (1)

(c) Using your line of best fit, or otherwise, estimate the height of a girl of
    mass 45 kg. (2)

12.2 Probability

Theoretical and experimental probability

- You need to be familiar with the probability scale from 0 to 1 and know the difference
  between experimental and theoretical probabilities.

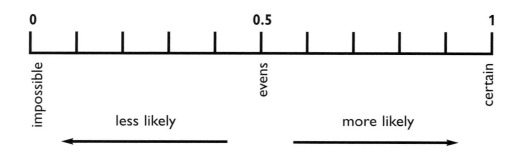

Theoretical probability

This is calculated using a simple fraction:

probability of A happening = $\dfrac{\text{number of ways A can happen}}{\text{total number of equally likely possibilities}}$

Example

What is the probability of rolling an even number with an ordinary die with six faces?

It can happen in three ways (2, 4 or 6).

There are six equally likely possibilities in total (1, 2, 3, 4, 5 and 6).

So the probability of rolling an even number is $\frac{3}{6}$, or 0.5 (50%).

Experimental probability

This is calculated using a similar fraction:

$$\text{probability of X happening} = \frac{\text{number of times X happened}}{\text{total number of experiments}}$$

Example

The drawing-pin experiment is a familiar example. Will the pin land point up or on one side? Try it and see!

Probability calculations

● You need to know that the sum of all probabilities in a situation is 1

First of all, why is the sum of all probabilities in a situation 1? Well, it goes back to page 176 where we saw that **certainty** had a probability of 1

When we say that the sum of all probabilities is 1, all we are saying in effect is that it is certain that **something** will happen. Quite obvious really!

Let's see now how useful that fact can be.

Example 1

The probability that Tom will be picked for the school hockey team is 0.7

What is the probability that he won't be picked?

The total probability (will + won't) is 1

The probability that he will be picked is 0.7

So the probability that he won't is 1 − 0.7 = 0.3

Example 2

When I phone my friend Anne, the probability that she will answer is 0.3 and the probability that someone else in her family will answer is 0.4

The probability that no one answers is 0.1; the only other possibility is that the line is engaged. What is the probability that the line is engaged?

The sum of all these probabilities is 0.8

So the probability that the line is engaged is 0.2

Listing outcomes systematically

● You need to be able to list systematically all possible outcomes of an experiment.

There are various ways of listing outcomes:

1. How many different four-digit numbers can you make using 7, 3, 1 and 4 once only?

   Well, there's 7314 and 3741 and 1743 and ...

   It would be difficult to carry on like this without missing numbers out or repeating earlier ones. Being systematic means being organised in your approach. Like this, for example:

1347	1374	1437	1473	1734	1743
3147	3174	3417	3471	3714	3741
4137	4173	4317	4371	4713	4731
7134	7143	7314	7341	7413	7431

   Read across the rows above. Can you see the method?

2. The table below shows all the possible outcomes when two dice are rolled and the scores added together. It then becomes very easy to see that a total of 7 can be reached in six different ways, making it the most likely total, but 2 and 12 can only be made in one way, making them the two least likely totals.

+	1	2	3	4	5	6
1	2	3	4	5	6	7
2	3	4	5	6	7	8
3	4	5	6	7	8	9
4	5	6	7	8	9	10
5	6	7	8	9	10	11
6	7	8	9	10	11	12

3. What are the possible outcomes when three coins are tossed onto a desk at the same time?

Possibility	1	2	3	4	5	6	7	8
Coin 1	H	H	H	H	T	T	T	T
Coin 2	H	H	T	T	H	H	T	T
Coin 3	H	T	H	T	H	T	H	T

Once again, careful listing shows all eight possibilities very clearly. What patterns can you find in the way the letters H and T have been written in the table?

Sample questions

Try these sample questions for yourself. The answers are given at the back of the book.

Some of the questions involve ideas met in earlier work which may not be covered by the notes in this chapter.

12.12 Samantha has a bag containing 10 sweets: 4 red, 1 yellow and 5 blue.
She picks one sweet at random.

  (a) (i) What is the probability that Samantha picks a red sweet? (1)
  (ii) Record this probability, with a letter R, on the probability scale below. (1)

```
|---+---+---+---+---+---+---+---+---+---|
0           R                              1
```

The sweet **is** red and Samantha eats it. She then picks another sweet.

  (b) What is the probability that Samantha picks a red sweet this time? (1)

12.13 The results of spinning a hexagonal spinner 100 times are recorded in this frequency table.

Score on spinner	Frequency
1	18
2	13
3	10
4	13
5	17
6	29

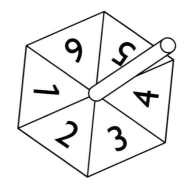

  (a) Do you think the spinner is **biased**? Explain your answer. (1)

  (b) Based upon the experimental results, suggest, as a percentage, the probability that this spinner will score 6 (1)

12.14 Stephen rolls two tetrahedral dice, one red and one green, each with faces numbered 1, 2, 3 and 4

He adds the scores together.

(a) Complete the table below to show all possible total scores. (2)

		Score on red die			
		1	2	3	4
Score on green die	1	2			
	2			5	
	3				
	4		6		

(b) What is the probability of Stephen's total score being:
   (i)   4 (1)
   (ii) more than 3? (1)

Stephen rolls the red die and scores 3

(c) What is the probability that his score on the green die will give him a total score of 5 or more? (2)

12.15 Marie and Clare are playing a game. Each girl has written the letters of her name on separate cards and placed the cards in her bag.

Each girl takes a card at random from her bag. Marie takes R and Clare takes L.

They replace the cards and repeat the process four times. The results are recorded in the table below.

	C	L	A	R	E
M	MC				
A			AA		
R		RL			
I					IE
E				ER	

(a) Complete the table above to show all the possible combinations. (3)

(b) What is the probability that the two cards taken will have the same letter? (2)

(c) What is the probability that the two cards taken will both have a vowel? (2)

Summary

Remember that you should be familiar with all of the material in Chapter 11.

You should also now be able to do the following:

1.	Compare two simple distributions, using the range and one of mode, median or mean.	5
2.	Interpret graphs and diagrams, including pie charts, and draw conclusions.	5
■■□ 3.	Construct and interpret frequency diagrams.	6
■■□ 4.	Construct pie charts.	6
5.	Draw conclusions from scatter diagrams, and have a basic understanding of correlation.	6
■■□ 6.	Draw a line of best fit on a scatter diagram, by inspection.	7
7.	Understand and use the probability scale from 0 to 1	5
8.	Find and justify probabilities, and approximations to these, by selecting and using methods based on equally likely outcomes and experimental evidence, as appropriate.	5
9.	Understand that different outcomes may result from repeating an experiment.	5
10.	Identify all the outcomes, using diagrammatic, tabular or other forms of communication, when dealing with a combination of two experiments.	6
■■□ 11.	Use your knowledge that the total probability of all the mutually exclusive outcomes of an experiment is 1	6

Use the glossary at the back of the book for definitions of key words.

Test yourself

Make sure you can answer the following questions. The answers are at the back of the book.

1. Gerry has recorded the shoe sizes of nine friends.

    | $6\frac{1}{2}$ | $8\frac{1}{2}$ | $7\frac{1}{2}$ | 6 | 7 | 9 | $8\frac{1}{2}$ | $9\frac{1}{2}$ | 8 |

    (a) What is the range of these shoe sizes?

    (b) Find the median shoe size of Gerry's friends.

    (c) What is the modal shoe size?

2. The mathematics examination marks for a class are shown below.

    | 64 | 79 | 53 | 45 | 63 | 78 | 66 | 77 | 47 | 67 |
    | 73 | 69 | 90 | 58 | 51 | 42 | 75 | 69 | 67 | 63 |

    (a) What is the range of marks for this set of results?

    Mr Hillard decides to sort the marks into groups: 40–49, 50–59 and so on.

    (b) Complete the tally and frequency columns in the table below.

Marks	Tally	Frequency
40–49		
50–59		
60–69		
70–79		
80–89		
90–99		
	Total	

    (c) What was the modal class of marks in the examination?

    (d) Draw a frequency diagram to show the results.

    Below is a frequency diagram showing the marks for the same class in an earlier mathematics examination.

    (e) By comparing the two graphs, comment on the performance of the class in the two examinations.

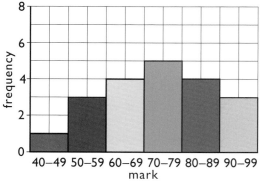

198

■■□ 3. A garden centre sells boxes of mixed bulbs. Each box of bulbs contains a gross (144) of which $\frac{1}{4}$ are daffodils and $\frac{1}{16}$ are hyacinths. In addition, there are three dozen snowdrops, twice as many tulips as hyacinths and the rest are crocuses.

(a) Draw a fully-labelled pie chart to show this information, marking each sector clearly with both angle and name of bulb.

A different garden centre also sells boxes containing a gross of mixed bulbs.

On a pie chart showing the selection of bulbs in these boxes, daffodils are represented by a sector of angle 135°.

(b) What percentage of the bulbs in this box are daffodils?

4. The conversion graph below can be used to change centimetres to inches.

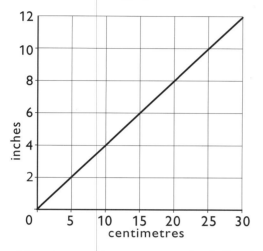

Use the graph to answer the following questions.

(a) How many inches are equivalent to 260 centimetres?

(b) There are 12 inches in 1 foot. Simon's height is 5 feet 10 inches.
What is his height measured in centimetres?

5. The science and mathematics percentages of nine pupils are recorded in the table below.

Science mark	56	48	50	65	54	78	91	55	87
Mathematics mark	63	55	58	64	49	72	80	64	92

(a) Plot points representing this information as a scattergraph.

■■□ (b) Draw, by eye, the line of best fit.

■■□ (c) Using your line of best fit, estimate the mathematics mark for a pupil who scored 60 in science.

6. In the National Lottery, the machine can choose at random any one of the first 49 counting numbers (1 to 49 inclusive) when selecting the first number.

   (a) What is the probability that the first number selected will be:
      (i) the number 23
      (ii) an even number
      (iii) a prime number less than 20?

   The first number chosen is 13 and the machine now chooses at random a second number.

   (b) What is the probability that the second number chosen will be 30?

7. On a snooker table there are 15 red balls and one each of white, yellow, green, brown, blue, pink and black.
   Hal, who is blindfolded, picks one ball at random from the table.

   (a) What is the probability that the ball is
      (i) yellow
      (ii) red
      (iii) not blue?

   Hal picked the green ball and put it in his pocket.
   Jenny now removes a third of the red balls, the blue ball and the pink ball.
   Hal then picks another ball at random.

   (b) What is the probability that he picks a red ball?

8. In the Venn diagram opposite,

   $\mathscr{E}$ = {integers from 40 to 50 inclusive}
   A = {odd numbers}
   B = {multiples of 5}
   C = {multiples of 7}

   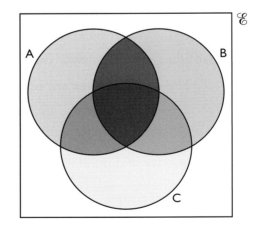

   (a) List all the members of
      (i) set A
      (ii) set B
      (iii) set C.

   (b) Complete the Venn diagram.

   (c) A number is chosen at random from $\mathscr{E}$. What is the probability that the number chosen is a multiple of both 5 and 7?

Glossary

11+ Vocabulary

Abacus	The predecessor of the electronic calculator: a device usually consisting of rows of beads on wires to assist with mental calculations.
Acre	A measurement of area in the imperial system of units (about 4000 m²).
Acute angle	An angle less than 90 degrees.
Add	Plus; find the total.
Addition	The process of adding; a 'sum'.
Adjacent	Next to; side by side; in a right-angled triangle the side which is not 'opposite' (to a given angle).
Algebra	The branch of mathematics using letters to stand for numbers.
am (am)	*ante meridiem* (Latin) which means 'before noon'; *see also* **pm (pm)**.
Amount	Quantity; how much or how many.
Angle	The amount in degrees by which two joined lines have been 'hinged open'.
Angle measurer	An instrument such as a protractor for measuring the sizes of angles.
Answer	That which was sought by the question.
Anticlockwise	An opposite direction to that in which the hands of a clock turn.
Area	The amount of space inside a flat shape, commonly measured in square centimetres (cm²), square metres (m²), hectares (ha) etc.
Arithmetic	The branch of mathematics dealing with numbers, especially with +, −, ×, ÷
Arrangement	A way of putting things in an order or an 'array' – a pattern.
Ascending	Going up; in order of increasing size.
Average	A calculation used to summarise a set of data.

Axes	Plural form of **axis**.
Axis	A line on a grid holding the numbers of scale, usually horizontal (*x*-axis) and vertical (*y*-axis).
Balance (1)	The remainder after a series of financial payments (in and out).
Balance (2)	An old-fashioned pair of weighing scales: if the scales balanced then the masses were equal.
Bank balance	The amount of money in the bank.
Bar chart	A diagram which shows data by the height or length of the bar.
Bar-line graph	As a bar chart, but using lines or sticks, usually to represent frequency (also called a 'stick graph').
Base	The bottom face of a solid shape or the lower edge of a plane shape.
Bearings	A three-figure direction measured clockwise in degrees from north.
Best estimate	The answer which is closest to the exact answer without having to work it out.
Between	Somewhere along the line from one to the other.
BIDMAS	*see* **BODMAS**.
BODMAS	**B**rackets, **O**f, **D**ivision, **M**ultiplication, **A**ddition, **S**ubtraction – a way to remember the priorities of arithmetical operations. (Some people prefer **BIDMAS**, where the second letter is for **I**ndices.)
Brackets	Another name for parentheses '(' and ')'; *see also* **Factorise** and **Multiply out**.
Calculate	Work out; evaluate. (It does not always mean use a calculator!)
Calculation	The process of finding the value of a numerical expression.
Calculator	Any machine which makes calculations easier.
Capacity	The amount of space taken up or enclosed by a solid; the volume.

Carroll diagram	A two-way table used to help with classification, e.g. Girls (G) / Boys (B) against Swimmers (S) / Non-Swimmers (N). (Named after Lewis Carroll.)
Celsius	The temperature scale, also known as centigrade, on which water freezes at 0 degrees and boils at 100 degrees.
Centilitre	One hundredth of a litre.
Centimetre	One hundredth part of a metre.
Centre	The middle.
Century	A period of time lasting one hundred years.
Certain	Having a probability of 1; impossible to fail; guaranteed to happen.
Chance	Another word for probability or likelihood.
Change (money)	The amount of money required to make up the cost of the purchases to the value of the cash offered.
Chart	A picture which helps to represent a set of data.
Circle	The round shape made by joining up all points a fixed distance from the centre.
Classify	Sort out according to the properties of the items; books can be classified by genre, shapes can be classified by number of sides etc.
Clear (display, entry)	Reset a calculator to receive the number again (C) or the whole calculation again (AC).
Clock (1)	12-hour clocks tell the time using only hours 1 to 12 but also with am or pm.
Clock (2)	24-hour clocks tell the time using hours 0000 to 2359; times after 1200 are pm times.
Clockwise	The same direction as that turned by the hands of a clock.
Column	The vertical in a table (up – down).
Compare	Put one thing against another to see how similar or different they are.
Compass	A direction finder marked as N, NE, E, SE, S, SW, W, NW.

Compasses	Geometrical instrument for drawing circles; also used to draw arcs when constructing triangles.
Congruence	The property of being congruent.
Congruent	Identical in size and shape.
Consecutive	Following on in counting order, e.g. 4, 5, 6 are consecutive numbers.
Continue	Carry on in the same way as before.
Conversion graph	A straight line graph used to convert between one unit and another, for example, metric and imperial.
Convert	Change from one into another, especially from one unit of measurement to another.
Co-ordinate pair	Two numbers (x, y) used to plot a point on a co-ordinate grid.
Co-ordinate point	The point plotted by a co-ordinate pair such as (2, 4).
Co-ordinates	Pairs of numbers used to indicate positions on a grid; (x, y) = (across, up).
Corresponding (points)	If a shape has been transformed (e.g. by translation) then each vertex has a Start and Finish position; these two positions make a pair of corresponding points/vertices.
Cube (solid shape)	A solid with six square faces.
Cube (number)	The result of multiplying a number by its square.
Cubed	A number which has been multiplied by its square, e.g. 2 cubed is 8 and 3 cubed is 27
Cubic centimetre	The volume of a cube which is one centimetre along each straight edge; a unit of volume, equivalent to one ml of liquid.
Cubic metre	The volume of a cube which is one metre along each straight edge; one cubic metre of water has a mass of one tonne.
Cubic millimetre	The volume of a cube which is one millimetre along each straight edge; about the size of a grain of sugar.
Cuboid	A solid shape which is a rectangular version of a cube.

Currency	The type of money (e.g. pounds, euros, dollars) used by a country.
Curve	A line between two points, not necessarily the shortest route; a line drawn through several points on a graph.
Data	Information, results etc. (often collected by a survey).
Data collection sheet	A table designed to collect the results of a questionnaire, observation or survey in an efficient manner.
Database	An information system, usually electronic, used to store and display details of a collection of things such as books, volcanoes or football players.
Day	A period of time lasting twenty-four hours.
Decade	A period of time lasting ten years.
Decimal number	A number with any number of figures after the decimal point e.g. 13.502
Decimal places	The number of digits after the decimal point, e.g. 3.1415 has four decimal places.
Decimal point	The dot between the units column and the tenths column. TU.t 1 0.5
Decrease	Make smaller.
Degree (°) (angles)	The unit of measurement for the size of an angle, e.g. 90 degrees make a right angle, 360 degrees make a full turn.
Degree (°) (temperature)	The unit of measurement for temperature.
Degree Celsius	The unit of temperature using a scale on which lie 0 °C (water freezing) and 100 °C (water boiling).
Degree Fahrenheit	The unit of temperature using a scale on which lie 32 °F (water freezing) and 212 °F (water boiling).
Denominator	The bottom number in a proper, improper or algebraic fraction. $\dfrac{3}{4}\ \dfrac{8}{5}\ \dfrac{ab}{3c}$
Deposit	A payment made at the beginning of a deal, which can either be returned later or count as a first payment.
Depth	How deep something is; usually a vertical measurement of distance starting at zero and increasing downwards.

Descending	Going down; numbers in decreasing order.
Diagonal	A line across a plane shape joining two vertices (corners).
Diagram	A picture used to illustrate a situation, especially to make a complex problem clearer.
Dice, die	One die, two dice: the (usually) cube-shaped solid used in games and probability experiments.
Difference	The answer to a subtraction.
Digit (1)	One of the symbols from 0 to 9 used in writing numbers.
Digit (2)	Another word for a finger, especially when used to help counting.
Direction	The way to be regarded as 'forwards', especially using the points of a compass or a three-figure bearing.
Discount	A reduction in the usual price.
Discrete	A measurement which can only take certain values, going up in 'jumps'.
Display (calculator)	The area on a calculator used to show the numbers entered and the calculation result.
Distance	The length of a line between two points.
Distribution	The way in which a set of data falls into groups in a frequency table.
Divide	Share; the **first** number is the one being shared.
Divisible	Can be divided by, e.g. 12 is divisible by 4
Division (1)	The operation of sharing one number equally into smaller parts.
Division (2)	The interval on a measuring scale.
Double (verb)	Multiply by two.
Double (noun)	The result of multiplying by two, as in '6 is the double of 3'.
Doubt	Includes the possibility of failure as well as success.
Draw (1)	To draw in mathematics requires pencil, compasses and ruler.
Draw (2)	An even score at the end of a game.
Draw (3)	Select a card (at random) from a pack.

East	Towards the direction of the rising sun, usually shown as towards the right on a map.
Edge (1)	The line joining two adjacent vertices in a polygon (also called a side); 'all the way around the edge' refers to the perimeter of the shape. 3 edges
Edge (2)	The line shared by two adjacent faces in a 3-D shape, running from one vertex to another. 12 edges
Eighths	The result when a whole is divided into eight equal pieces.
Enter (calculator)	Type in a calculation or command by a sequence of keystrokes; the final button pressed to obtain a result.
Equally likely	Having the same chance or probability.
Equals (=)	The expressions on either side have the same value.
Equilateral	All sides of equal length, e.g. equilateral triangle.
Equivalent	Two things which are the same in every way, especially fractions and ratios, e.g. $\frac{2}{4} \equiv \frac{4}{8}$ $\quad 4:12 \equiv 1:3$
Estimate	Make a reasonable guess at the answer without detailed calculation.
Even	A number which ends in 0, 2, 4, 6 or 8
Even chance	The probability of 50%, as in 'heads or tails'.
Explain	Give a reason for something, especially using the word 'because' in the answer.
Explore	Investigate an unknown area, problem or activity.
Face	A flat surface of a solid shape, e.g. a cube has 6 faces.
Factor	A small number which divides exactly into a bigger number, e.g. 4 is a factor of 12
Factor pairs	Two numbers which multiply to give the required product, e.g. (3, 20) is a factor pair of 60

Factor rainbow	Factors listed in order and joined in pairs can create a rainbow picture; if there is only one number in the middle then the original number was a square number, e.g. 16 1 2 4 8 16
Fahrenheit	The temperature scale on which water freezes at 32 degrees and boils at 212 degrees.
Fair	Not biased; a fair die has an equal chance of landing on any one if its six faces.
False	Not true; a lie; having a logical value of zero (on a spreadsheet).
Fifths	The result when a whole is divided into five equal pieces.
Fifty-fifty chance	Another expression for evens or 50% probability.
Flow chart	A chain of decision boxes or instruction boxes, useful for creating a logical process or organisation of ideas.
Fluid ounce (fl. oz)	An imperial measure of liquid capacity.
Fold (1)	Bend something over onto itself to double the thickness or make a crease.
Fold (2)	Suffix meaning 'many times' as in three-fold.
Foot	A unit of length consisting of 12 inches (about 30.48 cm) (pl. feet).
Formula	A 'recipe' for combining numbers, using words or letters (pl. **formulae**), e.g. $P = 2(l + w)$
Fraction	A quantity written as a numerator over (divided by) a denominator, e.g. $\frac{2}{3}$ (proper) $\frac{3}{2}$ (improper).
Fraction wall	A way of comparing fractions by splitting the same width into different equal quantities.
Frequency	The number of times something has happened.
Frequency diagram	A type of bar chart in which the vertical axis is frequency, indicated by the height of the bar.
Frequency table/chart	A table of collected data organised into categories and giving the total (frequency) in each category.
Function	A rule for changing one number into another, e.g. 'multiply by 4' or 'add 1'.

Function machine	A chain of one or more functions which features an input and output of numbers.	input $\triangleright$ $\boxed{\times 4}$ $\triangleright$ $\boxed{+1}$ $\triangleright$ output
Gallon	A unit of capacity consisting of 8 pints (about 4.5 litres).	
Geometry	The branch of mathematics dealing with shapes.	
Good chance	Having a probability above 50%.	
Gram	One thousandth part of a kilogram.	
Graph	A pictorial representation of data.	
Greater than (>)	Having a bigger value (note carefully which way the sign goes); the biggest number goes next to the big end of the sign, e.g. 5 > 3	
Greater than or equal to (≥)	Having a bigger value or just the same value, e.g. if $x \geq 2$ for the score on an ordinary die, then x could be 2, 3, 4, 5 or 6	
Greatest value	The maximum value obtained by a set of data or a line on a graph.	
Grid	A network of crossed lines, usually at right angles to each other.	
Grouped data	Data which has been sorted into groups (classes) of equal class interval.	
Half	The result when a whole is divided into two equal pieces (pl. **halves**).	
Halve	Divide by two.	
Hectare	A unit of area equal to 10 000 square metres (think of a square 100 m on each side); approx. 2.5 acres.	
Height	The vertical distance between the top and the ground or base.	height ←base→ height ←base→
Hexagon	A polygon with six sides.	
High	Having a large value; a measurement of the height of something.	
Horizontal	Parallel to the horizon; straight across.	
Hour	A unit of time equal to 60 minutes or one 24th of a day.	
Hundred, hundreds	The place value position to the left of the tens column.	H T U.t h

Hundredth, hundredths	The place value position to the right of the tenths column.	H T U.t **h**
Hundredweight	One twentieth of an imperial ton (112 lb).	
Identical	Exactly the same in all respects; congruent (shapes).	
Imperial	The measurement system in use before the metric system.	
Impossible	Not possible under any circumstance; probability 0; guaranteed to fail.	
Improper fraction	A fraction in which the numerator (top) is bigger than the denominator (bottom) – can be changed into a mixed number e.g. $\frac{3}{2} \rightarrow 1\frac{1}{2}$ $\frac{15}{4} \rightarrow 3\frac{3}{4}$	
Inch	Imperial unit of length (based originally on the length of part of a Roman thumb!).	1 inch
Increase	Make bigger.	
Input	A number which is 'fed into' a function machine; *see also* **Function**.	**input** — ×2 — output
Instruments	Mathematical equipment such as compasses and ruler.	
Integer	A whole number such as 35 or 108 or $^-2$	
Interpret	Give meaning to something, especially a set of results or a diagram.	
Interval	Any part of a scale, especially on a number line.	
Inverse	The opposite, e.g. × and ÷, + and –; square and square root.	5 →×3 →15 5 ←÷3 ←15
Inverse function	The function which does the opposite of the one given, e.g. '–3' is the inverse function of '+3'.	+3 –3
Inverse mapping	The reverse mapping, e.g. $x \rightarrow x - 3$ is the inverse mapping for the mapping $x \rightarrow x + 3$	
Investigate	Find out by asking one's own questions and looking for answers.	
Isometric	A grid of equilateral triangles, used for drawing solid shapes in two dimensions.	

Isosceles	Having two sides the same length to create a line of symmetry (especially isosceles triangle and isosceles trapezium).
Key (1)	Any one of the buttons on a calculator which can be pressed in the course of a calculation.
Key (2)	An indicator to provide essential information on a graph or scale drawing, e.g. scale 1 cm : 100 m; or a colour code for a pie chart.
Kilogram	One thousand grams; the standard unit for measuring mass.
Kilometre	One thousand metres; used for measuring long distances.
Kilometres per hour (kph or km/h)	Measure of speed obtained by dividing distance travelled (in km) by time taken (in hours).
Kite	A symmetrical quadrilateral with two adjacent pairs of equal sides.
Label	The description of an axis on a graph or chart, e.g. 'y-axis' or 'frequency'.
Least value	The minimum value attained by a set of data or a line on a graph.
Length	The distance between the two ends.
Less than (<)	Having a smaller value; note carefully which way the sign goes; the biggest number goes next to the big end of the sign, e.g. $3 < 5$ If $x < 3$ then x could be ... $-2, -1, 0, 1, 2$
Less than or equal to (≤)	Having a smaller value or just the same value. If $x \leq 3$ then x could be ... $-2, -1, 0, 1, 2$, or 3
Likelihood	Chance; e.g. in the phrase: 'the likelihood of winning the Lottery is very small'.
Likely	Describing something which has a good chance of happening.
Line	Originally the shortest distance between two points; in general, a line has infinite length but no breadth.
Line graph	A graph drawn by joining up plotted points.
Line of symmetry	One of the mirror lines on a diagram with reflection symmetry.

Line segment	A piece of an infinite line, with two end points.
Line symmetry	Another name for reflection or reflective symmetry.
Litre	One thousand millilitres; used for measuring quantities of liquid.
Long multiplication	A pencil and paper method of multiplying two numbers.
Lowest terms	Describes a fraction which cannot be cancelled down (simplified) any more, e.g. $\frac{1}{3}$ $\frac{3}{7}$ $\frac{10}{21}$
Map (1)	A scaled picture or scale diagram of an area.
Map (2) / mapping	A procedure for changing one number (input) to another (output).
Map (3)	The transformation of a shape mapped onto an image by means of reflection, rotation or translation.
Mass	The weight of an object, measured in grams and kilograms; *see also* **Weight**.
Maximum value	The greatest size a number can take in the given context.
Mean	The average found by adding the data and dividing the total by the number of items, e.g. the mean of 1, 2, 3 and 18 is 6
Measure	The value or size of something using standard units.
Median	The average found by writing data in order and finding the middle value, or the mean of the two middle values, e.g. the median of 1, 2, 3 and 14 is 2.5
Memory	The facility for storing numbers and half-way answers to assist in a calculation, when using a calculator.
Method	A procedure, process or 'recipe' for carrying out a calculation or operation, e.g. the method for constructing triangles needs a ruler, protractor and compasses.
Metre	The standard unit of length, equal to one hundred centimetres or one thousand millimetres.
Metric	The measurement system based upon powers of 10 with the metre as the basic unit of length.
Mile	A unit of length corresponding to 'a thousand paces' (5280 feet) or about 1609 metres (5 miles is approximately 8 km).
Miles per hour (mph or miles/h)	A unit of speed in which one mile is covered every hour.

Millennium	A period of time lasting 1000 years.
Millilitre	One thousandth part of a litre.
Millimetre	One thousandth part of a metre.
Minimum value	The smallest size a number can take in the given context.
Minus (negative)	A signed or directed number which is below zero; better known as 'negative numbers'.
Minus (subtract)	Take away; the second number is taken away from the first.
Minute (1) (time)	A period of time lasting 60 seconds or one 60th of an hour.
Minute (2)	Very small.
Mirror line	A line through the middle of a shape where one could place a mirror and still see all of it.
Mixed number	A number with a whole number part and a proper fraction part; can be converted into an improper fraction for multiplying and dividing calculations, e.g. $1\frac{1}{2} \rightarrow \frac{3}{2}$ $3\frac{1}{4} \rightarrow \frac{13}{4}$
Modal class/group	The class/group in a table of grouped data which has the highest frequency.
Mode	Occurring most often; most frequent or most common; the average represented by the most commonly occurring data item.
Month	A period of time lasting approximately four weeks (lunar month) or 28–31 days (calendar month).
Multiple	A product, e.g. multiples of 3 are all the numbers with 3 as a factor, i.e. numbers in the 3-times table.
Multiplication	The process of finding the product; i.e. multiplying.
Multiply	Find the product of two or more numbers; 'times', as in the times tables.
Nearest	Closest, especially when rounding numbers, e.g. 3467 is roughly 3470 to the nearest 10, or roughly 3500 to the nearest 100
Nearly	Almost, as in 'the value of pi is nearly 3 and one seventh'.
Negative	The opposite of positive; below zero, e.g. negative six is written as ⁻6
Negative numbers	Numbers which are below zero, occasionally referred to as 'minus numbers', e.g. ⁻3

Net (polyhedron)	A 'cardboard cut-out' design which can be folded up to make a solid shape.	
Ninths	The result when a whole is divided into nine equal pieces.	
No chance	Zero probability; impossible.	
North	Towards the North Pole.	
North-east	With north-west, south-west and south-east: the points of the compass in between the four main directions.	
Number line	Numbers in order on a marked line, usually either side of zero, (especially as an aid to mental or pencil arithmetic) for plotting points or for representing a solution set for a pair of inequalities.	
Numerator	The top number in a fraction, e.g. $\frac{3}{4}$ $\frac{5}{3}$	
Oblong	A rectangle which is not square.	
Obtuse	An angle greater than 90 degrees but less than 180 degrees.	
Octagon	A polygon with eight sides.	
Odd	A number which ends in 1, 3, 5, 7 or 9	
Operation	The four basic calculations done with numbers (+, −, ×, ÷).	
Opposite (1)	Facing; on the other side; in a triangle, the side furthest from the angle.	
Opposite (2)	An inverse, e.g. multiplication is the opposite of division.	
Order (1)	To list, e.g. a set of numbers according to size.	
Order (2)	The rules that say which of the various operations (e.g. +, −, ×, ÷) are to be given priority; also known as **BODMAS** or **BIDMAS**.	
Origin	The point with co-ordinates $(0, 0)$ on an (x, y) grid.	
Ounce	A unit of mass (abbreviated oz) which represents one sixteenth of a pound weight (about 28 g).	
Outcome	A possible result of a particular event.	

Outcome table	A systematic way of displaying all possible outcomes to an experiment.
Output	A number which 'comes out' of a function machine.
Parallel	Running in the same direction.
Parallelogram	A quadrilateral with two pairs of parallel sides.
Partition	Separating a number into its parts, e.g. 126 = 100 + 20 + 6 (the hundreds, tens and units parts).
Pattern (1)	An arrangement of objects, e.g. matches, counters or tiles, according to some rule which enables a sequence to be made.
Pattern (2)	A pattern of numbers enabling us to predict the next number in the sequence.
Pattern (3)	A geometrical design which is built by applying rules of symmetry.
Pentagon	A polygon with five sides. regular pentagon
Percentage (%)	A number which is a fraction of 100, e.g. $30\% = \frac{30}{100}$
Perimeter	The distance all the way around the edge of a shape.
Perpendicular	At right angles.
Pictogram	A diagram similar to a bar chart in which appropriate pictures are put in lines to make the (usually) horizontal bars. happy unhappy represents 2 children
Pint	A unit of capacity (usually liquid) consisting of 20 fluid ounces (about 0.6 litres).
Place value	Units, Tens, Hundreds etc; the size of a number depends on its position. H T U.t h
Plan	A bird's eye view of a solid, especially used to show floor layouts in buildings.
Plan view	The view from above.
Plane	A flat surface; two-dimensional, like a sheet of paper.

Plane shapes	Two-dimensional shapes which are drawn on paper, as opposed to solid shapes, which can be picked up.
Plot	Mark a small cross to indicate a position of a point.
Plus	The arithmetical sign (+) to indicate addition.
pm (pm)	*post meridiem* (Latin) which means 'after noon'; *see also* **am (am)**.
Point	A position often indicated by a cross; having no dimension.
Poor chance	Having a probability below 50%.
Position	Another name for place or location; in mathematics we describe positions precisely using co-ordinates.
Positive	Above zero on the number line, e.g. positive three is written as $^+3$ or simply 3
Possibility	One of the things which could happen.
Possible	Having a probability which is greater than 0
Pound (money)	£1; equal to 100 pence.
Pound (weight)	1 lb; equal to 16 oz (about 0.5 kg).
Prime	A number which has only two factors, 1 and itself.
Probability	The branch of mathematics which looks at the chance of things happening.
Probability scale	The number line from 0 (impossible) to 1 (certain).
Probable	Another name for possible, but usually used to mean with a probability greater than 50%.
Procedure	A sequence of instructions.
Problem	Any kind of question to which an answer is needed.
Product	The result of a multiplication.
Proper fraction	A fraction in which the numerator (top) is smaller than the denominator (bottom) – when written in decimal form it will be between 0 and 1, e.g. $\frac{3}{4} = 0.75$

Property	A characteristic of something, e.g. one of the properties of a kite is that it has one line of symmetry.
Proportion	Any of several ways (e.g. fraction or percentage) used to describe part of a whole, e.g. 'the proportion of girls in this room is about three-fifths'.
Protractor	Geometrical instrument used to measure angles, commonly made of a semicircle of clear plastic.
Pyramid	A solid with a flat (esp. square) base and the other faces sloping up to a point at the apex.
Quadrilateral	A polygon with four sides.
Quarters	The result of a whole divided into four equal pieces.
Questionnaire	A carefully planned set of unbiased questions used to collect information from people in a survey.
Range	The difference between the greatest and least values in a set of data.
Rate	The amount of one currency given in exchange for another ('exchange rate').
Ratio	A way of comparing the relative size of two or more whole numbers, e.g. 3 : 2
Reason	An explanation given in answer to the question 'why?'.
Reasoning	The process of clear thinking which uses logic and careful explanation.
Rectangle	A quadrilateral with four right angles; *see also* **Oblong**.
Reflect	Draw the result of a reflection in a given mirror line.
Reflection (1)	The image seen in a mirror or mirror line.
Reflection (2)	The transformation which maps an object onto its reflected image.
Reflection symmetry	The property of having matching halves either side of one or more mirror lines.
Reflex	Describes an angle which is bigger than 180 degrees.
Represent	Give in another form, especially as a diagram or graph.

Result (1)	The outcome of a survey or experiment, best displayed in a table.
Result (2)	The final answer to a numerical problem or calculation.
Result (3)	The effect of completing a transformation such as rotation or reflection.
Rhombus (diamond)	A symmetrical quadrilateral which has four equal sides.
Right (1)	Correct.
Right (2)	Describes an angle size of 90 degrees.
Right-angled	With one or more angles of 90 degrees.
Rotate	Draw the result of a rotation through a given angle and about a given point.
Rotation (1)	Turning around a fixed point.
Rotation (2)	The transformation which maps an object onto its rotated image.
Rotation symmetry	The property of having two or more 'right ways up'.
Rough	Approximate.
Roughly	Not given to a high degree of accuracy, e.g. an approximation.
Round	The shape of a circle.
Row	The horizontal in a table (left – right).
Rule (1)	The instructions for generating a sequence of numbers.
Rule (2)	A straight line, as drawn by pencil and ruler.
Ruler	Any instrument for drawing straight lines or measuring length.
Scale (1)	Measuring scales such as rulers, bathroom scales, electricity meters etc.
Scalene	All sides of different length, e.g. scalene triangle.

Sea level	A zero reference height defined by the average of high and low tides, so that all other heights can be compared with it (above and below).
Second (1)	The one after the first and before the third.
Second (2)	A unit of time equal to one sixtieth of a minute.
Sequence	A list of numbers following a logical pattern or rule, e.g. 1, 3, 5, 7, 9, ...
Set	A collection of things which all have something in common, e.g. {children who learn the piano}, {prime numbers}, {quadrilaterals} etc.
Sevenths	The result of a whole divided into seven equal pieces.
Shape	A geometrical figure; an enclosed space or form.
Share	Divide a given amount equally.
Side	A straight line between the vertices in a geometric shape.
Sign	The direction of a number, shown as $^+$ (which is often omitted) or $^-$ in front of the number.
Sign change key	The key +/− or (−) on a calculator which changes the sign of a directed number.
Sixths	The result when a whole is divided into six equal pieces.
Sketch	A diagram drawn more for convenience than accuracy.
Solid	A three-dimensional shape which can be picked up and handled, as opposed to plane shapes which can only be seen on paper.
South	Towards the South Pole.
Speed	The rate at which distance is travelled, commonly in metres per second or miles per hour.
Sphere	A ball-shaped solid.
Spinner	Anything capable of spinning, especially one which can indicate a variety of possible outcomes.
Square (1)	A regular quadrilateral.

Square (2)	To multiply a number by itself; the result obtained when this is done, e.g. $3 \times 3 = 9$
Square centimetre	A square, one centimetre on each side; a unit of area for small shapes and regions, such as those drawn in exercise books.
Square inch	A square, one inch on each side; an imperial unit for area occasionally seen in the measurement of pressures, e.g. pounds per square inch or p.s.i. as on some car tyres.
Square kilometre	A square, one kilometre on each side; a unit of area for very large shapes and regions, such as countries.
Square metre	A square, one metre on each side; a unit of area for large shapes and regions, such as playgrounds and tennis courts.
Square mile	A square, one mile on each side.
Square millimetre	A square, one millimetre on each side; a unit of area for very small shapes and regions, such as things seen under a microscope.
Square number	The result of multiplying a whole number by itself; can be drawn as a square of dots, e.g. 1, 4, 9, 16, 25 etc.
Square root	The number which when squared gives the one at the start, e.g. the square root of 64 is 8
Square yard	A square, one yard on each side.
Square-based pyramid	A solid shape with a square base, with the other four faces rising to a single point – the shape of the famous pyramids in Egypt.
Squared	Multiplied by itself, as in three squared is nine (written as $3^2 = 9$).
Statistics	The branch of mathematics dealing with understanding data.
Stone	A unit of weight equivalent, in Earth's gravity, to a mass of 14 pounds (6.35 kg).
Straight angle	Two lines which meet at an angle of 180°, thus making a single straight line.

Subtract	Minus, take away; the second number is the one being taken away.
Subtraction	The process of taking away one number from another.
Sum	The answer to an addition.
Surface	The outside of a solid shape.
Survey	A data collection exercise which usually involves a questionnaire of some kind.
Symbol	Any sign used in mathematics to give a particular meaning, such as the symbol used for pi (π) or 'less than' (<).
Symmetrical	Having symmetry of any kind.
Symmetry	Sameness, especially with reflection or rotation.
Symmetry lines	Mirror lines on a diagram which has reflection symmetry.
Table	Any two-way chart which helps to organise the information it contains.
Tables	Multiplication tables from 1×1 to 12×12
Tally	Counting via the 'five bar gate' method or using ticks, which are later totalled to give the frequency.
Tally chart	A diagram used to collect data by making marks in the appropriate row or column.
Temperature	Measured by a thermometer, usually in degrees Celsius.
Ten, tens	The place value position to the left of the Units column. H **T** U.t h
Tenth, tenths (1)	The place value position to the right of the decimal point. H T U.**t** h
Tenths (2)	The result when a whole is divided into ten equal pieces.
Tessellate	Fit together on a flat surface so that no gaps are left; rectangles tessellate but circles do not.
Tessellation	Shapes fitted together to cover a plane without gaps.

Tetrahedron	A regular triangular-based pyramid.	
Thermometer	An instrument used to measure temperature.	
Thickness	The measurement of height for solid objects which are almost flat.	
Thirds	The result when a whole is divided into three equal pieces.	
Thousand, thousands	The place value position to the left of the Hundreds column.	**Th** H T U.t h th
Thousandth, thousandths	The place value position to the right of the Hundredths column.	Th H T U.t h **th**
Three-dimensional (3-D)	Solid, such that it may be picked up or viewed from different positions.	
Through 90° etc.	A rotation needs a rotation centre to determine the point of turning, and an angle of rotation, e.g. 'through 180 degrees' to say through how much the object is to be turned.	
Time	Any interval along the line from past, through present, to future, or any fixed position on that line.	
Time graph (line graph)	Any type of graph which shows the way something is changing over time, e.g. a temperature graph, a travel graph, a happiness graph.	
Times	Multiply e.g. as in 'three times four'; *see also* **Multiply**	
Timetable	A schedule of times, usually of events through the day or week, e.g. bus, train, and school lessons.	
Title	A descriptive heading, especially important at the top of any graph, diagram, or new piece of work.	
Ton	An imperial unit for weighing very heavy objects; one ton is 160 stone (about twelve men) which is 2240 lb.	
Tonne	One thousand kilograms, used for measuring the mass of very heavy objects; a metric tonne is only slightly lighter than an imperial ton.	
Total	The result of adding; *see also* **Sum**.	
Transformation	A change, especially on a shape, for example, reflection, rotation, enlargement.	

Translate	A slide – the transformation which has no effect except a change of position.
Translation	The transformation by which a shape is translated.
Trapezium	A quadrilateral with one pair of parallel sides.
Triangle	A plane shape with three sides.
True	Not false; correct, straight, honest.
Two-dimensional (2-D)	Flat, such that it cannot be picked up; like a shadow or picture.
Uncertain	Having a probability which is less than one, and commonly used to mean with a probability less than 0.5
Unfair	Biased; not favouring both sides equally.
Units (1)	The place value position to the left of the decimal point. H T **U**.t h
Units (2)	The quantity being measured, e.g. cm, kg, min.
Unknown	Anything not known, especially the variable letter in an equation.
Unlikely	Having a low chance or likelihood.
Venn diagram	A diagram using overlapping circles to show how two or more sets are related.
Vertical	Perpendicular to the horizontal; straight up.
Vertex	A corner of a shape (pl. **vertices**).
Vertices	Corners of a plane or solid shape (sing. **vertex**).
Volume	The amount of space inside a solid shape, measured in cubic cm (cm^3), cubic m (m^3), etc.
Vulgar fraction	An ordinary fraction (proper fraction) with the numerator smaller than the denominator, e.g. $\frac{3}{5}$
Week	A period of time lasting seven days.
Weight	The force due to gravity exerted by something with mass; if there is no gravity, the mass stays the same but the weight becomes zero.

West	Towards the setting sun.	N W—┼—E S
Width	A measure of how wide something is.	
Word formula	A set of instructions or a flow diagram, which tells you what to do with the input.	
x-**axis**	The horizontal axis on a co-ordinate grid.	*y* ↑ —┼—→ *x*
x-**co-ordinate**	The first number of a co-ordinate pair, to indicate the distance to the right (negative means to the left), e.g. (**3**, 2).	
Yard	A unit of length consisting of three feet or 36 inches (about 91.4 cm).	
y-**axis**	The vertical axis on a co-ordinate grid.	*y* ↑ —┼—→ *x*
y-**co-ordinate**	The second number of a co-ordinate pair, to indicate the distance above the *x*-axis (negative means below the *x*-axis), e.g. (3, **2**).	
Year	A period of time lasting twelve months; the time taken for Earth to travel once around the sun.	
Zero (1) (place holder)	Nought; nothing, e.g. the zero in **3028** means 'no hundreds'.	
Zero (2)	The reference point on a measuring scale; when measuring a length or an angle, make sure you line up with zero on the ruler/protractor and not the edge of the plastic.	

13+ Vocabulary

Algebraic expression	One or more algebraic terms combined using + and − e.g. $5 + 2 - x$
Alternate angles	Angles in an angle diagram which are in a 'Z' or 'N' shape.
Angles at a point	Two or more angles sharing a common vertex with an angle sum of 360°. $a + b + c = 360°$
Angles in a triangle	The three angles in the same triangle always add up to 180°; in a right-angled triangle this is equivalent to saying that the other two angles always add up to 90°. $a + b + c = 180°$ $d + e = 90°$
Angles on a straight line	Two or more angles sharing a common edge with an angle sum of 180°. $f + g = 180°$
Apex	The highest point in a plane or solid shape.
Approximately	By way of an approximation; roughly.
Approximately equal to ($\approx$)	Roughly the same as; having used approximate rather than exact values.
Approximation	A 'rough' answer, often used as a check to a calculator result.
Arc	A section of the circumference of a circle.
Area factor	The old area was multiplied by this to obtain the new area; the area factor is the square of the scale factor. scale factor 2 → area factor 4
Arithmetic sequence	A sequence of numbers which goes up (or down) by the same amount each time, e.g. 1, 4, 7, 10, ...
Arrowhead	The only concave quadrilateral (a type of kite); delta or nested V-shape.

Average speed	The total distance travelled divided by the total time taken.
Axis of rotation symmetry	Imagine a CD spinning around a pencil – the pencil is the axis of rotation.
Axis of symmetry	Also known as the **line of symmetry**.
Base angles	Especially in an isosceles triangle – the two angles which are equal. (NB base angles are not necessarily at the bottom of the picture!)
Bias	A tendency to go one way more than another; favouritism.
Biased	A die, spinner or coin is biased if it is not fair.
Billion	One thousand million, written as 1 000 000 000
Bisect	Cut into two equal halves; the two diagonals of a rectangle, square, rhombus and parallelogram bisect each other.
Bisector	A line which cuts something in half, commonly an angle or another line.
Cancel	Cross out, usually in pairs, and especially when simplifying fractions or ratios. e.g. $\frac{4}{6} \to \frac{2}{3}$ $6:2 \to 3:1$
Cancellation	The process of simplifying which involves dividing by a common factor. $6x = 12 \to 6x = 2$
Centre of enlargement	The point from which the enlargement is constructed; the 'focus' or 'vanishing point'.
Centre of rotation	The part of the picture which does not move when the picture is rotated, e.g. the hub of a wheel.
Chord	A straight line joining any two points on the circumference of a circle.
Circumference	The perimeter of a circle.

Class interval	The size of the group (when data is grouped), e.g. 20 to 25 cm has a class interval (width) of 5 cm.
Coefficient	The number in front of a letter or term, especially in an equation, e.g. $\mathbf{3}x^2$ or $\mathbf{24}x$.
Collect like terms	Group together terms in algebra with the same letter part, e.g. $3ab + 4a + 2ab = 4a + 5ab$
Common factor	A factor which is shared by two or more numbers or terms, e.g. 5 is a common factor of 15 and 95, and 4 is a common factor of $4a$ and $8b$
Complementary angles	Two angles which add up to 90 degrees. $a + b = 90°$
Complements	Fits the gap left by the other, especially in the context of complementary angles.
Composite (1)	A shape made up from other simpler shapes.
Composite (2)	A number which is not prime.
Concave	Curving in (think 'caving in') like a letter C; the opposite to **convex**.
Conclude	Sum up the main points of a reasoned argument or proof.
Conclusion	The summary statement made from consideration of the statistics (figures and graphs) in the question.
Cone	A circular-based pyramid.
Conjugate	Two angles which add up to 360 degrees; compare with **complementary** and **supplementary**. $a + b = 360°$
Construct	Draw accurately a geometrical figure using ruler and compasses.
Construction lines	Lines left on a construction to show where the compasses and ruler were used.

Continuous	Without jumps or gaps; a measurement which allows 'in between' values.
Convex	Bulging outwards like a letter D; opposite to **concave**.
Correlation	Describes the way one measurement increases relative to another; see also **positive correlation** and **negative correlation**.
Corresponding angles	In an angle diagram, the equal angles formed by a straight line crossing a pair of parallel lines ('F-ANGLES').
Cosine (cos)	In a right-angled triangle, the cosine of an angle is equal to the ratio adjacent : hypotenuse or adjacent ÷ hypotenuse.
Counter-example	An example which breaks the rule; the rule 'all prime numbers are odd' has a counter-example in the number 2 which is prime but even.
Cross-section	The flat shape you get when you slice open a solid.
Cube root	The number which, when cubed, gives the number you started with, e.g. the cube root of 8 is 2 ($\sqrt[3]{8}$)
Cylinder	A solid shape which is a circular prism.
Decagon	A polygon with ten sides.
Decimal fraction (decimal)	A fraction expressed as a decimal, e.g. $\frac{1}{4}$ is 0.25 as a decimal fraction.
Decision tree diagram	A type of flow chart used for sorting or making decisions.
Deduce	Use logic to make a conclusion or deduction.
Definition	A precise explanation of a word or phrase.
Degree of accuracy	A way of describing the reliability of a measurement, e.g. 'to the nearest centimetre'.
Delta	Another name for an arrowhead or concave kite.

Density	A way of comparing the masses of the same volume of two substances; density = mass ÷ volume, e.g. water has a density of 1 g/cm^3, iron has a density of approx. 7 g/cm^3, lead has a density of approx. 12 g/cm^3
Diameter	A chord through the centre of a circle, cutting the circle in half.
Difference of two squares/cubes	A useful result in algebra which makes factorisation easier, e.g. $x^2 - y^2 \rightarrow (x + y)(x - y)$
Difference pattern	The way in which the differences between terms of a sequence change as the sequence continues; this process, known as the 'difference method' will show up almost every hidden pattern in a sequence.
Dimension	A measurement of length, width or height.
Distance–time graph	A graph used to illustrate a journey.
Dividend (1)	A big number which is being divided up by a smaller number (**divisor**).
Dividend (2)	A reward paid out to shareholders (investors) by a company when it wants to share out the profits.
Divisibility	The property of being divisible by a number other than one.
Divisor	When 24 is divided by 3 to get 8, 3 is called the divisor (24 is the **dividend** and 8 is the **quotient**; there is no **remainder**).
Dodecagon	A polygon with twelve sides; a regular dodecagon has twelve equal sides and twelve equal angles.
Dodecahedron	A solid with twelve faces.
Elements of a set	Members of a group which share the same property, e.g. in the set {vowels} are the elements {a, e, i, o u}.
Elevation	The view of a three-dimensional solid from either the front/back or sides.
Enlarge	Make bigger.
Enlargement	A transformation which changes the size of a shape to make a **similar** image.

Equal angles	One of many situations in geometry in which two or more angles in a diagram are the same.

Equal sides	Sides which are the same length, as in isosceles or equilateral triangles, many quadrilaterals and all regular shapes.

Equation	An expression with '=' in it, usually to be solved.
Equidistant	The same distance away.
Equivalence	Even better than being equal, e.g. $8x = 40$ is only true when $x = 5$; equivalence, however, is always true; e.g. $8x \equiv 5x + 3x$
Evaluate	Work out exactly, using a reliable method of calculation.
Event	One of any number of possible outcomes or future happenings.
Evidence	Supporting material for a generalisation, but evidence alone does not make a proof.
Exact	No further accuracy is possible.
Exactly	The true answer, with no inaccuracies or approximations.
Exchange rate	The figures used to convert one currency into another.
Exhaustive	Every possibility has been listed.
Experiment	Any trial which has at least one outcome.
Experimental probability	For example, the experimental probability of getting a head on a coin is (number of heads counted) ÷ (number of times coin was tossed); this gets closer to the **theoretical probability** the more trials are done.
Expression	A collection of terms, usually algebraic, e.g. $3x + 4 + 2x - 3$
Exterior angle	The angle through which a wire is bent at each vertex, when making a polygon from a straight piece of wire.
Factorise	Rewrite a number or algebraic expression as a product of two or more factors; numbers are written as a product of primes, while expressions are written with one or more brackets. $36 = 3^2 \times 2^2 \qquad 3y^3 = 3 \times y \times y \times y \qquad 3a + 6 = 3(a + 2)$

Finite	Having an end eventually.
Formulae	More than one formula (also known as formulas).
Fractional shape	A shape formed from a simpler shape by cutting parts away.
General term	The term in a sequence at any desired position, also known as the nth **term**.
Generate	Produce, or continue, a sequence using the given rule.
Gradient	A measurement of the steepness of a line, given by (height increase) ÷ (width increase).
HCF	See **Highest Common Factor**.
Hemisphere	Half of a sphere.
Hendecagon	A polygon with eleven sides.
Heptagon	A polygon with seven sides.
Highest Common Factor (HCF)	The biggest number which divides exactly into two or more larger numbers, e.g. 8 is the HCF of 16 and 24
Histogram	A type of bar chart where the area of each bar gives the frequency.
Hypotenuse	The longest side in a right-angled triangle.
Icosahedron	A regular solid with twenty equilateral triangle faces.
Identically equal to	Another way of saying 'equivalent to' i.e. always true.
Image	The result of a transformation on an object.
In terms of	A formula in terms of t will use only the variable t combined with numbers.
Index	The little number which indicates repeated multiplication, squares, cubes etc. e.g. 2^3
Index notation	Writing numbers in a form which shows the correct power of 10 each time, e.g. 3000 is 3×10^3
Indices	One index, two indices; see also **Power**.
Inequality	A statement featuring 'less than' or 'greater than'.
Infinite	Having no end, ever; you can never reach infinity.

Integer solution set	All the whole numbers which satisfy a pair of inequalities, e.g. $x \leq 2$ and $x \geq {}^-2$ gives the integer solution set $\{{}^-2, {}^-1, 0, 1, 2\}$
Intercept	'Cut across'; a useful word to describe where a straight line crosses the y-axis.
Interest	Money paid into a savings account by a bank or building society; usually a percentage of what was there before (compound interest).
Interior angle	An angle between two adjacent sides inside a polygon; in a regular polygon all the interior angles are equal.
Intersect (1)	The point at which two lines cross.
Intersect (2)	The point at which two sets overlap.
Intersection	The point at which two intersecting lines meet; this point of intersection is on both lines.
Irregular	Not regular (shapes), thus having two or more different sides and angles.
Justify	Give a reason for something, e.g. algebra as a powerful way to justify a statement such as 'odd + odd = even'.
LCM	*See* **Lowest Common Multiple**.
Least significant digit	The digit in a number which has least say in the size of the number, e.g. the 7 in 246.7
Like terms	Algebraic terms with the same letter part; these can be added or subtracted, e.g. $3x^2$, x^2 and $^-2x^2$ are all like terms.
Limit	The boundary beyond which the value cannot go; when you divide any number by the number just after it, you can get as close as you like to 1 but you will never quite get there; 1 is the limit.
Line of best fit	A straight line judged by eye to go through the majority of points on a scatter graph.
Linear	Like a straight line.

Linear equation	An equation containing only letters and numbers i.e. no squares or cubes of letters, e.g. $3x + 4 = 2x + 7$
Linear expression	A type of expression with no squares or higher powers, e.g. $3x + 5$
Linear function	A function which involves only $+$, $-$, $\times$ and $\div$ on the input number, which can be represented by a straight line, e.g. $y = 3x + 5$
Linear relationship	A mapping which uses only linear functions.
Linear sequence	A sequence of numbers which, if plotted as y co-ordinates for consecutive x values, would lie on a straight line; going up (or down) by the same amount each time, e.g. 15, 12, 9, 6 ...
Long division	A pencil and paper method of dividing one number by another.
Loss	A 'negative profit', where the money received in sales is less than the value of the goods sold.
Lowest common multiple (LCM)	The smallest number into which two or more smaller numbers will divide exactly, e.g. the LCM of 6 and 9 is 18
Mensuration	The process of measuring and calculating measurements.
Metres per second (m/s)	A unit of speed in which one metre is covered every second.
Metric/imperial approximations	Rough equivalents used to convert quickly between units in the metric and imperial systems.
Midpoint	The half-way point along a line, e.g. the point of intersection of the diagonals of a parallelogram.
Minuend	The number from which another (the **subtrahend**) is subtracted.
Mnemonic	An aid to remembering, e.g. '**N**aughty **E**lephants **S**quirt **W**ater' is a mnemonic for **N**orth **E**ast **S**outh **W**est.
Most significant digit	The digit in a number which has greatest say in the size of the number, e.g. the 2 in 246.7
Multiplicand	The number which is being multiplied by something else (the **multiplicator**).
Multiplicator (multiplier)	The number which is being used to multiply up another number (the **multiplicand**).
Multiply out	Multiply each term inside the brackets by the factor outside and then simplify the resultant expression.

Negative correlation	As one variable increases, the other decreases.
Net (without tax)	The value or price of something before VAT has been added on.
Nonagon	A polygon with nine sides.
Notation T(n) or T$_n$	Using algebra to write down a rule or expression in a convenient form.
n^{th} **term**	The general term of a sequence of numbers.
Object	The original shape before being transformed.
Octahedron	A regular solid shape with eight equilateral triangle faces.
Opposite angles (1)	When two lines cross, they make an X shape: the angles above and below the point of intersection are opposite and equal angles; left and right are also opposite and equal.
Opposite angles (2)	Two interior angles on opposite sides in a polygon; they can be joined by a diagonal which cuts the polygon in half.
Opposite sides	Sides in a polygon which are separated by the width of the shape – the polygon centre lies between them; a regular polygon with an odd number of sides has no pairs of opposite sides.
Order (of rotation symmetry)	The number of ways in which a plane shape appears the right way up (maps onto itself) while being turned through 360 degrees. order 2 order 3
Original value	The size of something at the beginning, commonly before a percentage change.
P(n)	For probability of event n, e.g. P(heads) is shorthand for 'the probability of getting heads'.
Per	Divided by; for each one; out of; as in **per**cent or metres **per** second.

Perpendicular bisector	A line which cuts another line in half, meeting it at right angles; the construction using ruler and compasses which creates this line.
pi (π)	The ratio of a circle's circumference to its diameter, approximately 3.14
Pie chart	A circular diagram in which the size of each sector shows the proportion of the whole.
Plane symmetry	The three-dimensional equivalent in solids of line symmetry in plane shapes.
Polygon	A shape with straight sides.
Positive correlation	As one variable increases, so too does the other.
Possibility space	A table listing systematically all possible outcomes of an experiment.
Power	The top right (index) number used in squares, cubes etc. to indicate repeated multiplying, e.g. 2^3 means 2 to the power of 3 (i.e. $2 \times 2 \times 2$).
Predict	Guess the outcome of a future event, usually choosing the outcome with the highest probability.
Prime factor	A factor which is prime; a number which divides exactly into a larger number but which does not itself have any smaller factors besides itself and 1, e.g. the prime factors of 14 are 2 and 7
Prime factor decomposition	Writing a composite number as a product of its prime factors, e.g. $180 = 2 \times 2 \times 3 \times 3 \times 5$
Prism	A solid which has the same shaped cross-section all the way through.
Probability sum	It is always certain that something will happen, so the sum of all probabilities at any time is 1
Probability tree	The branching diagram used to keep track of multiple-event probabilities.
Product of prime factors	A way of writing any whole number as a product of its component primes, e.g. $60 = 2 \times 2 \times 3 \times 5$
Profit	The overall gain made by the seller when something is sold; profit = selling price − cost price.

Proof	A logically strong argument which explains why something is always true (note that an example does not make a proof!).
Proportional to (in proportion to)	Where one number multiplied by another number requires the second to be multiplied by the same number, e.g. adapting a recipe for a different number of people.
Proportionality	The property of being in proportion.
Prove	Provide an argument which leaves no room for doubt.
Pythagoras	The mathematician whose theorem calculates sides of right-angled triangles. $$c^2 = a^2 + b^2$$
Pythagorean triple	Any set of three integers which could be lengths in a right-angled triangle, e.g. (3, 4, 5) or (5, 12, 13). $$3^2 + 4^2 = 5^2$$
Quadrant	One of the four areas separated by the x- and y-axes; quarter of a circle; (the 'First Quadrant' is the one where x and y are both positive, and they are then counted anticlockwise).
Quadratic	A type of equation or expression which has an x-squared term, but not higher. e.g. $x^2 + 3x$ (expression); $x^2 + 3x - 2 = 0$ (equation)
Quadratic function	A function which includes squaring as well as the other arithmetical functions.
Quadratic sequence	A sequence of numbers which, if plotted one after the other, would lie on a curve such as $y = x^2$
Quotient	The (whole number) answer to a division; a ratio or fraction which gives this answer; *see also* **Remainder** e.g. $13 \div 5 \rightarrow$ **2** remainder 3
Radius	The distance from the centre of a circle to the circumference (pl. **radii**).
Random	Occurring by chance alone; unpredictable; any one of several possibilities.
Range of values	When grouping data, each category is a suitable range of values, the same width as all the others.
Rate	The measure of progress or increase with time, metres per second; litres per hour etc.

Raw data	Data as gathered in a survey, before being 'processed' by grouping, averages, graphs etc.
Record (noun and verb)	Information gathered in a survey and written down carefully in a table; an entry in a database.
Recurring decimal	A fraction converted into decimal form which continues in a repeated pattern for ever, e.g. $\frac{2}{9} = 0.222 \ldots$
Reduce/reduction	The opposite of increase/enlargement.
Region (1)	A part of a surface, e.g. one marked out by lines on a grid or in a shape.
Region (2)	Part of a Venn diagram which illustrates a subset of the universal data set.
Regular	Having all the sides the same length and all the angles equal (regular polygons).
Relationship	The connection between two or more numbers, including unknown numbers, often written as a formula.
Remainder	Division gives a whole number part (quotient) and a remainder, either of which can be zero, e.g. $13 \div 5 \rightarrow 2$ remainder **3**
Risk	A gamble; an experiment where failure has a non-zero probability.
Round	Simplify or approximate an answer so that fewer figures are required to write it down.
Sale price	The new price of an item after a reduction or discount has been applied.
Sample	A selection, preferably random and unbiased, for the purpose of a survey or experiment.
Sample space	An organised list of all the possible samples that could be made, also called an 'outcome' space.
Satisfies	A value satisfies an equation if the equation can be shown to be true when the value is substituted.
Scale (1)	A unitary ratio, e.g. 1 : 20 000 which means that 1 cm on the drawing represents 20 000 cm (200 m) in real life.
Scale (2)	Used when drawing a graph; choose the right scale on the axes so that all the numbers can be plotted on the paper clearly.

Scale drawing	A drawing accurately drawn from scaled measurements from the original.
Scale factor	Used to reduce or enlarge the original, e.g. on a diagram or map.
Scatter graph	Points of paired data (e.g. height, weight) plotted as (x, y) co-ordinates in order to test whether or not there is a relationship (**correlation**) between the two.
Section	A piece, especially when referring to a part of a line or part of a shape; also used to mean 'cross-section'.
Sector	Part of a circle cut out by two radii, e.g. 'a pie slice' in a pie chart.
Segment	Part of a circle cut out by a chord
Semicircle	Half of a circle, cut out by a diameter.
Service charge	The extra charge on a bill to pay for services, e.g. in a restaurant, the charge for the waiter or waitress.
Set notation	The collection of symbols used to describe things in sets.
Set square	Triangular device used to draw/measure angles of (45, 45, 90) degrees or (30, 60, 90) degrees.
Side	Reference to either left or right of the = sign in an equation.
Significant figures	Those figures which, in a form of rounding, are concerned more with the order of magnitude of the number than with the number of decimal places.
Similar	Having the same shape, but of a different size, e.g. an enlargement.
Similarity	The property of being similar, i.e. the same shape (not to be confused with its non-mathematical meaning of 'being nearly the same').

Simplest form (lowest terms)	Most commonly used to refer to fractions after they have been cancelled by removing common factors above and below; also used for ratios e.g. $\frac{3}{6} \rightarrow \frac{1}{2}$ $9:12 \rightarrow 3:4$
Simplify	Reduce to a simpler form, especially with fractions, ratios and algebraic expressions, e.g. $\frac{2}{6} \rightarrow \frac{1}{3}$; $4:2 \rightarrow 2:1$; $3x + 4x \rightarrow 7x$
Simultaneous equations	Two or more equations which need to be solved at the same time, e.g. $\left.\begin{array}{l} x + y = 10 \\ x - y = 4 \end{array}\right\}$
Sine (sin)	In a right-angled triangle, the sine of an angle is equal to the ratio opposite : hypotenuse or opposite ÷ hypotenuse.
Slope	Gradient; sloping.
Solution	The answer to a problem, equation or inequality.
Solve	Find the value of the variable, by a systematic method, which will make the equation correct.
Spin	Turn (usually fast) especially to determine an outcome, e.g. coin, spinner etc.
Standard (index) form	*See* **Index notation**.
Steepness	A measure of the slope or gradient of a line; (very steep lines are almost vertical).
Straight edge	Any kind of ruler or similar which is used only to assist with drawing diagrams and constructions.
Straight-line graph	A graph of a linear function, such as $y = 5x + 2$
Subset	A set of related objects which forms part of a larger set, for example: {girls in Year 7} is a subset of the set {girls in the school}.
Substitute	Replace the letters in an algebraic expression with numerical values.
Substitution	The process of changing letters into numbers in order to evaluate an expression.
Subtrahend	The number which is being subtracted from the larger number (**minuend**), e.g. $24 - \mathbf{15} = 9$

Summand	One of the numbers being added together to make the sum.
Supplementary angles	Two angles which add up to 180 degrees. $\quad a + b = 180°$
Surface area	The total area of each surface of a solid shape.
Systematic	Having an organised approach, especially with regard to the creation of lists.
Tangent (1)	Any straight line which just touches the circumference of a circle; it touches in one place and is always at right angles to the radius at that point.
Tangent (2) (tan)	In a right-angled triangle, the tangent of an angle is equal to the ratio opposite : adjacent or opposite ÷ adjacent.
Tax	Any form of duty added on to the price of something.
Term (1)	A sequence made of a list of numbers generated by a rule; each number in the list is called a term.
Term (2)	A component of an algebraic expression, separated by + or − signs, e.g. 'like terms' or 'x^2 terms'.
Terminating decimal	A fraction converted into decimal form which terminates (stops), e.g. $\frac{3}{4} = 0.75$
Theoretical probability	Assuming all outcomes are equally likely, the theoretical probability is (the number of ways of getting what you want) ÷ (the total number of equally likely outcomes).
Theory	Any idea which has support or evidence, but needs proof before it is accepted as true fact.
Therefore	As a result; following on from which; my conclusion is etc.
Three-figure bearing	A direction given as degrees clockwise from north. $\quad$ N $\quad$ 040°
To one decimal place (to 1 d.p.)	A form of rounding which is accurate to the nearest tenth. U.th $\quad$ U.th 0.36 $\quad$ 0.4 $\quad$ to 1 d.p.
To the power of n	Repeatedly multiplied by itself n times ($n = 2$ for squaring and $n = 3$ for cubing).

Transform	Change, especially on a shape, for example reflection, rotation, enlargement.
Trial and improvement	A method for solving equations by improving on each earlier trial.
Triangular number	One of the numbers which can be drawn as an equilateral triangle of dots; a number in the sequence 1, 3, 6, 10, 15 … the nth triangular number is given by $\frac{1}{2}n(n + 1)$.
Triangular prism	A solid shape with a continuous triangular cross-section which remains congruent between the two ends.
Trigonometry	The branch of mathematics dealing with the measurement of triangles.
Two-way table	Used for sorting into rows and columns, e.g. a bus timetable, football results sheet.
Unit fraction	Any fraction with a numerator of one, e.g. $\frac{1}{2}, \frac{1}{3}, \frac{1}{5}, \frac{1}{23}$
Unitary method	Calculating with ratios in which you find out the value of one item before multiplying by the number required.
Universal set	The greatest set of all; contains everything in the question ('the universe').
Value	The arithmetical result of substituting given values into an algebraic expression and evaluating the expression which remains.
Value added tax (VAT)	A legally-required tax added on to the price of certain items.
Variable	The letter in an equation representing the value to be found; the letters used in a formula or algebraic expression.
Verify	Check that something is true.
Vertically opposite angles	In an X formed by two lines crossing, angles facing each other rather than side by side are 'vertically opposite'.
View	The picture you get of a three-dimensional shape when seen from the side (elevation view) or the top (plan view).
Volume factor	The old volume was multiplied by this to obtain the new volume; the volume factor is the cube of the scale factor.

Sample questions answers

Chapter 1 (11+ Number)

1.1   (a)   15, 36, 45, 114, 1011   (2)

      (b)   12, 16, 24, 36, 52   (2)

      (c)   all of them!   (2)

1.2   2, 3, 5, 13, 17   (2)

1.3   (a)   6, 12 or 18   (1)

      (b)   3 or 6   (1)

      (c)   4   (1)

      (d)   3, 7   (2)

      (e)   12   (1)

      (f)   3, 7   (1)

      (g)   6, 7, 12 or 3, 4, 18   (2)

1.4   (a)   40, 45   (1)

      (b)   42, 39   (1)

      (c) $-3, -7$ (2)

1.5   (a)   21, 28   (2)

      (b)   16, 26   (2)

      (c) $7, 3\frac{1}{2}$ (2)

1.6   (a) -5 m   (1)

      (b) -0.9 m   (2)

1.7   (a) $-7\,°C$ (1)

      (b)   4 degrees   (1)

1.8   (a)   309   (1)

      (b)   one hundred and forty-seven   (1)

1.9   (a)   7 (7 units)   (1)

      (b)   300 (3 hundreds)   (1)

      (c)   100 times greater (7 tens as opposed to 7 tenths)   (2)

1.10 21.3   5.30   78.35   (3)

1.11 (a)   3070   (1)

      (b)   3.07   (1)

1.12 (a)   100 times   (1)

      (b)   1000 times   (1)

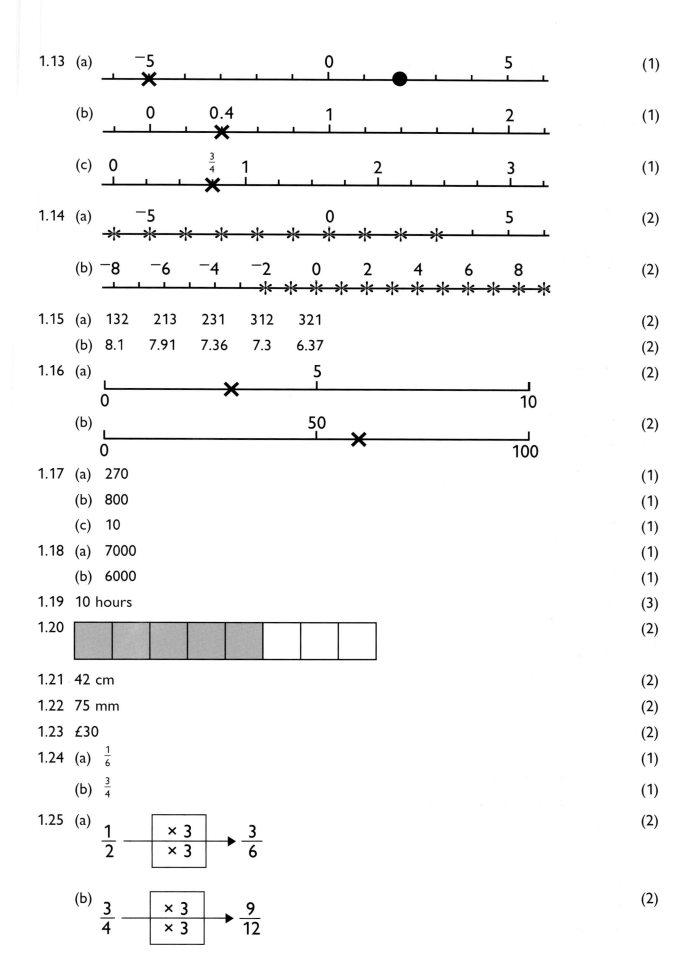

1.13 (a)   (1)

(b)   (1)

(c)   (1)

1.14 (a)   (2)

(b)   (2)

1.15 (a) 132   213   231   312   321   (2)

(b) 8.1   7.91   7.36   7.3   6.37   (2)

1.16 (a)   (2)

(b)   (2)

1.17 (a) 270   (1)

(b) 800   (1)

(c) 10   (1)

1.18 (a) 7000   (1)

(b) 6000   (1)

1.19 10 hours   (3)

1.20   (2)

1.21 42 cm   (2)

1.22 75 mm   (2)

1.23 £30   (2)

1.24 (a) $\frac{1}{6}$ (1)

(b) $\frac{3}{4}$ (1)

1.25 (a) $\frac{1}{2}$ ⟶ [× 3 / × 3] ⟶ $\frac{3}{6}$ (2)

(b) $\frac{3}{4}$ ⟶ [× 3 / × 3] ⟶ $\frac{9}{12}$ (2)

1.26 (9)

Fraction (in simplest form)	$\frac{1}{2}$	$\frac{3}{4}$	$\frac{2}{5}$	$\frac{7}{10}$	$\frac{3}{10}$
Decimal	0.5	0.75	0.4	0.7	0.3
Percentage	50%	75%	40%	70%	30%

1.27 (a) 5 : 2 (2)

(b) 2 : 7 (2)

Chapter 2 (13+ Number)

2.1 (a) 42 (1)

(b) 16 (1)

(c) 72 (1)

(d) 3 (1)

(e) 64 (1)

(f) 4 (1)

(g) 64 (1)

(h) 2 (1)

(i) 81 (1)

2.2 (a) 39 (1)

(b) 1 or 3 (1)

(c) 56 (1)

(d) 3 (1)

(e) 1 (1)

(f) 3 (1)

2.3 (a) 31, 37, 41, 43, 47 (3)

(b) 120 (1)

(c) $2 \times 3^2 \times 5 \times 31$ (3)

2.4 (a) $^-3$ $^-2$ $^-1$ 0 3 5 7 (2)

(b) (i) 2 (1)

(ii) $^-3$ (1)

(iii) $^-3$ (1)

(iv) 7 (1)

(c) (i) −10 (1)

(ii) −20 (1)

(iii) 12 (1)

(iv) −2 (1)

(v) $-\frac{1}{2}$ (1)

(vi) 3 (1)

2.5 (a) (i) 50.7 (1)

(ii) 0.0507 (1)

(iii) 507 (1)

(b) (i) 110.7 (1)

(ii) 11.07 (1)

(iii) 1.107 (2)

(iv) 820 (2)

2.6 (a) 1.32   2.13   2.31   3.12   3.21 (2)

(b) (i) < (1)

(ii) > (1)

(iii) ≥ (1)

(iv) ≤ (1)

2.7 (a) (i) 500 (1)

(ii) 400 (1)

(b) (i) 81.5 (1)

(ii) 81.5 (1)

■■□ 2.8 (a) 40 (1)

(b) 9 (1)

2.9 (a) $\frac{5}{8}$ (1)

(b) $\frac{2}{5}$ $(\frac{8}{20} = \frac{4}{10} = \frac{2}{5})$ (1)

(c) In $\frac{2}{3}$, 2 is the numerator and 3 is the denominator (1)

2.10 (a) (i) $\frac{6}{10}$ (1)

(ii) 0.6 (1)

(iii) 60% (1)

(b) $\frac{3}{5}$ (1)

2.11 (a) (i) $3\frac{2}{5}$ (1)

(ii) $\frac{12}{5}$ (1)

(b) (i) 1.75 (1)

(ii) 175% (1)

245

2.12 (a) $\frac{10}{13}$ (1)

■■□ (b) $1\frac{1}{6}$ (1)

■■□ (c) $2\frac{1}{12}$ (2)

(d) $\frac{1}{2}$ (1)

■■□ (e) $\frac{1}{6}$ (1)

■■□ (f) $\frac{7}{12}$ (2)

■■□ 2.13 (a) $\frac{1}{2}$ (1)

■■■ (b) $\frac{5}{6}$ (2)

■■□ (c) $\frac{3}{4}$ (2)

■■■ (d) $\frac{16}{33}$ (3)

2.14 (a) (i)   6 : 11 (1)

(ii) 6 : 5 (1)

(iii) 5 : 6 (1)

(b) 2 : 3 (1)

2.15 **To make 24 crunchies**

Cornflakes   600 g

Chocolate   500 g

Honey   40 ml

Sultanas   100 g (4)

Chapter 3 (11+ Calculations)

3.1   6 + 11 = 17 (2)

3.2   16 − 9 = 7 (2)

3.3   7 × 2 = 14 (2)

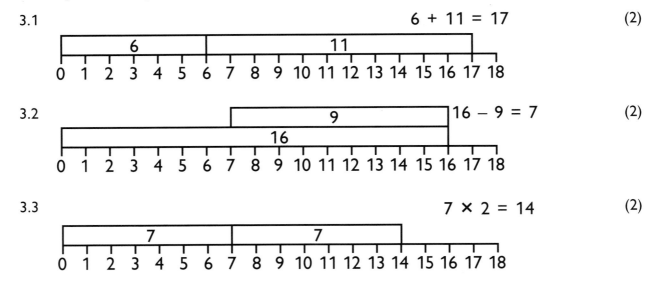

3.4 $18 \div 6 = 3$ (2)

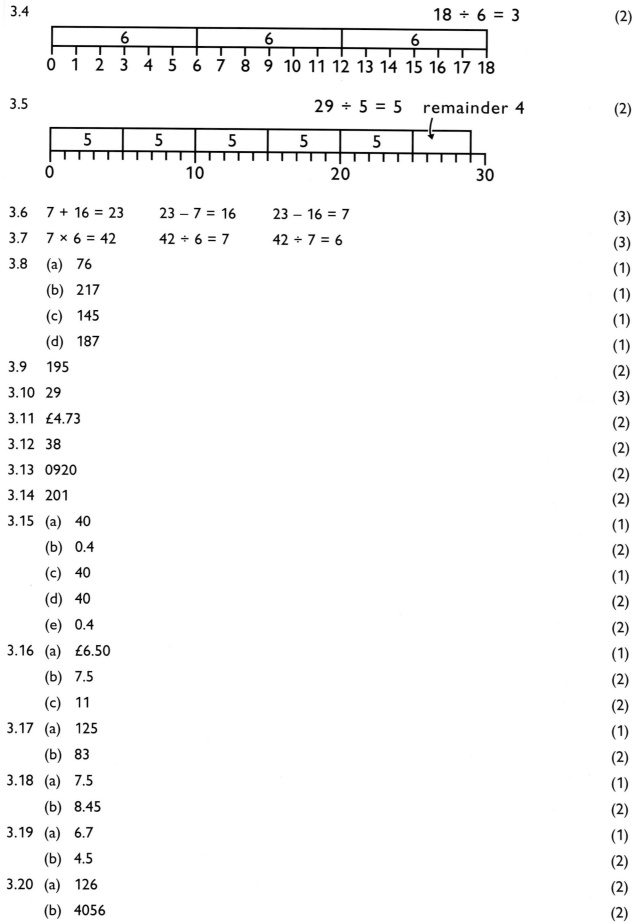

3.5 $29 \div 5 = 5$ remainder 4   (2)

3.6 $7 + 16 = 23$ $23 - 7 = 16$ $23 - 16 = 7$ (3)

3.7 $7 \times 6 = 42$ $42 \div 6 = 7$ $42 \div 7 = 6$ (3)

3.8   (a)   76   (1)

     (b)   217   (1)

     (c)   145   (1)

     (d)   187   (1)

3.9   195   (2)

3.10   29   (3)

3.11   £4.73   (2)

3.12   38   (2)

3.13   0920   (2)

3.14   201   (2)

3.15   (a)   40   (1)

     (b)   0.4   (2)

     (c)   40   (1)

     (d)   40   (2)

     (e)   0.4   (2)

3.16   (a)   £6.50   (1)

     (b)   7.5   (2)

     (c)   11   (2)

3.17   (a)   125   (1)

     (b)   83   (2)

3.18   (a)   7.5   (1)

     (b)   8.45   (2)

3.19   (a)   6.7   (1)

     (b)   4.5   (2)

3.20   (a)   126   (2)

     (b)   4056   (2)

3.21 (a) 241 (2)

(b) 143 (2)

3.22 1.23 1.32 2.13 2.31 3.12 (2)

3.23 (a) £16.50 (2)

(b) (i) 28 pence (2)

(ii) 4 pence (2)

Chapter 4 (13+ Calculations)

4.1 (a) 3100.1 (2)

(b) 2719.1 (2)

(c) 26 280 (2)

(d) 503 (2)

4.2 (a) 4.421 (2)

(b) 3.479 (2)

(c) 3.56 (2)

(d) 14.24 (2)

4.3 (a) 13 (1)

(b) 31 (1)

(c) 23 (2)

(d) −1 (2)

4.4 (a) 1275 (1)

(b) 51 (2)

(c) 150 (2)

(d) 150 (2)

■■□ 4.5 (a) 8 (3)

(b) 1 (3)

4.6 (a) £455.40 (3)

(b) £17.95 (3)

4.7 (a) 11.78 (1)

(b) 3.871 794 872 → 3.87 (1)

(c) 7.413 793 103 → 7.41 (1)

(d) 12.378 553 44 → 12.4 (1)

4.8 (a) 195 364 (1)

(b) 3.383 784 863 → 3.38 (1)

(c) 1.181 665 75 $\rightarrow$ 1.18 (1)

(d) $2\frac{8}{11}$ (1)

4.9 (a) 105.683 176 9 $\rightarrow$ 106 cm² (1)

(b) 3 760 000 000 (1)

4.10 (a) £10.80 (1)

(b) 15 min 12 sec (1)

(c) 4 hr 45 min (1)

(d) 4 (1)

(e) $\frac{2}{7}$ (1)

4.11 (a) $1\frac{3}{5}$ (1)

(b) 4 500 000 000 (1)

(c) 0.005 07 (1)

(d) $1\frac{1}{3}$ (1)

(e) 10 (1)

4.12 (a) 5.763 157 895 (2)

(b) 5.76 (1)

(c) 5.8 (1)

4.13 (a) 61.76 (1)

(b) 60 (2)

(c) 17.9 (2)

4.14 (a) (i) 0.017 913 253 01 (2)

(ii) 0.02 (1)

(b) (i) $^-$0.364 470 588 2 (2)

(ii) $^-$0.364 (1)

■■□ 4.15 (a) (i) $\dfrac{300}{30 + 10}$ (2)

(ii) $7\frac{1}{2}$ (1)

(b) (i) 7.058 968 059 (1)

(ii) 7 (1)

(iii) 7.06 (1)

4.16 (a) £40 (1)

(b) 10 (1)

(c) 10 kg (1)

(d) £25 (1)

(e) £2.10 (1)

4.17 (a) £550 (1)

    (b) 9 yrs (1)

    (c) 1.5 m² (1)

    (d) 64 (1)

    (e) 4000 (1)

4.18 (a) £29 (2)

    (b) £29.27 (2)

4.19 (a) Megan is correct. Julian did think of 6 (3)

A suitable flow chart might look like this.

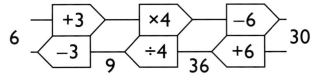

    (b) John is not correct. Moira thought of 106 (3)

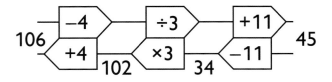

Chapter 5 (11+ Problem solving)

5.1 Probable answers:

    (a) M (1)

    (b) PP (1)

    (c) PP (1)

    (d) PP (1)

    (e) MJ (1)

5.2 Probable answers:

    (a) measuring tape or metre rule (2)

    (b) measuring tape or string and metre rule (2)

    (c) thermometer (2)

    (d) measuring jug or cylinder (2)

    (e) stopwatch (2)

    (f) beam balance or scales (possibly find mass of a hundred and then divide by 100, depending on accuracy of scales) (2)

    (g) centimetre squared paper (probably draw round your foot and count squares) (2)

5.3   50 and 59   (2)

5.4   (a) 50p, 10p, 2p   (1)

       (b) 5p, 2p   (2)

5.5   35   (3)

5.6   13 (the numbers are 4 and 9)   (3)

5.7   (a) (i)   A   (1)

            (ii) C   (1)

            (iii) B   (1)

       (b) For example: (4)

5.8   £1.50 each (John has £5.60 at the start; together they have £9.80 before
       buying the DVD)   (3)

5.9   £6.05 (milk £1.29, bread £1.56, cheese £1.10; total £3.95)   (3)

5.10   (a) $\frac{1}{5}$ (2)

       (b) 54%   (1)

       (c) 11 g   (2)

5.11   (a) 192   (2)

       (b) (i)   1280 g   (2)

            (ii) 720 g   (2)

       (c) 520 g   (2)

       (d) 442 g   (2)

       (e) 6p   (1)

       (f) £4.80   (2)

Chapter 6 (13+ Problem solving)

6.1 Probable answers:

   (a) Try a simpler example first or try a practical approach   (1)

   (b) Make an organised list   (1)

   (c) Guess and check   (1)

   (d) Look for a pattern   (1)

   (e) Try a simpler example first   (1)

   (f) Find a formula and then test it before using it   (1)

6.2 (a)   (2)

Year	Number of flowers
1	3
2	5
3	7
4	9
5	11

   (b) 15 flowers   (2)

   (c) year 15   (2)

6.3 (a) 36   (2)

   (b) (i) 10   (2)

      (ii) 16   (2)

      (iii) 8   (2)

      (iv) 2   (1)

6.4 (a) 28 or 91   (2)

   (b) (i)   (2)

      (ii) kite   (1)

      (iii) 1   (1)

6.5 (a) 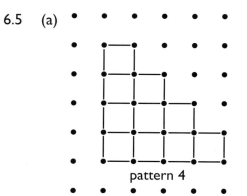 (2)

pattern 4

(b) (6)

Pattern Number	Number of squares	Total number of dots	Perimeter (cm)
1	1	4	4
2	3	8	8
3	6	13	12
4	10	19	16
5	15	26	20

(c) (3)

6	21	34	24
7	28	43	28
8	36	53	32

6.6 (a) £50 (2)

(b) 50 litres (2)

6.7 (a) £41.93 (2)

(b) (i) £27.95 (2)

(ii) £22.05 (2)

(c) £16.95 (division by factors recommended) (2)

6.8 (a) flour 12 ounces; margarine 9 ounces; sugar 6 ounces (3)

(b) she will use: flour 10 ounces; margarine $7\frac{1}{2}$ ounces; sugar 5 ounces

She can bake at most 15 cakes ($\frac{5}{6}$ of 18) (2)

Chapter 7 (11+ Algebra)

7.1   (a)   6   (1)

     (b)   23   (1)

     (c)   3   (1)

     (d)   1   (1)

     (e)   9   (2)

7.2   (a)   9 years   (1)

     (b)   6 cm   (1)

7.3   (a)   3   (1)

     (b)   −1   (2)

     (c)   10   (1)

7.4   (a)   9   (1)

     (b)   23   (1)

     (c)   6   (1)

     (d)   54   (1)

7.5   (a)   7   (1)

     (b)   −2   (2)

     (c)   2   (2)

7.6   (a)   2   (2)

     (b)   5   (2)

7.7   (2)

7.8   (a)   12, 14   (1)

     (b)   22, 26   (2)

     (c)   5, 0   (2)

     (d) $1\frac{1}{2}$, $1\frac{3}{4}$ (2)

7.9   (a)   10, 8   (2)

     (b)   16, 22   (2)

7.10   (a)   ×5 machine   (2)

     (b)   ×3 machine   (2)

7.11   (a)   (2)

input		output
0	+2	2
1		3
2		4
3		5

(b) 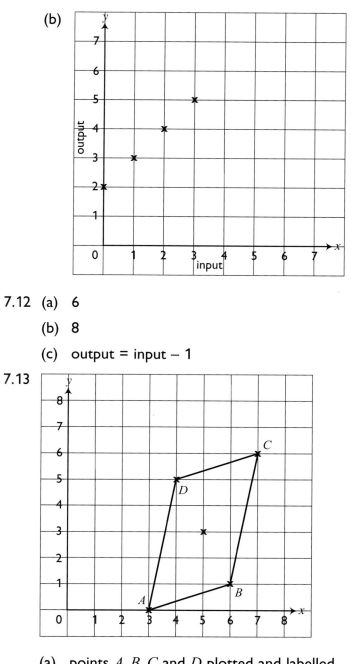 (2)

7.12 (a) 6 (1)

(b) 8 (1)

(c) output = input − 1 (2)

7.13

(a) points A, B, C and D plotted and labelled (2)

(b) points joined to form parallelogram $ABCD$ (1)

(c) (5, 3) (1)

Chapter 8 (13+ Algebra)

8.1 (a) $8c$ (1)

(b) d^2 (2)

(c) $15e^3$ (2)

(d) $3f$ (2)

■■■ (e) 2 (2)

8.2 (a) $3(h - 4)$ (2)

(b) $5(4e - 3f)$ (2)

(c) $2e(e + 2)$ (2)

(d) $4p(p - 2q)$ (2)

8.3 (a) $4a + 12b$ (1)

(b) $6q + 4r$ (2)

(c) $2m + 3n$ (3)

8.4 (a) $^-2$ (2)

(b) 120 (2)

(c) 2 (2)

(d) $^-9$ (3)

8.5 (a) 1 (1)

(b) $^-8$ (1)

(c) $^-18$ (2)

(d) 12 (2)

8.6 (a) $t + 3$ (1)

(b) $4t$ (1)

(c) $t - 5$ (1)

(d) $\dfrac{t}{2}$ (1)

(e) t^2 (1)

8.7 (a) $b + 2$ (1)

(b) $3b$ (1)

(c) $5b + 2$ (2)

(d) $5b + 2 = 22$, leading to $b = 4$ (2)

8.8 (a) $5x$ (1)

(b) $x + 3$ (1)

(c) $7(x + 3)$ or $7x + 21$ (2)

(d) $3x + 4(x + 3)$, leading to $7x + 12$ (2)

(e) $7x + 12 = 467$, leading to $x = 65$ (3)

(f) £7.34 (2)

8.9   (a) $q = 4$ (1)

       (b) $p = 4$ (1)

       (c) $n = 3$ (2)

       (d) $y = 2$ (2)

       (e) $x = -7\frac{1}{2}$ (3)

■■□ 8.10   (a) $s = 4$ (2)

         (b) $a = \frac{1}{2}$ (2)

         (c) $r = 1\frac{1}{2}$ (2)

         (d) $y = 15$ (3)

         (e) $m = 26$ (2)

         (f) $s = 7$ (3)

■■■ 8.11   (a) $a = 7$ (2)

         (b) $u = 2$ (3)

         (c) $v = -1$ (3)

         (d) $c = 28$ (2)

         (e) $v = \frac{8}{3}$ or $2\frac{2}{3}$ (3)

■■■ 8.12   6.57 (when x is 6, y is 24; when x is 7, y is 35 so it is reasonable to suppose that when y is 30 the value of x must be a little more than 6.5)   (5)

■■■ 8.13   (a)   (i) $x < 2\frac{1}{5}$ (2)

               (ii)   1, 2   (1)

         (b)   (i) $n \leq 6$ (3)

               (ii)   6   (1)

8.14   (a)   31, 27   (2)

       (b)   21, 31   (2)

       (c)   50, 25   (2)

       (d)   23, 28   (2)

       (e)   256, 1024   (2)

       (f)   1, 0   (2)

8.15   (a)   6, 16, 36, 76   (2)

       (b)   'add 3'   (1)

8.16   (a)   299   (1)

       (b) $n = 334$ gives $T_n = 1001$ (2)

■■☐ 8.17

x	−1	0	1	2	3	4
y	3	4	5	6	7	8

(2)

■■■ 8.18

x	−2	−1	0	1	2	3
y	4	1	0	1	4	9

(2)

8.19

(a) graph of $x = 4$ drawn (1)

(b) graph of $y = 5$ drawn (1)

(c) graph of $x = -3$ drawn (1)

■■☐ 8.20

(a) points plotted and graph drawn of $y = 2x + 3$ (2)

(b) graph of $y = x - 4$ (2)

258

■■■ 8.21

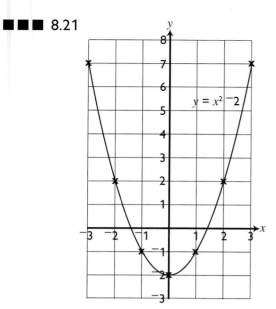

(2)

■■■ 8.22 (a)

x	−4	−3	−2	−1	0	1	2
x^2	16	9	4	1	0	1	4
$2x$	−8	−6	−4	−2	0	2	4
y	8	3	0	−1	0	3	8

(3)

(b)

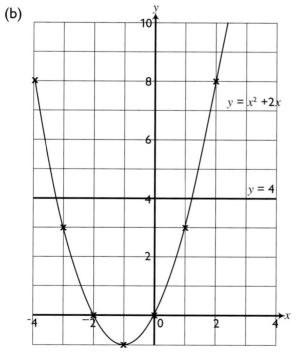

(3)

(c) $x = 1.2$ and $x = -3.2$

(2)

(d) $x = -1$

(1)

■■■ 8.23 (a) (2, 4)   (1)

   (b) 4 = 2 + 2 and 4 = 6 − 2   (2)

■■■ 8.24 (a) $2x − 3 = x + 1$ (1)

   (b) $x = 4$ (2)

   (c) $y = 5$ (1)

   (d) check   (1)

■■■ 8.25 (a) $4y = 8$ (1)

   (b) $y = 2$ (1)

   (c) $x = 1$ (2)

■■■ 8.26 (a) $3x + 2y = 110$ (1)

   (b) $5x = 4y$ or $5x − 4y = 0$ (1)

   (c) $x = 20, y = 25$ (4)

   (d) 10 apples and 1 pear, 5 apples and 5 pears, just 9 pears   (3)

Chapter 9 (11+ Space, shape and measures)

9.1 (a) 23   (2)

   (b) 94   (2)

9.2 (a) 700 ml   (2)

   (b) 225 ml   (2)

9.3 (a) (i)   1230 mm   (1)

        (ii) 1.23 m   (1)

   (b) (i)   40 000 g   (1)

        (ii) 88 pounds (40 × 2.2)   (2)

9.4 (a) 22 cm   (1)

   (b) 30 cm²   (1)

9.5 (a) 12 cm³   (2)

   (b) 36 cm³   (2)

9.6 (a) (i)   1310   (1)

        (ii) 0735   (1)

   (b) (i)   2.30 pm   (1)

        (ii) 9.45 pm   (1)

9.7 (a) (3)

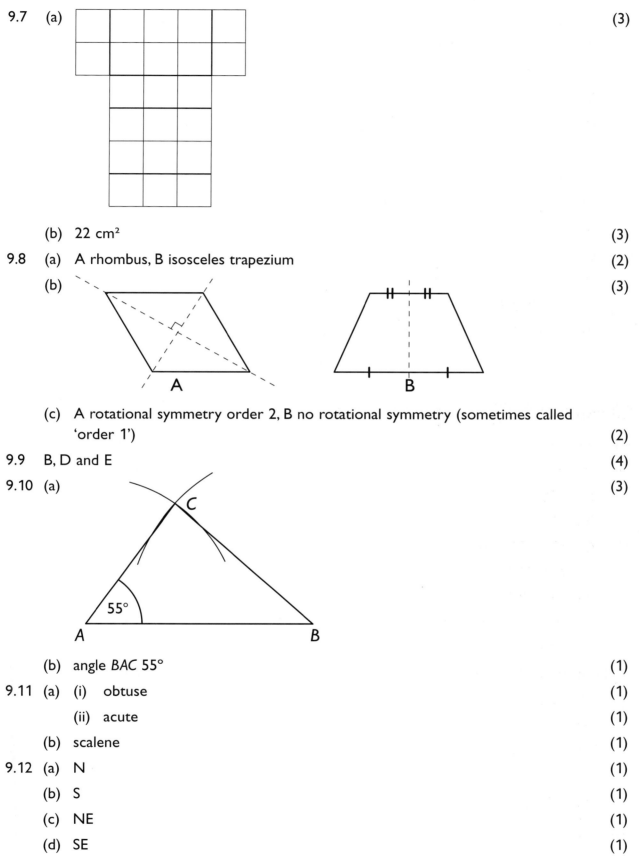

(b) 22 cm² (3)

9.8 (a) A rhombus, B isosceles trapezium (2)

(b) (3)

(c) A rotational symmetry order 2, B no rotational symmetry (sometimes called 'order 1') (2)

9.9 B, D and E (4)

9.10 (a) (3)

(b) angle *BAC* 55° (1)

9.11 (a) (i) obtuse (1)

(ii) acute (1)

(b) scalene (1)

9.12 (a) N (1)

(b) S (1)

(c) NE (1)

(d) SE (1)

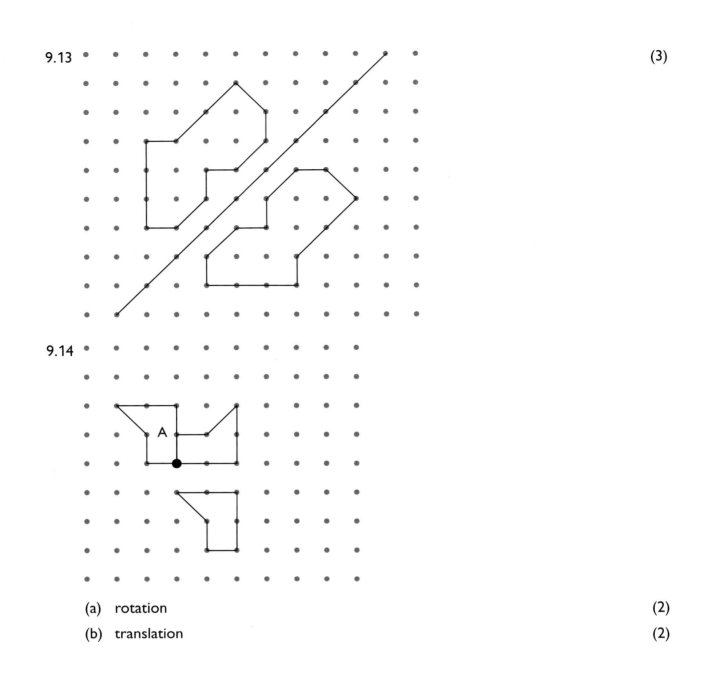

9.13 (3)

9.14

(a) rotation (2)

(b) translation (2)

Chapter 10 (13+ Shape, space and measures)

10.1 (a) (i) 130 mm (1)

(ii) 0.13 m (1)

(iii) 5 inches (1)

(b) 1.8 m (1)

(c) 960 km (2)

10.2 (a) 5 ha (1)

(b) (i) 100 cm² (1)

(ii) 1000 cm³ (1)

10.3 (a) (i) 12 cm/minute (1)

(ii) 0.2 cm/s (1)

(iii) 720 cm (7.2 m) (1)

(b) (i) 10.5 miles (2)

(ii) 0920 (2)

10.4 (a) (i) (4)

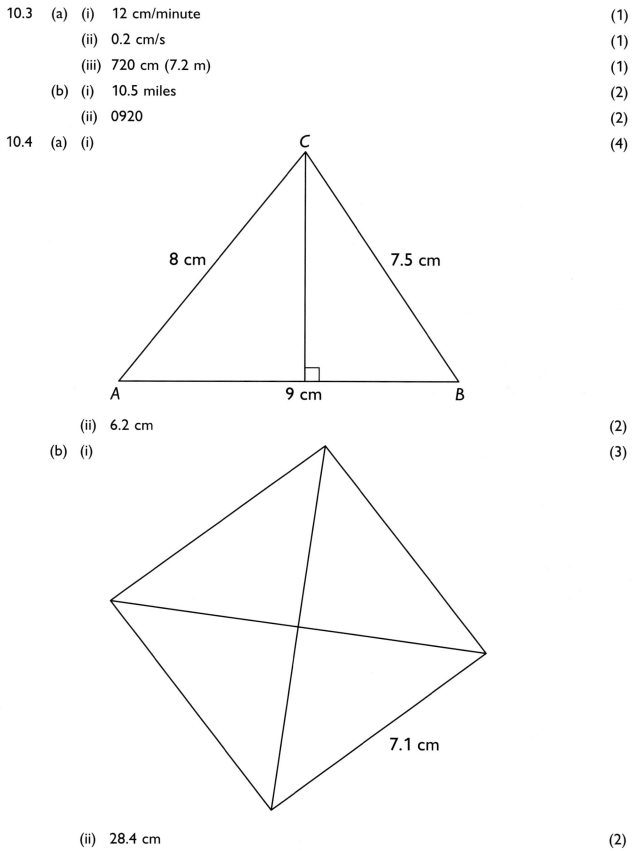

(ii) 6.2 cm (2)

(b) (i) (3)

(ii) 28.4 cm (2)

10.5 (a) (2)

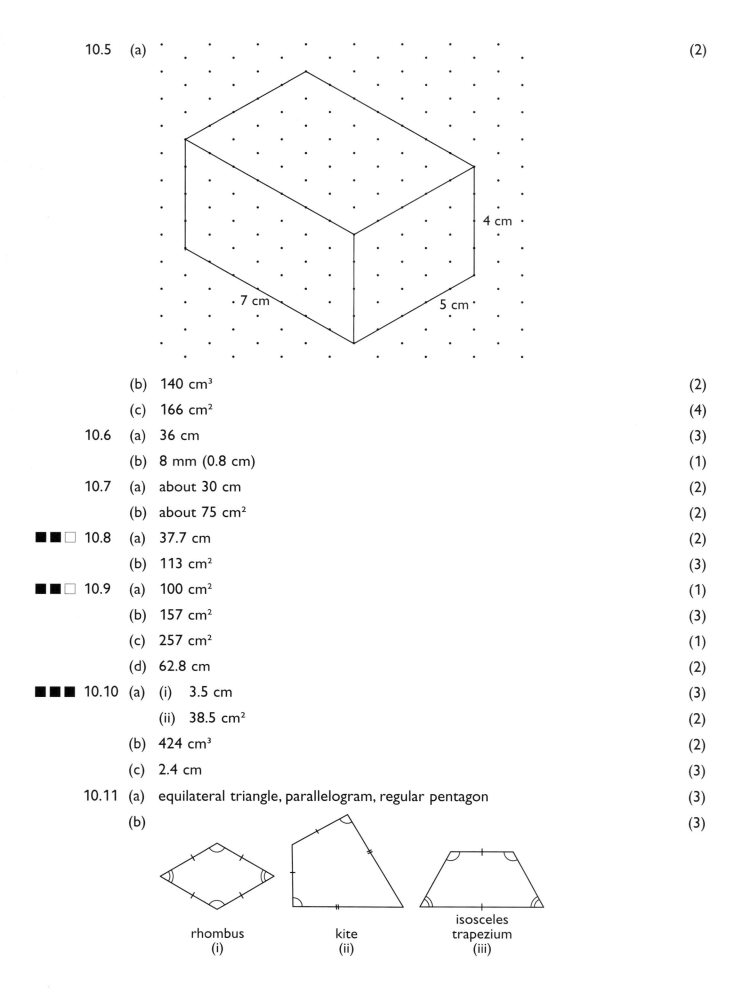

(b) 140 cm³ (2)

(c) 166 cm² (4)

10.6 (a) 36 cm (3)

(b) 8 mm (0.8 cm) (1)

10.7 (a) about 30 cm (2)

(b) about 75 cm² (2)

■■□ 10.8 (a) 37.7 cm (2)

(b) 113 cm² (3)

■■□ 10.9 (a) 100 cm² (1)

(b) 157 cm² (3)

(c) 257 cm² (1)

(d) 62.8 cm (2)

■■■ 10.10 (a) (i) 3.5 cm (3)

(ii) 38.5 cm² (2)

(b) 424 cm³ (2)

(c) 2.4 cm (3)

10.11 (a) equilateral triangle, parallelogram, regular pentagon (3)

(b) (3)

rhombus
(i)

kite
(ii)

isosceles
trapezium
(iii)

264

(c)

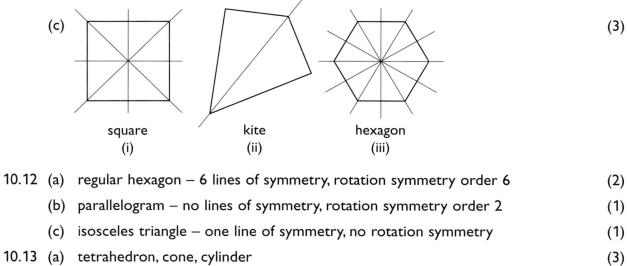

square
(i)

kite
(ii)

hexagon
(iii)

(3)

10.12 (a) regular hexagon – 6 lines of symmetry, rotation symmetry order 6 (2)

(b) parallelogram – no lines of symmetry, rotation symmetry order 2 (1)

(c) isosceles triangle – one line of symmetry, no rotation symmetry (1)

10.13 (a) tetrahedron, cone, cylinder (3)

(b) (1)

■■□ 10.14 (a) square, rhombus (2)

(b) square, rectangle, rhombus, parallelogram (2)

(c) square, rhombus, kite (2)

(d) square, rectangle, isosceles trapezium (2)

(e) parallelogram (2)

(f) kite, isosceles trapezium (2)

■■□ 10.15 (a) 120° (1)

(b) (i) 24° (1)

(ii) 156° (1)

(iii) 2340° (2)

■■□ 10.16

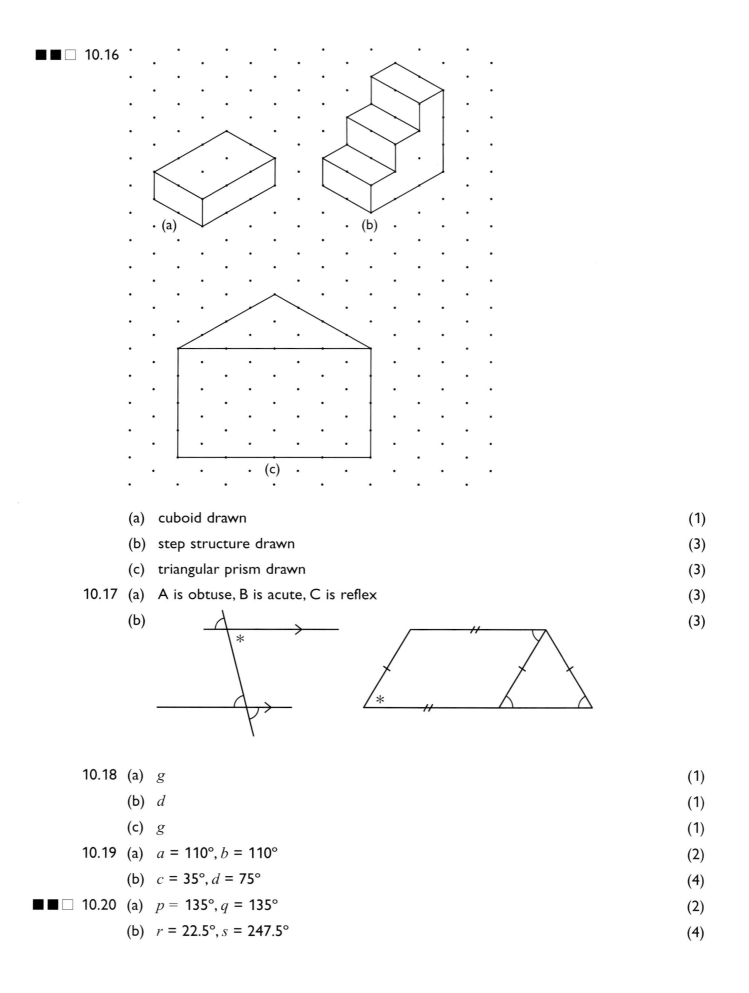

    (a) cuboid drawn   (1)

    (b) step structure drawn   (3)

    (c) triangular prism drawn   (3)

10.17 (a) A is obtuse, B is acute, C is reflex   (3)

        (b)   (3)

10.18 (a) g (1)

        (b) d (1)

        (c) g (1)

10.19 (a) $a = 110°, b = 110°$ (2)

        (b) $c = 35°, d = 75°$ (4)

■■□ 10.20 (a) $p = 135°, q = 135°$ (2)

        (b) $r = 22.5°, s = 247.5°$ (4)

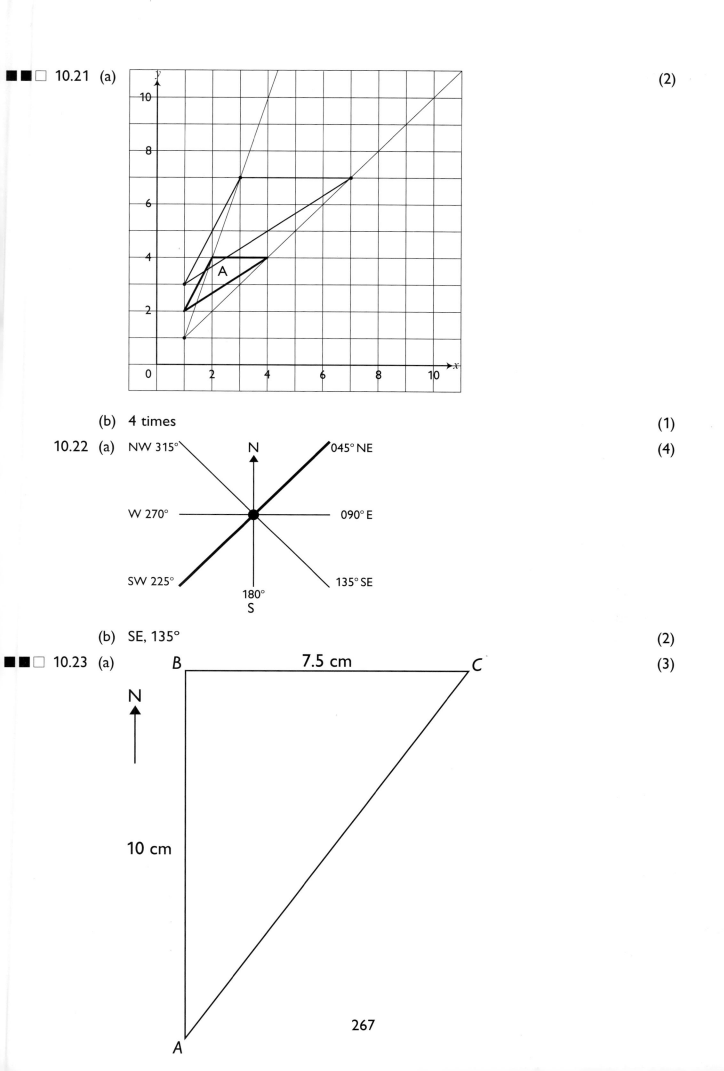

■■□ 10.21 (a)   (2)

         (b) 4 times   (1)

10.22 (a)   NW 315°   N   045° NE   (4)

             W 270°   090° E

             SW 225°   135° SE
                           180°
                            S

         (b) SE, 135°   (2)

■■□ 10.23 (a)   B   7.5 cm   C   (3)

             N

             10 cm

                                        267

             A

	(b)	(i)	037°	(1)
		(ii)	217°	(2)
		(iii)	25 m	(2)

■ ■ ■ 10.24 (a) 6.40 cm (2)

(b) 7.21 cm (2)

(c) 5.66 cm (3)

Chapter 11 (11+ Handling data)

11.1 (a) (4)

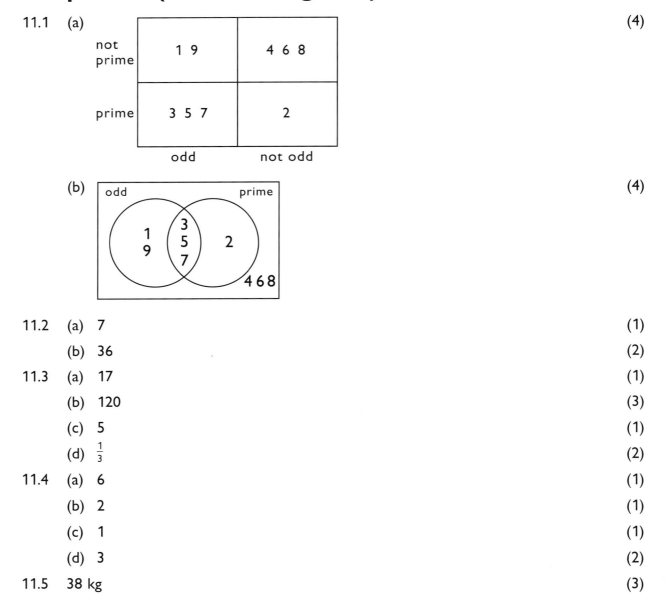

11.2 (a) 7 (1)

(b) 36 (2)

11.3 (a) 17 (1)

(b) 120 (3)

(c) 5 (1)

(d) $\frac{1}{3}$ (2)

11.4 (a) 6 (1)

(b) 2 (1)

(c) 1 (1)

(d) 3 (2)

11.5 38 kg (3)

11.6 (a) (4)

Height (m)	Tally marks	Frequency
1.25 to 1.29	I	1
1.30 to 1.34	II	2
1.35 to 1.39	II	2
1.40 to 1.44	̶I̶I̶I̶I̶	5
1.45 to 1.49	̶I̶I̶I̶I̶ I	6
1.50 to 1.54	III	3
1.55 to 1.59	I	1
	Total	20

(b) (4)

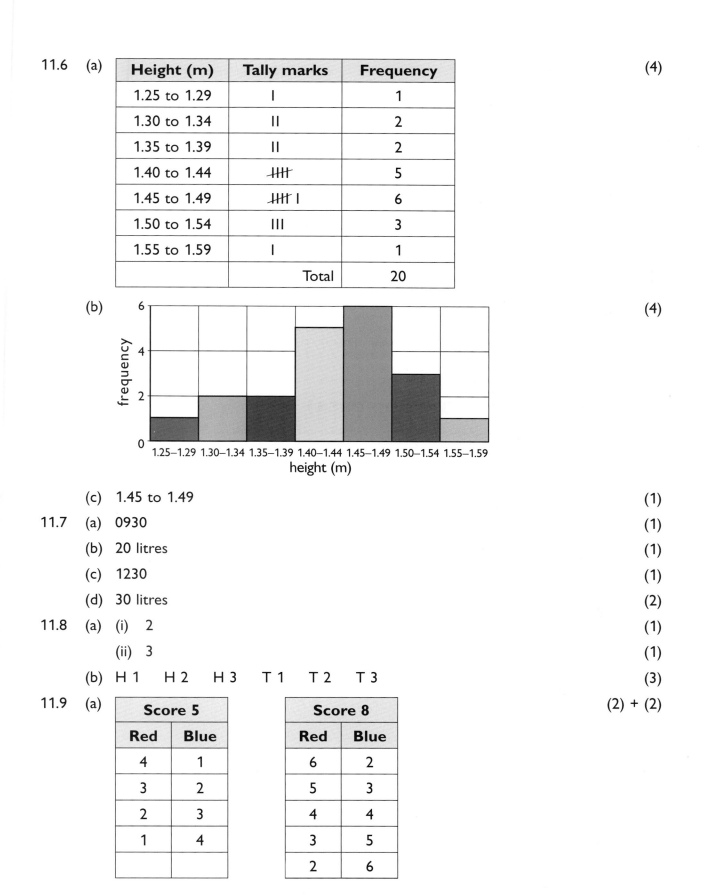

(c) 1.45 to 1.49 (1)

11.7 (a) 0930 (1)

(b) 20 litres (1)

(c) 1230 (1)

(d) 30 litres (2)

11.8 (a) (i) 2 (1)

(ii) 3 (1)

(b) H 1   H 2   H 3   T 1   T 2   T 3 (3)

11.9 (a) (2) + (2)

Score 5	
Red	Blue
4	1
3	2
2	3
1	4

Score 8	
Red	Blue
6	2
5	3
4	4
3	5
2	6

(b) Minnie is not right. There is an equal chance of rolling two sixes as rolling two of any number. (1)

11.10 (a) even chance (1)

(b) impossible (1)

(c) unlikely (1)

(d) likely (1)

(e) even chance (2)

11.11 (a) (1)

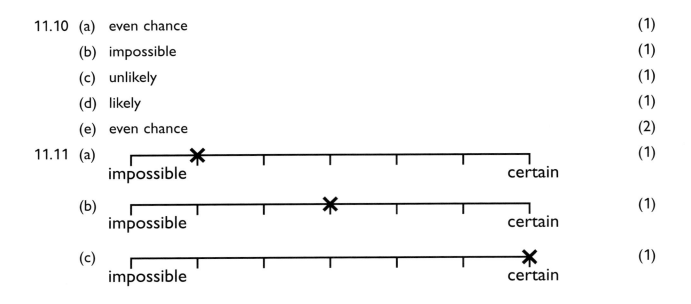

(b) (1)

(c) (1)

Chapter 12 (13+ Handling data)

12.1 (a) (2)

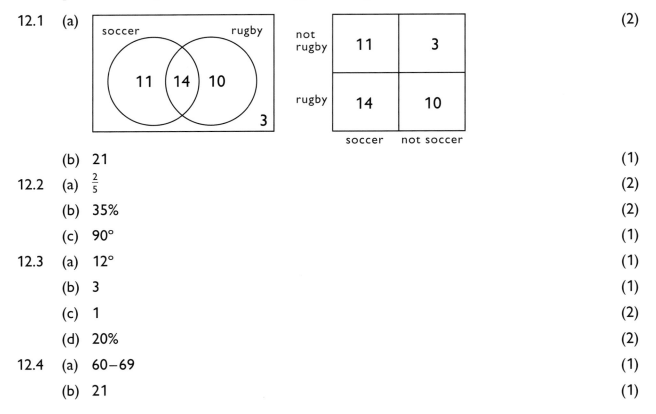

(b) 21 (1)

12.2 (a) $\frac{2}{5}$ (2)

(b) 35% (2)

(c) 90° (1)

12.3 (a) 12° (1)

(b) 3 (1)

(c) 1 (2)

(d) 20% (2)

12.4 (a) 60−69 (1)

(b) 21 (1)

12.5 (a)

Score	Tally	Frequency
1	III	3
2	IIII	4
3	II	2
4	III	3
5	III	3
6	ЩH	5
	Total	20

(3)

(b)

(3)

(c) 6 (1)

(d) 3.7 (3)

(e) 4 (2)

12.6 (a) 25 (1)

(b)

Number of peas	Tally	Frequency
20–22	III	3
23–25	ЩH	5
26–28	ЩH II	7
29–31	III	3
	Total	18

(3)

(c) 26–28 (1)

12.7 (a) (i) 6 (1)

(ii) 3 (1)

(iii) $2\frac{1}{2}$ (2)

(b) Rovers had the larger range of scores. Wanderers scored in every match, were more consistent and scored the highest number of goals overall (35 compared to 29 scored by Rangers). (2)

12.8 (a) 362 kg (2)

(b) 280 kg (1)

(c) 41 kg (2)

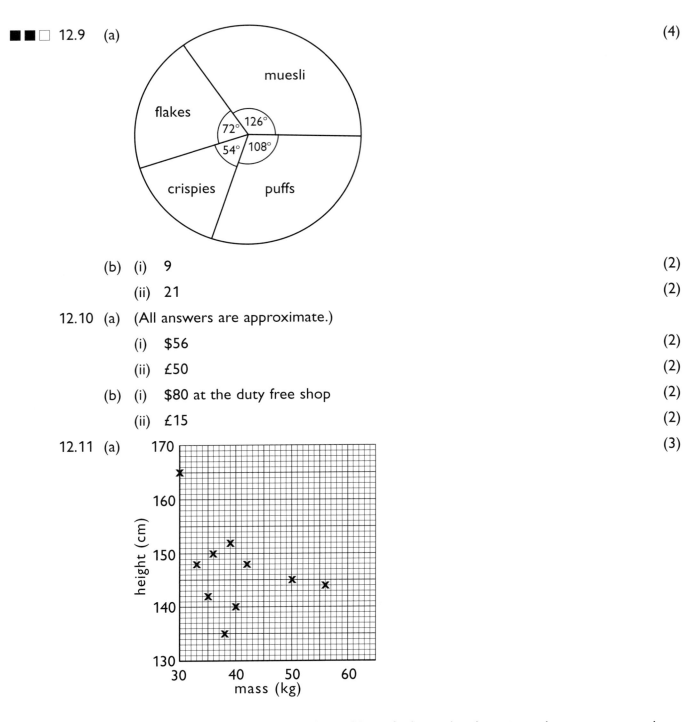

■■□ 12.9 (a)   (4)

        (b) (i) 9   (2)

             (ii) 21   (2)

12.10 (a) (All answers are approximate.)

             (i) $56   (2)

             (ii) £50   (2)

        (b) (i) $80 at the duty free shop   (2)

             (ii) £15   (2)

12.11 (a)   (3)

■■□   (b) It is not possible to draw a line of best fit from the data since there appears to be
             little or no correlation – the sample of girls includes one very tall girl with low
             mass, for example.   (1)

■■□   (c) It is possible to make a guess, based upon the data – perhaps about 145 cm. (2)

        Note: This question is not typical of scattergraph examination questions, but is included
        here to make you think!

12.12 (a) (i) $\frac{2}{5}$ (1)

(ii) (1)

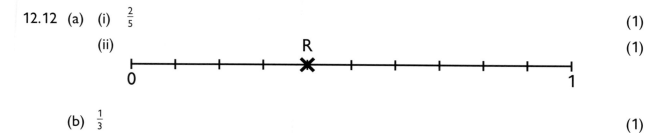

(b) $\frac{1}{3}$ (1)

12.13 (a) Yes, possibly – the spinner appears to be biased towards 6 (and 1 and 5 which are adjacent to 6). This could be because the spindle is slightly off centre (nearer to 3) or there could be a 'weight' under the 6
To be sure, it would be necessary to investigate with a larger number of spins. (1)

(b) about 30% (1)

12.14 (a) (2)

	Score on red die			
	1	**2**	**3**	**4**
1	2	3	4	5
2	3	4	5	6
3	4	5	6	7
4	5	6	7	8

(Score on green die)

(b) (i) $\frac{3}{16}$ (1)

(ii) $\frac{13}{16}$ (1)

(c) $\frac{3}{4}$ (2)

12.15 (a) (3)

	C	**L**	**A**	**R**	**E**
M	MC	ML	MA	MR	ME
A	AC	AL	AA	AR	AE
R	RC	RL	RA	RR	RE
I	IC	IL	IA	IR	IE
E	EC	EL	EA	ER	EE

(b) $\frac{3}{25}$ (2)

(c) $\frac{6}{25}$ (2)

Test yourself answers

Chapter 1 (11+ Number)

1.

1	2	③	4̷	5	⑥
7	8̸	⑨	10	11	⑫̸
13	14	⑮	1̷6	17	⑱
19	2̷0	㉑	22	23	㉔̸
25	26	㉗	2̷8	29	㉚
31	3̸2	㉝	34	35	㊱̸

(a) 3 and every third number circled

(b) 4 and every fourth number with a cross

(c) the numbers which are circled and have a cross are multiples of 12 (common multiples of 3 and 4)

2.

×	2	3	4	5	6	7	8
2	④	6	8	10	12	14	16
3	6	⑨	12	15	18	21	24
4	8	12	⑯	20	24	28	32
5	10	15	20	㉕	30	35	40
6	12	18	24	30	㊱	42	48
7	14	21	28	35	42	㊾	56
8	16	24	32	40	48	56	㊽

(a) multiples of 9 shaded

(b) square numbers circled

(c) 12 and 24 (4 times each); 16 appears 3 times

3. (a) a prime number is a number with no factors except itself and 1

(b) 2, 3, 5, 7, 11, 13, 17, 19, 23, 29, 31, 37, 41, 43, ...

4. (a) (i)   345   354   435   453   534   543

(ii) 350   350   440   450   530   540

(iii) all of them! – the digits add to a multiple of 3

(iv) 345 and 435

(v) 54 300

(vi) 34.5

(b) (i) $\frac{3}{5}$

(ii) $\frac{4}{5}$

Chapter 2 (13+ Number)

1.

×	4	9	2	5	8	6	1	3	7
3	12	27	6	15	24	18	3	9	21
9	36	81	18	45	72	54	9	27	63
8	32	72	16	40	64	48	8	24	56
2	8	18	4	10	16	12	2	6	14
6	24	54	12	30	48	36	6	18	42
5	20	45	10	25	40	30	5	15	35
4	16	36	8	20	32	24	4	12	28
7	28	63	14	35	56	42	7	21	49
1	4	9	2	5	8	6	1	3	7

With practice, a time of just under a minute is possible. Answers do not need to be neat, just legible!

2.   (a) 19

(b) 4

(c) 5

(d) 8 or 32

(e) 16

(f) 8 or 27

3.   (a) 9

(b) −4 and 4 or −5 and 5

(c) 8 and −5

(d) (i)   −4 + 5 = 1

(ii) 6 − 4 = 2

(iii) −3 × −5 = 15

(iv) 8 ÷ −2 = −4

4. (a) $2 \times 3^2 \times 5 \times 7$

   (b) 17 640

5. (a) 6   6.066   6.6   6.606   6.66

   (b) 0.66

■■□ 6. (a) 300

   (b) 4

7.

Fraction	Decimal	Percentage
$\frac{7}{20}$	0.35	35%
$\frac{1}{4}$	0.25	25%
$1\frac{1}{5}$	1.2	120%
$\frac{3}{20}$	0.15	15%

8. (a) $\frac{13}{50}$

   (b) 0.65

   (c) £3.20

   (d) $\frac{27}{50}$

   (e) £6

9. (a) 44

   (b) 84 kg

   (c) $\frac{1}{5}$

   (d) 10 days

10. (a) £9

   (b) 20%

   (c) £32.40

   (d) 28%

■■□ 11. (a) (i) $\frac{5}{12}$

      (ii) $\frac{7}{12}$

   (b) (i) $\frac{1}{4}$

      (ii) $\frac{4}{9}$

12. 7.2 m

13. (a) 60°   120°   60°   120°

   (b) rhombus

14. (a) Brazilian 120 g, Honduran 80 g

(b) £20

(c) £3.00

Chapter 3 (11+ Calculations)

1. (a) Answer should be about 3000; answer should end in 5

(b) 2955

(c) Forgot about place value and didn't put a zero in the units column when multiplying by ten

2. 361

3. 245

4. (a) 45 × 3 is 135

(b) 43 × 5 is 215

(35 × 4 is 140, 34 × 5 is 170, 53 × 4 is 212, 54 × 3 is 162)

5. The total cost of the items was £20.03 (3 pence more than £20).

Chapter 4 (13+ Calculations)

1. (a) 9.54

(b) 2.54

(c) 21.14

(d) 1.51

2. (a) 49.05

(b) 13.89

(c) 2.3765

(d) 19.4

3. (a) 34

(b) 60.3

(c) 8

4. (a) (i) 4.92

(ii) −1

(b) 5.92

■■□ 5. (a) (i) $\dfrac{40}{9 \times 9}$

        (ii) 0.5 ($\frac{1}{2}$)

    (b) (i) 0.490 183 973 3

        (ii) 0.49

        (iii) 0.490

6. (a) (i) 7.391 975 309

        (ii) 7.39

    (b) (i) 3.057 607 09

        (ii) 3.058

7. (a) 26 points

    (b) £115

    (c) £135

    (d) 360 ml

    (e) 9801

8. (a) 25%

    (b) 50 g

    (c) £120

    (d) 4.5 ha

    (e) 0820

Chapter 5 (11+ Problem solving)

1. Answers vary

2. 43

3.

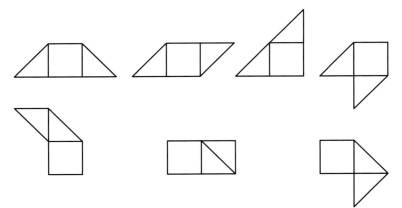

4.   (a) (i)   Brenda

          (ii)   Angus

    (b) 2 minutes 19 seconds

    (c) second

5.   (a) 60 green balls

    (b) (i)   10p

          (ii)   £10

    (c) green

    (d) equally likely

Chapter 6 (13+ Problem solving)

1.   27   (You probably found first that there are 6 diagonals from each vertex and then halved 9×6)

2.   5   (You probably made an organised list)

3.   5.5   ($\sqrt{25}$ is 5 and $\sqrt{36}$ is 6, so it can be assumed that the square root of 30 is a little less than 5.5; 5.4×5.4 gives 29.16 and 5.5×5.5 gives 30.25 so, to 1 decimal place, the answer is 5.5)

4.   76, 156

5.   16   (You probably tried a simpler – shorter – maze)

6.   498

7.   (a) $\frac{5}{12}$

    (b) $\frac{1}{6}$

    (c) 24

8.   (a) £224

    (b) £292

    (c) 45 hours (13 extra hours)

■■■ 9.   (a) 2 cm

    (b) (i) x cm

          (ii) $x - 4$ cm

          (iii) $x^2 + 4x - 16$ cm^2

    (c) (i)   464 cm^2

          (ii)   640 cm^3

10. (a) (i)   24.61

(ii)   26.20

(iii)   26.11

(b)   Beatrice and Colin

(c)   85.56 kg

Chapter 7 (11+ Algebra)

1.   (a) 7

(b) 28

(c) 8

(d) 4

2.

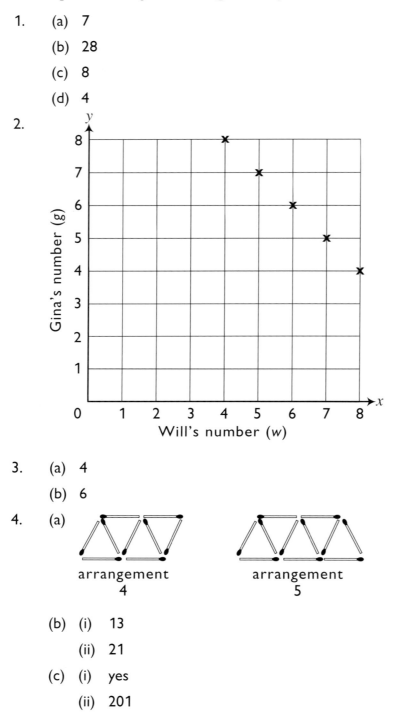

3.   (a) 4

(b) 6

4.   (a)

arrangement 4   arrangement 5

(b) (i)   13

(ii)   21

(c) (i)   yes

(ii)   201

5.

0	1	2	③	4	5	⑥	7	8
⑨	10	11	⑫	13	14	⑮	16	17
⑱	19	20	㉑	22	23	㉔	25	26
㉗	28	29	㉚	31	32	㉝	34	35
㊱	37	38	㊴	40	41	㊷	43	44
㊺	46	47	㊽	49	50	㊿	52	53

6. (a) (i) points A, B, C, D plotted and labelled

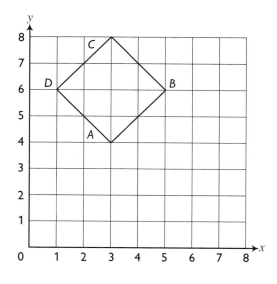

(ii) ABCD drawn; square

(b) Isosceles triangle PQR with co-ordinates

Chapter 8 (13+ Algebra)

1. (a) $6k$

(b) $6k$

(c) $3k^2$

(d) $9k^2$

(e) $9c^3$

(f) $20t^6$

2. (a) $4a - 8$

(b) $6a + 15$

(c) $11a - 10$

(d) $10t + 15u - 2v$

(e) $e - 6f$

■■□ 3.   (a) $2rs + 5r^2$

       (b) 0

       (c) $5b + 23$

■■■   (d) $\dfrac{4}{5c}$

■■■   (e) $5b$

■■■   (f) $8n$

    4.   (a) $3(a + 2)$

       (b) $2(2b - 5)$

       (c) $2(a + 2b - 4)$

■■■   (d) $a(a + 2)$

■■■   (e) $3r^2(2r - 1)$

    5.   (a) 12

       (b) 8

       (c) 18

       (d) -30

    6.   (a) $c + 4$

       (b) $c - 2 = 2(c - 6)$ leading to $c = 10$

       (c) 17

    7.   (a) (i) $y - 4$

           (ii) $3y$

       (b) $\dfrac{5y - 4}{3}$

       (c) $y = 14$

       (d) 10, 14, 42

    8.   (a) $d = 19$

       (b) $w = 3$

       (c) $c = 3$

       (d) $a = -1$

       (e) $e = 2$

       (f) $b = 6$

■■□ 9.   (a) $d = 12$

       (b) $r = 20$

       (c) $y = 8$

■■■   (d) $x = -1\tfrac{1}{2}$

■■■   (e) $x = 24$

(f) $x = 0$

10. (a) x is 8.45 (or x is 3.55) gives y as 29.9975

(b) x is 3.55 (or x is 8.45)

(c) x could be 2 or 10 since $2(12 - 2) = 20$ and $10(12 - 10) = 20$

11. (a) 9, 6

(b) 10, 2.5

(c) 18, 29

12. (a) 18, ... , 24

(b) 36, ... , 64

(c) 26, ... , 50

13. (a) 10, 28, 82, 244

(b) 12, 30, 84, 246

14. (a) multiply by 2 and then subtract 1

(b) $T_n = 4n - 1$

15. (a) (i) $T_1 = -1$, $T_{100} = 9998$

(ii) $n = 21$

(b) (i) $T_1 = \frac{1}{4}$, $T_{100} = \frac{199}{301}$

(ii) T_n approaches $\frac{2}{3}$

16. (a)

x	−3	−2	−1	0	1	2	3
x^2	9	4	1	0	1	4	9
$2x^2$	18	8	2	0	2	8	18
y	13	4	−1	−2	1	8	19

(b)

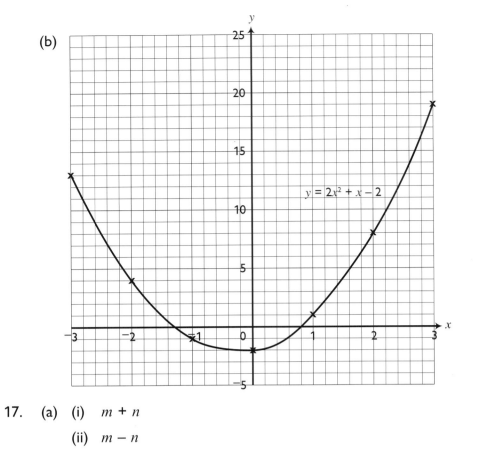

$y = 2x^2 + x - 2$

17. (a) (i) $m + n$

   (ii) $m - n$

(b) $m + n = 20$

(c) Natascha is 7 years old ($m - n = 6$, so $2m = 26$, leading to $m = 13$)

Chapter 9 (11+ Space, shape and measures)

1. A 140 g

   B 125 g

2. (a)

3. (b)

3. (a) 9 cm³

    (b) For example:

4. (a)

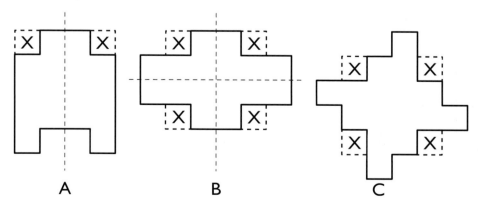

    (b) (i) 110°

         (ii) 6.9 cm

5. (a) congruent – the same shape and size

    (b) (i) B

         (ii) C

         (iii) E

6. For example:

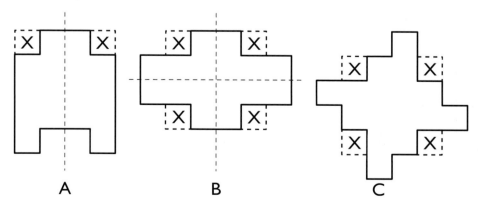

Chapter 10 (13+ Shape, space and measure)

1. Note: All answers are rounded. The official rules for sports usually give a range of measurements.

    (a) (i)   70 mm

       (ii)   40 mm

       (iii) 25 cm

    (b) (i)   160 g

       (ii)   3 g

       (iii) 120 g

    (c) (i)   300 ml

       (ii)   180 litres

■■□ 2. (a) approximately 625 mm² (661 mm² – 36 mm²) or 6.25 cm²

    (b) approximately 1250 mm³ or 1.25 cm³

3. (a) 8 minutes 24 seconds

    (b) 2 minutes 6 seconds

    (c) 7 seconds

4. A (a regular hexagon) 6 lines, rotation symmetry order 6

    B (a rhombus) 2 lines, rotation symmetry order 2

5. $a = 72°, b = 36°, c = 72°, d = 54°, e = 54°$

6.

(e) (ii) 9

7.

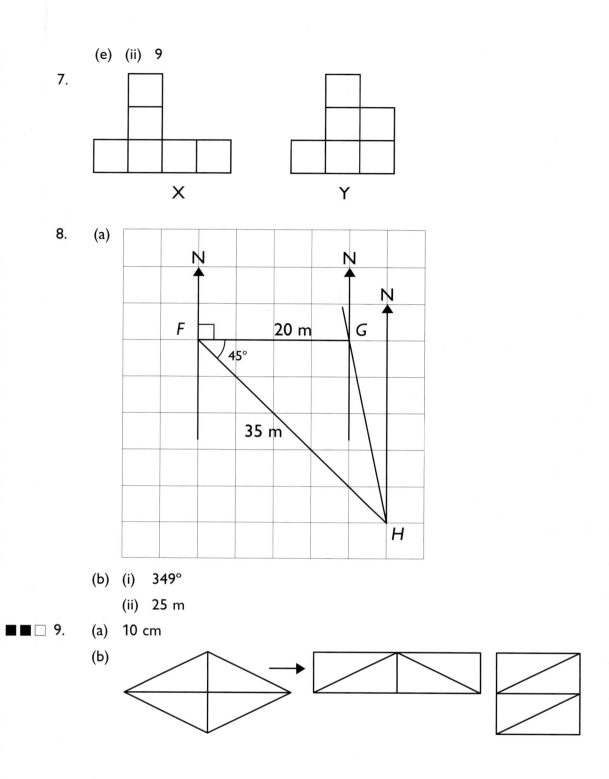

X   Y

8. (a)

(b) (i) 349°

(ii) 25 m

9. (a) 10 cm

(b)

(c) 17.1 cm

Chapter 11 (11+ Handling data)

1. (a) (i)   13

    (ii)   17

    (iii) 13.5

    (b)

Grade	Scores	Tally	Frequency
A	17–20	‖‖	5
B	13–16	‖‖ ‖	7
C	9–12	‖‖ ‖	6
D	5–8	‖	2
E	1–4		0

    (c)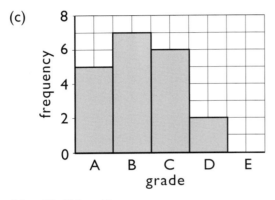

    (d) 18 (90 ÷ 5)

2. (a) 1130

    (b) 10 km

    (c) 1330

    (d) $1\frac{1}{2}$ hours

    (e) 30 km

    (f) 5 hours

3. (a) $2\frac{1}{2}$ miles

    (b) about 1500 m

4. Answers vary. It could be a good idea to discuss your answers with a friend.

5. (a) (i)   This was **not** a good strategy since there were insufficient trials.

        (ii) No

    (b) No – this die would **appear** to be biased towards 1

    (c) A large number of trials is needed.

    (d) The stallholder could:

        • make sure that any biased die looks attractive

        • make sure that other people cannot watch what happens.

Chapter 12 (13+ Handling data)

1.   (a) $3\frac{1}{2}$

    (b) 8

    (c) $8\frac{1}{2}$

2.   (a) 48

    (b)

Marks	Tally	Frequency
40–49	III	3
50–59	III	3
60–69	IIII III	8
70–79	IIII	5
80–89		0
90–99	I	1
	Total	20

    (c) 60–69

    (d)

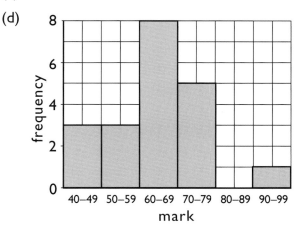

    (e) The second paper was probably more difficult; only one pupil achieved more than 79% compared to 7 pupils in the earlier exam, etc.

■■□ 3.   (a) 2.5° each bulb; 36 daffodils (90°); 9 hyacinths (22.5°); 36 snowdrops (90°); 18 tulips (45°); 45 crocuses (112.5°)

    (b) 37.5%

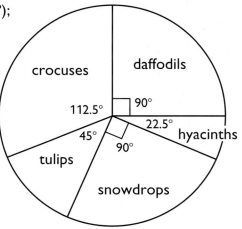

4. (a) about 100 inches

    (b) 175 cm

5. (a)
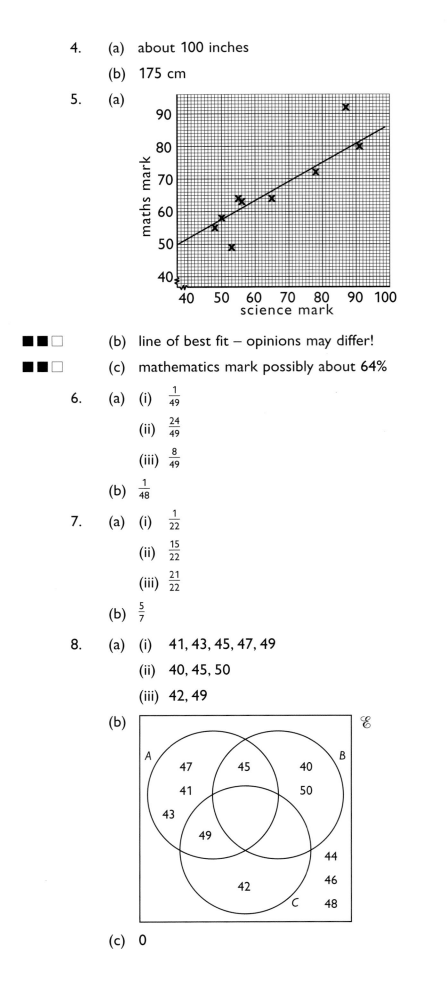

    (b) line of best fit – opinions may differ!

    (c) mathematics mark possibly about 64%

6. (a) (i) $\frac{1}{49}$

        (ii) $\frac{24}{49}$

        (iii) $\frac{8}{49}$

    (b) $\frac{1}{48}$

7. (a) (i) $\frac{1}{22}$

        (ii) $\frac{15}{22}$

        (iii) $\frac{21}{22}$

    (b) $\frac{5}{7}$

8. (a) (i) 41, 43, 45, 47, 49

        (ii) 40, 45, 50

        (iii) 42, 49

    (b)

    (c) 0

290